Notebooks 1924–1954

Notebooks 1924–1954

Wilhelm Furtwängler

Translated by Shaun Whiteside
Edited and with an Introduction by Michael Tanner

Quartet Books
London New York

First published in English in Great Britain by
Quartet Books Limited 1989
A member of the Namara Group
27/29 Goodge Street
London W1P 1FD

The German-language edition was originally selected and
edited by Günter Birkner and Elisabeth Furtwängler

British Library Cataloguing in Publication Data
Furtwängler, Wilhelm, *1886–1954*
Notebooks 1924–1954.
1. Music, 1924–1954. Biographies. Collections
I. Title II. Tanner, Michael III.
Aufzeichnungen, 1924–1954. *English*

ISBN 0-7043-2697-3

Typeset by AKM Associates (UK) Ltd Southall, London
Printed and bound in Great Britain by
The Camelot Press plc, Southampton

Contents

Notebooks 1924–1954

Introduction

Wilhelm Furtwängler (1886–1954) was not only the greatest conductor of his time. He was also a composer whose works have far more interest than those of other conductor-composers such as Weingartner and Klemperer; several of them would certainly survive without the interest of being by a supreme interpreter. Furtwängler thought continuously and hard about music throughout his life. The published results can be found in two substantial books of essays and lectures, *Ton und Wort* and *Vermächtnis*, two books of *Conversations*, and some pamphlets. They are all remarkable, though uneven, containing some pieces that are as fine as anything written on their subjects, such as the magnificent 'The Case of Wagner: freely after Nietzsche' (in *Ton und Wort*). But they are written in a style which is often tortuous, abstruse and convoluted. Furtwängler's education, mainly conducted privately, was in the German tradition of philosophizing as it was practised by Kant, Hegel and Schopenhauer among other giants of the late classical and early romantic periods. And though Goethe was for him, as for all educated Germans, perhaps the central figure of European letters and is referred to frequently in his writings, that great poet and thinker's concreteness and directness of expression was not something that he found it possible to emulate. Furtwängler's intellectual training was enviable in its width and thoroughness, a great deal of his adolescence being spent in Greece and Italy. But he was not, in the usual sense of the word, an intellectual. His responses to life and to art, above all to music, were passionate and intuitive. He was not a naturally articulate man, and though his writings served the purpose, for him, of helping to clarify his feelings about the things that he cared most about, he had neither the time nor the inclination, in his fantastically busy life, to cultivate a style that makes for easy understanding.

It is for this reason that the *Notebooks* are often a better guide, or at any rate a more accessible one, to his thoughts than his formally composed essays and lectures. His widow tells us that he deplored ostensibly private writings that were in fact composed with one eye on publication, such as many of Rilke's letters, and the *Notebooks* show all the signs of being written in haste and only for himself, to the extent that sentences sometimes peter out, and it isn't always clear to whom or what he is referring, using pronouns without there being a proper name in the vicinity. They still provide, however, many passages of illumination, both of his own thought processes and more important, because he was so representative a cultural figure, of the attitudes of educated Germans during the first half of this century. Most significantly, they contain a great deal that sheds light on those aspects of his life and work that were, and remain, most controversial: his feelings about the key-figures in his performing repertoire, and the reasons for its particular circumscriptions and limitations; his attitudes towards contemporary music and musicians; and (though not to as great an extent as one could wish) his views on the position of art and the artist under a totalitarian and criminal regime.

It is clear throughout the *Notebooks*, as in everything he wrote, that Furtwängler regarded the music he cared most about – roughly speaking, the German tradition from Bach to Pfitzner (whose name crops up, for the English reader, surprisingly often) – as an activity akin to a religious practice, or to contemplation and meditation. For him its purpose was no more internal to it ('Art for art's sake') than it was for Beethoven. For him, as for Beethoven, it was the central element in a spiritual journey to a world of eternal values, a journey best portrayed, musically, in sonata form, in which elemental conflicts lead to a final, transcending unity. Furtwängler seems to have been a Christian, but he also seems, like Beethoven, more concerned to express and elicit spiritual states untethered to any particular set of dogmas. Just as Beethoven, in setting the Christian Mass in his *Missa Solemnis* (a work which Furtwängler regarded as so great as to be virtually unperformable, and in fact hardly ever performed), found that the text was, for most of the time, serviceable for the expression of his own highly idiosyncratic and vague religious yearnings and beliefs, so Furtwängler found in the works he felt closest to a medium for his most urgent, even desperate intensities of feeling about human destiny. This resulted in the seemingly paradoxical combination, in his finest performances, of extremely 'personal' readings which frequently gave, and still give, offence to purists, and the sense which his admirers have that no other interpretation than his is possible, that he alone does the fullest justice to composers when he finds in them what no one else has or could.

Such an approach to music is clearly unfashionable – it has been for most of the century. So it isn't surprising that Furtwängler's writings, including the *Notebooks*, are characterized by an embattled tone. He combined, in his life, intense personal insecurity with an extremely strong sense of having a mission, and a passionate feeling of being misunderstood. This led, often, to displays of vanity and nervously defensive reactions to rivals, even to conductors who didn't have reputations that he needed in any serious way to fear. Anton Dermota, the great tenor who frequently performed under him, tells a revealing story in his autobiography *Tausendundein Abend*. In 1953, when he was singing Don Ottavio with Furtwängler in a series of performances at the Salzburg Festival, he told Furtwängler that he was going to Bayreuth between *Don Giovanni*s to take part in Beethoven's Ninth Symphony under Hindemith, not a distinguished or celebrated interpreter of the classics. Furtwängler insisted that he should report back immediately on his return, and when Dermota told him that it had been a passable performance, but no more, of the Ninth, Furtwängler expressed great relief. It must seem inconceivable to us that Furtwängler could have been so concerned, but it shows a great deal about how isolated he was aware of being on the contemporary musical scene, when anyone who represented 'objectivity' could be felt by him as a threat.

In the *Notebooks*, the most elaborate, indeed the longest single entry, though still tactfully abridged by the editors from its original form (in which it has never appeared), is devoted to his lifelong rival Toscanini. As published here (pp. 39–46) it still amounts to a pretty strident attack. It wasn't simply, though it certainly was partly, a matter of personal jealousy and wounded vanity in the face of Toscanini's triumphant appearance in Berlin in 1930, following on his prodigious success with the La Scala company there the previous year. In his piece 'Toscanini in Germany', Furtwängler attempts to convey, until his patience runs out, what he felt was wrong in detail with Toscanini's interpretation, not only of Haydn and Beethoven but also of Debussy. In the original version, Furtwängler speaks of having heard Toscanini conduct 'at least fifty times'. He was clearly fascinated by what Toscanini could get an orchestra to do, at the same time as he was in fundamental disagreement with his aims. What the great Italian stood for, as the leading 'modern' conductor (in style, of course, not in repertoire), was what the Germans refer to as *Werktreue*, fidelity to the work. And what Furtwängler was concerned with, in an idiom that had not yet come into existence, was deconstructing that concept. Had the two of them been alive now, they might have found that they were united in hostility to our contemporary vogue for 'authentic' performances, which it is just as hard to imagine

Toscanini approving of as Furtwängler. Yet while Furtwängler had already, in the *Notebooks* and some of his essays and conversations of fifty years ago and more, mounted his attack on the notion of authenticity, Toscanini might well have found himself in an awkward position. For he did adhere to naïve ideas of what a musical work was, and therefore of what fidelity to it amounted to, as in his celebrated remark, apropos of the first movement of the Eroica Symphony, that 'Some people say it is Napoleon, some Mussolini, some Hitler, but for me it is *allegro con brio*.' Evidently there are other possibilities which Toscanini overlooked and which Furtwängler didn't. For it is clear, on page after valuable page of the *Notebooks*, that Furtwängler recognized that at every moment, in conducting or otherwise performing a musical work, the interpreter is confronted with choices, while Toscanini appears to have denied that, in his insistence that music be played 'as it is written'. Since he was a great artist, Toscanini actually made his own set of choices, which means that a recording by him is as instantly recognizable as one by Furtwängler. Nor did Toscanini scruple to amend the orchestration of a work if he felt that the composer had failed to realize his intentions; so that his most intelligent admirer, Spike Hughes, in his excellent book *The Toscanini Legacy*, is to be found praising his hero time and again for playing music 'as it is', except that when he doesn't, that is because, in Hughes' opinion, he can improve it; then Hughes praises him for his flexibility and sensitivity for *not* playing it 'as it is'. That is obviously to give the whole argument away. Furtwängler's performances of Bach, which were notorious in his lifetime, and are not less so now, have recently been described by Reinhard Goebel, the leader of the 'authentic' group 'Musica Antiqua Koln' as 'disgusting' (Gustav Leonhardt has said the same) and 'not worth talking about'. He even goes so far as to refer to 'Mr Furtwängler', which is as insulting as a musicologist can get. But if he listened to Toscanini's performance of the Second Brandenburg Concerto (or, for that matter, to Klemperer's recording from the 1950s of the same work, with saxophones substituted for trumpets), Goebel might move from insult to speechlessness.

So the claim, which is sometimes advanced in contemporary discussions of authenticity, that Toscanini was a forerunner of the authentic performance movement, seems not to survive casual scrutiny, and if the current champions of that movement were to read the *Notebooks* they would find powerful arguments to be countered – and in my view they would only be able to counter them to their own satisfaction. That is one reason for reading this book. The fact that

Furtwängler's arguments are usually stated *ad hominem* adds to their force; one can generally check up on what he is talking about. Since he seems never to have been able to state his views to his own satisfaction – hence the exraordinary number of entries on the same subjects, and the impressive improvements in the ones from the later years – it is useful to be able to fill in his meaning by playing records which illustrate his points. But although he genuinely felt his position as spokesman for German music threatened by his eminent contemporaries, with the exception of Bruno Walter whom he greatly admired, it was the general tendencies of musical performance that most alarmed him. Remember that the entries for the first nine years were written in the context of 'die neue Sachlichkeit' ('the new objectivity') which was regarded by many people as the distinguishing feature of the musical culture of the Weimar Republic (by far the best account of it in English is to be found in Volume I of Peter Heyworth's biography of Klemperer). Furtwängler, taking over the Berlin Philharmonic at Arthur Nikisch's death in 1922, saw himself as the bearer of a great tradition in which justice had been done to the German classics. And although it is false to claim that he showed no interest in contemporary, even avant-garde, music – he performed 'Le Sacre du Printemps' (which Klemperer never did) and gave the first performance of Schoenberg's Orchestral Variations opus 31, as well as a good deal of Bartók, Debussy, Ravel and many lesser figures – one feels, reading these notes, that it was in most cases more from a sense of duty than from conviction of their enduring worth. His references to Schoenberg and Stravinsky are never complimentary, and in the case of the latter often downright hostile. He rapidly characterized Stravinsky as an ironist – a mode of consciousness utterly alien to Furtwängler – and one can see why he should have done that during the 1920s and 1930s, though 'Le Sacre' itself evidently doesn't fit into that category. But the narrowness of his vantage-point, as well as the intensity and depth with which he felt it, emerges in such remarks as this, from 1940:

> Has it ever occurred to anyone that the great 'earthly' artists of the nineteenth century, Brahms, indeed Wagner and Verdi, were the *only* ones who were able to put truly religious content into music? The acid test is whether or not one is capable of this. Imagine R. Strauss or Stravinsky writing a 'Mass'! Thus we can see what is wrong with them. Distanced from real content. But . . . virtuoso. (p. 122)

Actually Stravinsky did write a Mass, and a very fine one, in 1948; and religious works, in the fullest sense, dominate his last years. But already in 1930 he had produced the sublime 'Symphony of Psalms', the greatest of all his religious works, and one with which Furtwängler ought certainly to have been acquainted. But even if he had been, he might well not have appreciated it for what it is – it answers too few of Furtwängler's preconceptions of what is required of religious music.

His attitude to Richard Strauss was less straightforward. Strauss' works featured in his Berlin Philharmonic programmes, at least from 1922 to 1941, more often than those of any other composers except Beethoven and Brahms. And yet his attitude towards Strauss in the *Notebooks*, which never found expression in any of his published writings, is almost as hostile as to Stravinsky, and shows, as one would expect, a much fuller comprehension. In 1939, for instance he writes typically:

> The playful trait in Strauss: not the playing of a child, which is actually in deadly earnest, but the conscious play of an irresponsible person, of the person devoid of content, the redundant person. As he never means it quite truly, quite warmly, quite seriously, he is never heard or felt quite truly, quite warmly, quite seriously. He is, of all of them [contemporary composers], the one who 'can' do the most and who 'is' the least. (Incidentally, the two depend causally on one another). (p. 116)

That strikes me as shrewd, just and final. Why, then, the frequent performances? If Furtwängler was passionately intent on analysing contemporary musical decadence, as he was, Strauss was obviously the best case to take. So his name recurs frequently in these pages, almost always as part of Furtwängler's campaign against technical virtuosity which, as the last quotation makes plain, Furtwängler profoundly distrusted. So the frequent performances seem to have been a case of yielding to 'popular demand'. Strauss was the last German composer to achieve wide acceptance in his homeland, and for Furtwängler not to have conducted him would have been to take a very evident stand. But it was the kind of stand that he was in a unique position to take.

When one surveys Furtwängler's work as a conductor, many such questions arise. It is odd, for example, that in one respect his temperament should have been so restlessly exploratory – in respect, that is, of his perpetual dissatisfaction with his performances and interpretations of the repertoire; while in another – that of his repertoire itself – he should have been so unadventurous, even by the standards of star conductors. Why, one wonders, did he play the same tiny handful of Haydn symphonies over and over again, leaving all the rest unexplored? Why did he wait until 1943 to 'discover' Bruckner's Sixth Symphony, proclaim how lucky he was to have made so exciting a discovery so late in life, and then drop it after four performances? Neither his *Notebooks* nor anything or anyone else tells us. Such questions may seem trivial in themselves, but they point to that combination of boldness and timidity in Furtwängler which seems to have been a pervasive feature of his personality.

As with other geniuses, one is so grateful for what they did that one become ungrateful that they didn't do more. Still, he does remain a deeply puzzling figure. The greatness of the vast majority of his preserved performances is so overwhelming that not to have him performing far more works is a lifelong deprivation. It seems as if, for the most part, he felt that the works he got to know during his formative years were as comprehensive a canon as he needed to know, and that his sole duty as interpreter was to probe ever deeper into them. Even so, anomalies, and many of them, remain. Why, for instance, so few performances of the Jupiter Symphony? There are so many ways in which he seems to have been uniquely qualified to bring out and draw together all its many facets, it is so triumphant a summation of the tradition in which he worked and to which he ascribed supreme value, welding together a vast diversity of materials into an affirmation of unity without equal. Yet he seems to have dropped it halfway through his career. Perhaps all one can say, in the face of such bewildering and exasperating facts, is that like other great creative figures *manqués*, he settled on the works in which he felt he could best simultaneously recreate and express himself. Radically dissatisfied with himself, unable to renounce the immediate fame and prestige of a conductor's career for the solitary life of a composer writing music of a kind which he knew was bound to be condemned as old-fashioned (the life of Hans Pfitzner, which may be one reason why Furtwängler is so obviously fascinated and made uneasy by him, as the *Notebooks* repeatedly show); simultaneously intent on proving to the world the inherent spiritual greatness of the German heritage while the country was in the hands of a popularly supported gang of thugs – supported by some of the same people who rapturously applauded Furtwängler's concerts; broken in will by the pressure of international hostility during and after the

Second World War, yet still managing to keep up a hair-raising schedule of conducting on three continents – all told, we must be amazed and grateful that as much remains to us as it does. In one of the few purely personal entries in the *Notebooks* he asks himself, early in 1945, 'Is it through coldness, decadence, poverty of feeling that I work, that I can work in these terrible times?' The answer seems to me to be a clear 'No'. But the cost was a frightful one and in the end Furtwängler was no longer able to go on paying it. He died through a combination of overwork and lack of the will to go on living. He had been an heroic fighter, all the more so because his personality contained so many unheroic elements. These *Notebooks*, which provide many insights and also reveal, in their shortcomings, the areas where Furtwängler's vision failed to reach, are an invaluable if not indispensable aid to understanding him and the culture of which he was so late a representative.

Michael Tanner
Cambridge
November 1988

I have footnoted references to names when it seems to me likely that the reader won't know anything much about them and when it is worth knowing something more than the context provides. I have not given away information on major cultural figures, nor on a few very minor ones about whom I wasn't able to discover anything. I have nearly always refrained from glosses on what Furtwängler says, despite severe temptation, since they would double the length of the book. But there are one or two corrections of fact.

1924

Only twice in history has art existed with the exclusion of the standard of individual forces: in classical antiquity and the Gothic age. In both cases the level as a whole is indisputably higher than it has been subsequently. Why should this be the case? How did Homer come about, or the 'Nibelungenlied'? Was it because of the ignorance surrounding art, the lack of any accompanying aesthetic? For in these periods too, individual genius, as ancient tragedy reveals, was not unknown. Only now, perhaps, do we understand the immense profundity of the work of Marées.* It is the work of every artist, every living person. But we exchange life and the health of the soul for grey theory, for history! There are only two types of art: bad art and the work of genius – but the work of genius is correct, simple. Today it is unknown that simplicity is the fruit of genius; that fruit is held to be progress. Of course every artist has a historical situation into which he is born, the language, the milieu allocated to him. But the meaning of art always lies in moving from the individual to the general, with each individual situation; that is the eternal aspect of art, immediately and always abundantly clear to simple people, to everyone, but closed for ever to the historian. What capital has been made out of the opposition between the Gothic age and classical antiquity – instead of understanding that the two are the same, but with their premises reversed. Spengler† was right to see the ancients as pertaining to the surface, the Faustian to depth. But the ancients do not lack the Faustian, and we, thank God, do not lack surface. We came close to forfeiting all relation

---

* Hans von Marées (1837–87), German painter who produced a large number of allegorical paintings with titles such as 'Praise of Modesty'. They are most reminiscent, for the English spectator, of the work of Burne-Jones. Furtwängler's ascription to them of 'immense profundity' is one of his most dated judgements.

† Oswald Spengler (1880–1936), philosopher of culture, whose most famous work was *The Decline of the West*, which had an immense vogue in the earlier part of the century, but was too much the product of intellectual dilettantism to have survived, except as a curiosity.

to living sensuous culture. (Goethe's dislike of the telescope!)* Certainly, these statements of mine, in so far as they are understood at all, will be challenged. For through them, three-quarters of all art-historical strivings lose their meaning.

The artist always tends to underestimate the significance of history – the historian, the significance of individual achievement.

On theatrical matters

Wagner's stylization in the orchestra: seeking to repeat this *independently* on the stage is a pleonasm (at best!). What does stylization mean? Michelangelo and beautiful form. Organization instead of organism. A musical and an unmusical director.

Leader type. Psychology of the man of the theatre. Importance of the director grows with the importance of the decorative. The decorative, that which comes from outside, the suppression of representation.

Frankfurter Zeitung

'A few things about the contemporary public'

The artist within the art-work and the artist *outside* it. Definition of temperament.

Temperament in the sense of the audience: 'Overflowing' of the personal over the artistic, that is, 'overheated'. (Hildebrand, problem of form, and 'idea of the relief'.)† Form, from a human point of view, an ethical matter, especially today. It is possible to say that the artist today is *forced* into having an unartistic effect within today's public. Structure of the audience. Essence of *true* temperament. Rarity of this, inner fatigue and nervousness today. The performance of Beethoven's symphonies, for example (Wagner and Beethoven). Essence of the self-contained organic art-work.

The mania for progress means progress in terms of machinery. Progress, a journalistic concept.

---

* This refers to the great thinker's alarm at the way in which he saw the natural ciences, especially as pursued by those influenced by Newton, as leading to a fatally prosaic way of seeing the world.

† Adolf von Hildebrand (1847–1921), sculptor and art-historian, who played a considerable part in Furtwängler's education. Furtwängler's first serious love-affair was with his daughter Bertel.

Verdict on productions

Always devoting oneself to the new, without asking too many questions (Wagner, *Meistersinger*, Act I), etc.

Mediocre, for Beethoven, equals bad. The real reason for jadedness is the large number of mediocre performances.

The theory of progress is the emergency bridge used by the evolving communal feeling of the contemporary age.

Pannwitz:* Full of great and deep thoughts. The overall position, like Nietzsche's, threadbare. What undermines it is the boundless ambition that springs from fleshless intelligence, opposing any kind of creation.

Want what you are capable of, and what you are capable of wanting, and be *completely* clear on the matter and: live according to it.

Either remaining steadily in the tonic (in the minor, in any case) or hovering in the dominant, moving towards the subdominant. The latter only possible with a well-established tonic. Otherwise always aim for a tonic foundation.

Missa Solemnis

The essential thing about the *impulse of the will* is the accent; this is why performance of the chorus is almost impossible.

The sufferings of the soul can only be overcome by knowledge, by the will and morality. Knowledge brings the purification of passion. Asceticism is *incomplete, half*-knowledge.

I have become *far too* accustomed to composing solely with a *driving rhythm*!

Inadequate organization and sense of form! That is, one should not turn a question of power into a question of 'the age' or 'history' or 'progress' and degrade it as such.

---

* Rudolf Pannwitz (1881–1969), philosopher of culture, who owed a great deal to Nietzsche; but Furtwängler's bracketing of them has not stood the test of time.

Meister Eckart (From the Kingdom of Heaven!)*
This sermon is meant only for those who already call it their own, as their own lives, or who at least possess it as their heart's desire.

The present age tends towards the Absolute! But the 'Absolute' is 'prattle', merely imagined; any act is always relatively limited.
The combination of deed and prattle: 'Liebestod'.

Anyone not driven to self-knowledge today is not cut out for it. Only intellectualism and naïveté have no need of it. The former, because it thinks it possesses everything (pride as a surrogate for the lack of possession), the latter because it has not yet reached that point. Both are what they are without self-knowledge – they have no need of it. Everyone else today is that much more forced towards self-knowledge. It is branded into them as if with glowing irons.

Form of life and form of effect in music, in performance as well.

Society

Unironic (ironic is antisocial) and active. Never to see oneself as an object and talk about oneself. Always discuss things or works (especially when tired). Do not linger over negative judgements. Never allow (passive) repercussions through the speeches and judgements of others. Always active and steady. *Always seriously being the way you are.*

Always aggressive!

Above all: Never reflect with others on the impression of measures intended or taken!

Toch†

The ending good in itself, in all rather long. Second part better than the first. Themes brilliantly worked, fluid, well-contrasted in its way, but

* Meister Eckart (c. 1260–1328), German mystic who developed quasi-pantheistic views which were posthumously condemned as heretical. Furtwängler thought of his world-outlook as being comparable to that of Anton Bruckner.
† Ernst Toch (1887–1964), Austrian composer who emigrated to the United States. I haven't been able to ascertain which of his works Furtwängler is waxing lukewarm about in this entry. He did conduct one work of Toch's in a Berlin Philharmonic concert in 1927, and another in 1931.

rather lacking in content. Would perform it, if nothing better at the time.

General symptoms of fatigue. The musical *ars amandi* wears itself out in all kinds of perversion, instead of asking whether it is not perhaps the most important thing, love, that is missing.

1925

The two methods of classification

1) From an understanding of the whole, the sign taken symbolically. Classical composers (Brahms – Reger).

2) Realistic, pragmatic (Mahler – Wagner).

Europe, Christ: sublimation (intensification) of instinct. India, Buddha: overcoming (real) of instinct.

For us today: discovering, penetrating the relation between sublimation and the overcoming of instinct. Where it cannot be sublimated it must be overcome. If it is not overcome at times, it cannot at times be sublimated. Sublimation is the end, overcoming the means. (To such an extent in the East that it becomes genuine overcoming; this has never been striven for in the West.)

1927

The age is our curse; the unproductive its very basis. That which lies on the surface is illuminated, the depths are left in darkness.

This means that everything that is a part of the surface is stressed just as the other is hidden, repressed.

This process has been extraordinarily intensified in the last few years, both in Europe and America.

The surface includes technical matters. The technique of instrumentalists and orchestras keeps improving. Technique is primarily that which is learnable. Also the method through which this learning occurs, the training, has become very much better. One can see how art and sport converge. Or even more, the two are more or less identical.

Here America still has an advantage over Europe. It gives the greatest instrumental and vocal technicians the resonance they require. Its orchestras are technically the best.*

So for decades it saw individuality only as the motive and opportunity for technical perfection. The soloist only for his intrument and the possibilities inherent within it – not the other way round – the conductor only for his orchestra – not the other way round; having the best orchestra was the pride of America.

The corollary, here, was that soon the instrument had to exist for the person of the instrumentalist and the orchestra for the person of the conductor. High technical attainments and personality cult are inseparable. But neither has anything to do with art itself.

It appears as if art itself – America in particular seems to show this – steps back into view the more technique reveals itself in its true essence.

This essence is its *learnability*. This learnability is its democratic trait. It is something anyone can learn. But this is not true of art.

One can say that what is not part of the surface is not part of technique. That which does not belong to technique is negated by it. It has to do a lot of work – in contrast to art, which is inspiration and grace

---

* The notes on this and the following pages are clealy inspired by Furtwängler's contacts with American orchestras, which began in 1925.

whichever form it takes. It therefore seeks to take control, and to eliminate from its domain everything that is not accessible and comprehensible to it.

Technique includes: apart from technical mastery of the apparatus in the narrower sense, the technique of historical contemplation and the study of the various styles. The correct reproduction of a classical work, a work by Wagner or Stravinsky in terms of tempo, construction, development, in such a way that the public guardians of the consecrated traditions have nothing to complain about, is entirely learnable. Just as one can learn to make 'varied and good programmes'.

Also, all of these techniques have recently been learned very well, and their methods improved.

Like any technique, all of this can become an artistic device. But in itself it has nothing to do with art and everything to do with more or less good entertainment.

But it is certain in the long term that people want art, and not technique in any of its forms. That is something that can be better obtained from sport.

The whole person can only be freely and really devoted to art; everything else is only a partial interest.

That is why artists, i.e. the experts, are seldom competent judges of artistic achievements.

There is nothing unfortunate about this. The only unfortunate thing is if the wider audience, the influential public, shares and follows these interests. Then the thing that is called art will increasingly disappear from public life, to be replaced by a changeling.

This whole process has been intensified through the increased intellectual control to which modern man has become accustomed, and which is typical of him. The more the capacity for thought has increased, the more the ability to feel has declined. Man cannot with impunity become one-sided and over-exploitative.

So what is not 'technique'? What is not 'learnable'? This would be easily said, precisely if it were 'learnable'. It can only be shown, not spoken.

Technique is infertile knowledge. Above all, then, literal rendering. Like the whole of the 'classical tradition', this is a part of what is learnable.

There is a difference between treating a masterpiece as a living plant resplendent in its natural colours, allowing it to grow and unfold in front of the audience, or in its dried condition, in alcohol, etc.

The thing to be avoided is not dissection, but dissection without a consistent awareness of the living and natural context.

The experience of this context is the true artistic experience. It is and must always be unique and new, and has as little to do with the score as —

It is not the detail *per se* that places obstacles in the way of understanding, but only the point where the detail is supposed to be integrated within the whole.

This is why literal rendering has become the motto of infertile, unimaginative people. It comes about as follows: first subjectivity and then the abandonment of personality, resignation. And that is the lamentable condition of the contemporary public.

Classical art, a Pompeii.

Break between classical and modern music stemming from this.

Difference between being faithful to the score and faithful to the sense. The sense must be understood: one piece needs to be expressed loudly, another quietly. The score does not differentiate. A *sfz* varies from one place to another – in the score, there is no difference. One work like a painting with a Dürer-like form – cleanness – another like Rembrandt – colour.* The performers' lack of imagination sees the same correctness and cleanness everywhere. Why the classics, which are certainly so extraordinarily demanding, are lost to such an extent.

Even the same uniformly beautiful tone. As if an instrument, an orchestra, only had to sound beautiful. It has to sound the way its creator demands.

Tradition connects with that which is already current. Like this, it is the tradition of mediocrity.

Conducting means free creation. Everything else must be preparation. That is what the good orchestras are there for, not for their own sake, that is why technique exists in the first place. Technique must make free regulation of the rhythm possible, and go beyond this to influence the tone. A technique which is rhythmic and precise to the detriment of the freedom of breathing, at the cost of those 1,000 little traits that turn life into musical life, into music, creates discipline, in my opinion, but not art. But discipline must be a *precondition*!

There are conductors who remain teachers throughout their lives.

---

* The contrast between Dürer and Rembrandt – line and colour – is one that Furtwängler frequently returns to in his essays and interviews, for obvious reasons.

They are schoolmasters, parade-ground strategists. A well-rounded life creates different demands.

It is impractical, indeed impossible to create this through rehearsals. Twenty rehearsals would not be enough to achieve what the establishment of the proper contact can do . . . But there are always people who are more interested in the number of rehearsals than in what it sounds like. Even within orchestras. They want to be impressed; of course they are incapable of hearing.

Where does one come across the most difficult tasks? Unquestionably among the classics. Has it not struck you that any beginner can produce tolerable performances of Strauss, Stravinsky, Beethoven symphonies, hardly even a master.

Yes, I introduce few innovations. It also seems to me that the demand for the obligatory innovation at every concert in New York is far too closely related to the jadedness of the place. You yourself will have realized how little of any value can be involved in this, and that what is more important for the conductor is reproduction and renewal and not simple reference. Only the great are capable of that. The greater the work, the greater the task of the conductor – indeed also that of the audience. It is a mistake to think that new works are more difficult, greater achievements, etc.

It is all very satisfying. One must differentiate between the development and slow blossoming of an audience that really does understand art, and the fantastic surface agitation of the metropolis, a ball to be tossed around by a thousand non-artistic motives, politics, etc., always moving in extremes and never knowing what it wants apart from one thing: perfection! But this has the backing of an audience, perhaps not overly large, but reliable. Curious that the wide selection significantly benefits the technical standards, which are higher than the European average but not without a level of self-overestimation. An accurate assessment and evaluation of intellectual qualities is made difficult in a number of ways: 1) The excessive variety that is on offer, too often leading to comparison rather than understanding. Competition between German and French music, i.e. the concept of style is unknown. 2) The haste and proliferation of musical life, which is even greater than that of Berlin and makes concentration impossible, thereby rendering any decisive judgement difficult. 3) The lack of any uniform type of feeling in an audience flung together on colonial soil, something which one still bears in mind, even if progress on this is being made by the day and the hour, and agreement being reached on technical matters.

Everything organizational is excellent.

Orchestras.

My orchestra is the one which satisfies me entirely, and which is without a doubt one of the best orchestras in the world. A difference in the system. The orchestra more important than the conductor – and also often more so than the music. The orchestra is actually a luxury. Concerns which are fed with the largest imaginable amount of money and rehearsal time. For the artist who can make use of the rehearsals this has many advantages, so that we have every reason to see in America a model for ourselves. So we are just as little justified in our habitual underestimation of American musical cuture, which has come about among conditions quite different from our own, as we are in speaking of the naïve self-overestimation of the Americans. *Each of us* has every reason to learn from the other. Our superiority in the artistic and intellectual sphere is met, on the American side, by an unquestionable superiority in all organizational matters. But there is no point in either country constantly harping on about 'How wonderfully far we have come', as this will get us nowhere.

The restriction to technique in America has similar consequences to the restriction to science in modern thought. Tendency towards the 'definitive' method. Through impersonal objective thought, personal and productive values are eliminated.

Attempt at metaphysical organization on the part of the artist. Philosophers in recent times not universal enough. One wonders whether it is necessary – only because this universality among people is missing – for all culture to fall apart. At this point a few remarks on the basic observable artistic types: 1) the transcendental (Bach), 2) the individual, the hero, the superman (Beethoven), 3) instinct (Wagner). Everything becoming impersonal. Combination, etc. – which must of course remain an inadequate theory, but still a guiding principle in the chaos of today's opinions. Particularly in that ridiculous struggle – very German – between the adherents of the great artists, and the struggle of the vulgar against anything great, the latter combining in a curious way with the former days, a farce, also for anyone who has long been used to seeing through the psychology of opinions and the triviality of all literary dilettantism – even that of Nietzsche, on this point, a sorry sight.

To some extent Wagner always instinct, even when he approaches the hero (Siegfried's turning-point, fear) or the religious (*Parsifal*, *Tannhäuser* – chastity).

I know that true greatness is just as rare as true universality. Of course the two depend upon one another. Common as greatness and universality are *between* people, they are extraordinarily rare in reality, i.e. in individual characters.

The structure of opinions always reveals the wretchedness and poverty of human thought;

1) Working hypothesis
2) Mass hysteria, politics
3) The personal (Nietzsche, Hugo Wolf)
4) Fanaticism in the individual interest
5) Vulgarity, i.e. science of the concept of the audience, etc.

Experts (such as Bernard Shaw) will concede to me that today's unparalleled narrow-mindedness, fanaticism, etc., are more painful and disagreeable than in the darkest of the Dark Ages.

Progress has changed as little as the human organism changes. A symphony by Haydn will always be alive, for it is an organism, and we are organisms! It is the blood of our blood, flesh of our flesh. Machine-music is a theory, politics, in my opinion, and nothing more.

Progress in the arts, an aspect of modern theories, to which politics therefore attaches itself with the greatest ease. Unlike the *new*, supplied by every new work (*Meistersinger*). This work is the example which precisely reveals that progress is unrelated to medium.

Progress. *Tristan*, the greatest example so far, here also the penetration of morality. So it is progress that has produced it? Later Wagner, *Meistersinger, Parsifal*, has been average, etc. The embodiment of the world of *Tristan* (the terrible tragedy partly in lyricisms, partly in the stimulation of struggle) is its appropriate expression, hence the life of Tristan goes beyond sensation. Progress is politics and politics is stultifying. If is is appropriate anywhere, the repetition of the natural act of creation is out of place in art.

Community

The need for community as a basis for art lies deeper than any manufactured progress. In any case it comes from a realization – unfortunately only a realization *post festum*. If Wagner in *Tristan* . . .

Tristan world, etc. —; in old-fashioned terms, he found himself confronted with his God. He felt he was an individual, but felt around him the community of the whole of the modern world. This gave him his strength and gave his work its meaning. Today it is true in many ways that the individual does not experience his isolation proudly, as individuality (Goethe's *Persönlichkeit*), but as a curse. He *seeks machine-music.*

Programme

First to practical matters. Aesthetic errors, so that Bruckner's Ninth Symphony and Liszt would be cause for complaint, for instance, but not Bruckner's and Beethoven's *Fifth* Symphonies together. The latter combination in particular is wrong. It depends on the sequence, in which the interval break is still important.

Just as combination according to intellectual standards is nonsense, the same is true of *programmes* organized from historical or other external viewpoints. Only relevant if the individual work comes into its own. It is a fact that a modern work can successfully follow a classical one, but seldom the other way around. (The deeper reasons behind this will not be discussed here.) If I place a work by Stravinsky after one by Mozart – followed immediately by a Bach concerto, that puts both Stravinsky and Bach in a bad light – it will do nobody any good. General theories, opinions on programmes, are cheap these days, two a penny.

Other external points of view come into play. As director of the Berlin Philharmonic Concerts I play a part in contemporary life. It is clear that the effect of contemporary composers deserves particular attention, to the extent that one cannot apply the same unconditional standards in the selection of new works as in the selection of the works of the past. That involves consideration for the people responsible for them. The flightless eagle type is unfortunately not so rare today. He deserves real sympathy, even if this is mixed with a feeling of irritation. Which is secretly even greater with regard to the sparrow, who can only fly past disguised as an eagle. There are considerations involving the general public which extend to the point where one may need to include a work simply in order to have it discussed, and to reveal that it is *not* as it has previously been performed. It goes without saying that the *reductio ad absurdum* in my intended sense demands the best imaginable performance as well as the greatest work of art. So it is nonsense to believe that I am committed to all the works that I perform. That cannot be asked of any modern conductor; neither is it the job of the custodian of a modern institution. So his character is in no way required to deny itself, to level itself out. The correct emphasis lies naturally in his effectiveness as a whole. Of course, if he submits to the agitated politics of the day in our contemporary cities . . .

Progress becomes more and more of a theory. Increasingly it is becoming distanced from the centre, from 'man'. Hence the curious fact that for some time, in contrast to earlier ages, the most progressive works bear the least fruit. As the public [has been] completely ruined by politics, i.e. is still concerned with politics rather than judgement, it chases after progress instead of art.

The professional ethics of the conductor

Real professional ethics is not technical ability but a spiritual attitude. (Doctor, priest. Everything at the service of magic, of the magical effect.)

We have come so far today that we are gradually recognizing *life* in its deeper forms; how far have we come now? – We sit and watch.

Science means: turning charisma into an educational commodity.

Baring the soul – old art.
Intellectual unassailability – new art.

Art, continuation of the natural act of creation. Ever greater control. Naturalism, etc. – until in Expressionism the awareness of the other side breaks through once more, the awareness of community. From a mixture of 'community' and 'creation', 'organism' is produced.

Progress is politics. Everything not progressive is reactionary. But as the real world is non-political, it is reactionary as well. Yes, nature is reactionary. All real 'vitality' is reactionary. Surface value – voluble. Depth – wordless, because organically connected.

We are becoming aware of just as great a decline in reproduction as in production. Why: the categorization of composers – a defence, as it were, against the world, which functions almost automatically – is becoming increasingly contrived, less and less understood.

If, finding no heroism in his own life, a person denies the existence of heroism, then that is his own shortcoming. Art does not come from 'life', but from nature, from 'vitality'. Also, that other life contains just as much heroism – generally – as one gets out of it.

Back-door psychology

E. Newman* has – I do not know the books – apparently taken it upon himself to unmask the characters of Wagner and Beethoven once and for all. Adolf Weismann has written an article on it in the *Vossische Zeitung* and gone on, for his part, to make connections with contemporary opinions about the great musicians. The general question is not without interest in so far as it throws up the connection between music and life, which has been a problem since Nietzsche. Psychoanalysis is a great scientific discovery – but only in the possession of the very finest minds. In those of the rest it becomes stupidity of sometimes grotesque dimensions, chiefly because it distracts from the main issue and makes it all too easy, using apparently cryptic information, to explain that which in no way seeks to be 'explained', but primarily to be *recognized*.

Because Beethoven is said to have had syphilis, *hence* his 'moralism'.

Now psychoanalysis is certainly not designed to explain people of mythical stature such as Beethoven and Wagner, especially since in today's conditions it is only designed to understand the average stimuli of the average person, and not those who are expressive of a deeper collective will. It remains superficial and can therefore only say to what extent Wagner and Beethoven were *also people*. That they were people is something we know already, for we know, for example, that they ate and drank like everyone else.

Wagner had no right to egoism because he had something to defend that he alone was actually able to provide throughout the centuries. And *Mein Leben*, certainly not an agreeable read, is attributed to him rather than his wife. Psychoanalysis has the attribute of also turning against those who use it. Above all, it can speak of their *intentions*, and there are people who . . .

---

* Ernest Newman (1868–1959), English music critic and biographer, above all of Wagner. Furtwängler is referring here to *The Unconscious Beethoven* in which Newman combined biographical data and psychological speculations to produce a kind of 'physiology' of Beethoven's works. Furtwängler's strictures seem just. Newman, incidentally, kept up a relentless campaign against Furtwängler from the time of his first London appearance in 1924 onwards, even finding his performances of Wagner unacceptable.

Essays 1927

1) Composers – opinions!!
2) Machine, soul, art.
3) Literarization of music (relation of theory and reality).
4) Music of the future!
   a) Progress
   b) Community
5) New programmes.
6) Being a conductor.
7) Universality (Goethe).

Wagner's remark about the *Pastoral* is accurate. The *Pastoral* is above all a religious work, the expression of Beethoven's piety towards nature. Hardly ever has an artist been able so accurately to portray the unity and harmony of the human soul with the whole of nature. All the more curious that for a long time this symphony, which was held to be *bürgerlich*, was declared to be Beethoven's weakest work.

Conductor's lament!

It should be an art, and it is an exhibition, a spectacle.

1928

I have refrained from speaking out against the less than objective stance that your expert Alexander Berrsche* has for many years held towards me. This is not the place to contradict his statements, always just as correct theoretically as they are incorrect in practice. But if he now claims that in the *Andante* of Schubert's C Major Symphony I beat sprightly crotchets (he twice refers to this), when in reality I never beat it anything but *four-eight* and, on average, take the tempo of this movement slower than other conductors, one can only wonder whether this is deliberate falsification or boundless dilettantism on his part. I refuse to be exposed any further to the judgement of such a critic, and request your assurance that in future he will cease to discuss my concerts. If this assurance is not forthcoming, I shall publicly declare an end to my visits to Munich, as I cannot see why, as an artist, one should, on top of everything else, also be subjected to the extreme falsification of situations.

Kitsch

Kitsch is the intellectual half-man's fear of complete dedication – the fear of being duped. The concept of kitsch arose at the same time as false values – sentimentality, etc. It is modern man's reaction against . . . which was needed. It is surely suspicious that kitsch today is taken to include not only Raphael and Praxiteles but also Michelangelo and Beethoven. This cannot simply be explained as a trivial exaggeration, and we can see there is a problem concealed here, the problem that is seen one-sidedly, in the blindness of monstrous arrogance [on the part of] today's intellectuals, as a crisis of production, whereas it is also the crisis of perception that is involved here.

---

* Alexander Berrsche (1883–1940) was a Munich music critic who took the unusual line of applauding Furtwängler's compositions and condemning his conducting. This entry would appear to be the draft for a letter to the newspaper for which he reviewed, but I don't know whether it was sent. At any rate, Furtwängler continued to appear in Munich.

1928

The modern art-historian returns from Greece, saying, with visible satisfaction (that is also part of the picture): Olympia – kitsch. Now there have been generations capable of revering the wonderful, sensuous culture of Praxiteles. The Berliner goes on, he makes generalizations, there are people who declare all of Vienna and Paris to be kitsch, and people who place Verdi, Chopin, Beethoven and Michelangelo under the same heading (the fact that much that is contemporary is swallowed out of enthusiasm and only afterwards recognized as kitsch, is generously passed over in silence). If one were to ask these gentlemen, on their word of honour, they would also have to admit that natural coitus is kitsch, and that real life only begins with the variations (like Romeo and Juliet, Faust's Gretchen, etc.). But joking aside: we can see that there is another problem concealed here. One of the decisive modern problems, in fact. In the age of psychoanalysis anything and everything is analysed – so why not oneself? There is as yet no modern Nietzsche who would not only use psychology to demolish what exists, but also provide a psychology of the very person doing the demolition; only then would one become aware of just how little the revaluation of all values is a problem for the values themselves and how much, instead, it is a problem for the revaluator. Of course that takes more than scientific method, it takes the gift of feeling and establishing values, the gift needed for real greatness.

The word 'kitsch' is of recent coinage. In my youth, around thirty years ago, they began to recognize that Raphael was kitsch – and high time, too* – (some people thought the same of Mozart, and that has happened in the meantime). At the same time, *Zarathustra* or *Heldenleben* by Strauss, and Tchaikovsky, which are now declared to be kistch, were taken deadly seriously. Also, people's opinions, of course, particularly the fashionable views of intellectuals, are by no means as interesting as those who hold or communicate them generally think. For us the only issue is the problem itself.

In classical antiquity – let us take literature for example – there is much that is weak, but little kitsch. Emotion was not yet in fashion – so neither was false emotion. In the first Christian age too, into the High Renaissance (until Beethoven's day in the history of music), kitsch is barely encountered. Only with the destruction of religious bonds, the

---

* The remark about its being high time that Raphael was recognized as kitsch is one of the most startling in the *Notebooks*, all the more so in the light of Furtwängler's tastes in painting.

emptying and the abuse of form – with the emergence of sentimentality, in a word – do we see the emergence of kitsch. The word contains a *defence* against false emotion, against everything that is contrived, calculated, therefore exaggerated and, despite all its beauty, powerless, surrogate. With the creation of the word 'kitsch' the age begins to defend itself against false values (hence its coincidence with the effect of Nietzsche's last work). That is the positive side; and it was high time; false values, gushing, contrived sentimentality were pouring out in a terrible deluge to flood the age, and authenticity was being left far behind. The concept of kitsch was an evaluative one, then, a reaction of higher, pure, essential man against mediocrity. But it was still based on the rejection of something that one had experienced, to which one had been dedicated, i.e. one ceased to experience it, to be affected by it. If this happens spontaneously, as, for example, the human body is capable of spontaneously rejecting poison, it is fine. But what happens if, as the result of the peculiar intellectual training into which the spirit of the age forces everyone (especially in Germany and France), the whole thing becomes an intellectual process, a method, so to speak. So that everything that creates a self-sufficient impression aimed only at the whole of people's emotions, is rejected as kitsch for precisely that reason. So that any kind of dedication becomes an object of mockery! Some all-two-human qualities also urge this development onwards. For example the superior attitude, brought to a fine art in the cities, the inevitable tendency of the intellect (no longer burdened by any connection with the deeper forces of life) to act in an increasingly judgemental fashion: judging and, in the process, feeling superior both to others and to the object of one's judgement, the apparent intoxication of power that results (in fact made up only of negative factors), and, bound up with this, the lack of that respect which late Goethe saw as the core of all education. A lack which is not only presumptuousness and impudence but equally unreality, a lack of knowledge about reality, although it imagines itself to be precisely the opposite. Wherever one goes nowadays one can often experience grotesque examples of this. Those who are no longer capable of uninterrupted dedication are now beginning to seek out everything that does not call for such respect. The new objectivity, the extremely craft-oriented trend of one part of the most recent production is just as bound up with this as the preference for ages and artistic periods to which we do not have real access, since we do not share their preconditions (particularly those of a religious nature). This is all easy to talk about and write fat books about, but unfortunately this is not the case for true art. Let us define: if the concept was originally a necessary expression of the reaction against falsity, an expression of real and living evaluation (which, in the individual case, it can still be, even today), it is nowadays the characteristic expression of anyone who, wary of being duped, dare not show dedication. The dried-up modern 'expert', never able to escape the control of his intellect, is the one for whom the greatest things, Beethoven, Brahms, etc., become kitsch; to whom knowing everything has become his life's pleasure, second nature, a need – even, and above all, when it is directed against himself. He always wants to be cleverer with his head than his heart. At any rate, one acknowledges the *Hammerklaviersonate* (because one does not know it), but everything that belongs to simpler, harmonic, sensuous areas is frowned upon. Naturally the Hermes of Praxiteles must go. But it is remarkable that when sensuousness is at issue, all evaluations, in fact all *capacity for evaluation*, come to an end and the most dreadful *kitsch* appears. But that is in no way remarkable, because precisely that insecurity that always results from a lack of fullness in life and the prejudiced evaluations of the intellect, and which has become the true sign of our age, is responsible for the modern concept of kitsch with all its degenerations.

Crisis of judgement

The influential critic of a leading city newspaper writes: Beethoven's Fifth Symphony is starting to become fragile to us, etc. (I am taking a mild example, in Germany it was read quite differently). What does he mean, 'is starting . . . to us'? What is he talking about, the Fifth Symphony or 'us'? And who are 'we'? But according to the gentleman's statement, so characteristic and naïve, there seems to be no doubt on this matter. It never occurs to him that the question might in fact be reversed, and that it could be our fault if the Fifth Symphony begins 'to become fragile'. If a head and a book collide, it is not only the book that rings hollow, says Lichtenberg.

I was much more inclined to feel that, if he rejects Beethoven so easily, perhaps his admiration for him had not been so very deep. And in fact, when dealing with various performances of the same work, I was forced to notice that he was not blessed with the ability to judge an adequate or even a good performance, or the ability to tell this performance from a bad one.

This is a classic example not only of the unparalleled conceit that can result from a lack of the fullness of life and fullness of responsibility in modern man, but of the trend of fashion in general.

(I should clearly state here that I am not talking about the serious work that is done for and against Beethoven, such as the works of Halm and Kurth,* etc.; their position also has its weakness, but it lies elsewhere and I shall not touch upon it here.)

If we went so far as to reject Tchaikovsky, it was an act of sincerity, of the will to recovery. But if one throws all of Wagner and Brahms after him without further ado, that is called 'throwing the baby out with the bathwater'; it is infantile foolishness.

As far as the world is concerned, there is a terrible presumption in someone explaining that he is there because of Beethoven's symphonies and not because of the Gewandhaus.†

The attitude of Marées, Hildebrand, etc. (functional spectatorship), has much in common with the tendencies of modern science and hygiene. Not from within, but from outside, through 'knowledge of the correct functions', does one seek to rebuild the disturbed whole. The reason for being involved in authentic and consummate art.

---

* Ernst Kurth (1886–1946) was an immensely distinguished Swiss musicologist, whose masterpiece, *Romantic Harmony and its Crisis in Wagner's 'Tristan und Isolde'* (untranslated, alas), remains of fundamental importance for the understanding of the pivotal position that *Tristan* holds in the history of music.

† The Gewandhaus refers, of course, to Leipzig's great orchestra, of which Furtwängler was for a time the principal conductor; it is the oldest symphony orchestra in Germany.

1929

The great diversity in weight and power which one may observe in the playing of different conductors is too much of a tangible fact for one to be able to ignore it, however much one might have the laudable wish not to fall into the trap of overrating the conductor. To understand all this we should first of all ask ourselves what the conductor actually has to do.

It is a fact that the effectiveness of a conductor, although most visible, is the most hidden and, so to speak, the most mysterious of all the kinds of musical reproduction. Not mysterious in the sense of suggestion, i.e. irrational factors, being more involved than in the case of singers or pianists, but in the sense that his relation to his instrument, the orchestra, the way in which he controls and masters it, is a figurative, an indirect and consequently a more complicated one. We know, for example, that this singer has such and such a voice, this violinist has such and such a tone. Even in the case of the pianist we speak of an individual touch, although he is not close to his instrument in the way that the violinist is to his own Stradivarius, which he takes everywhere, or the singer to his voice, which he has had from birth. In reality, however, every real conductor has just as much his own tone, his own touch, his own voice as those mentioned above, and, indeed, not only with 'his' orchestra – although it is here that he can develop it the most – but with *any* orchestra. Indeed, the importance of the true conductor depends on the extent to which, from the first down-beat – whichever orchestra it may be – he can give his tone to the orchestra, impress his intentions upon it.

If there are repeated tests where the audience does not know the conductor and then has to guess his name after the performance, with negative results, this does nothing to contradict the above apart from the fact that truly original conductors, i.e. those who can really and completely communicate their intentions to the orchestra without stopping halfway, are very rare – much rarer than the general public thinks and would like to believe.

Also, in cases such as these, one may also question the competence of those who are judging, even when they are members of the 'press'; for the capacity for judgement in musical matters is generally much more limited and specialized than one thinks. One critic knows something about songs and is at a complete loss when faced with a pianist or a violinist, another knows something about composition and is helpless when faced with the reproductive work of the conductor. But the critic, because of his position, has to understand everything. (A case of: To whom God granted office, did he also grant intelligence?) Incidentally, such tests would, even with violinists and pianists of my acquaintance, often turn out badly in any case.

The importance of technique in art – often underestimated in former times which were more inclined to irrationality – is today rather overrated. Accordingly, one might expect more insight into technical conditions. This is not true for the conductor; a certain plan of conducting, an academic concept of how to conduct, has certainly emerged in recent times, as it has with the violinist and the pianist – and, incidentally, not to the benefit of the music. But it is striking that precisely the true conductors, Toscanini, Bruno Walter, correspond to this 'plan' only to a very small degree. The fact is that these conductors can immediately impress their own sound on *any* orchestra, while with a didactically correct conductor all orchestras sound the same. In cases such as these, even musicians make use of the slogan of suggestion which is available as a substitute for fuzzy thinking. Not that I do not properly recognize the importance of suggestion, of personality as a complex of central importance; but here, in this case, it is a question of technical matters, of the way in which, through certain movements, a certain sound is mechanically transferred to the orchestra. It is certainly not a question of something mechanical and technical, the end-in-itself sense of certain contemporary theories (which have even taken hold of composition), but rather of the point where technique begins to communicate the spiritual, where consequently, to stay with our subject, it is not the conductor's beat that shapes the sound and artistic intuition, but intuition that shapes the beat.

Discussions of the technical problem of conducting would take us too far from the subject at hand. Also, the relatively young art of conducting is itself too little established to have been theoretically grasped to any extent. What has been written on the subject so far is, where it does not deal with questions of interpretation (Wagner, Weingartner),*

* Felix Weingartner (1863–1924) was a highly influential interpreter of the Austro-German classics, which he performed in a sober, anti-Romantic style. He was the first conductor to record all the Beethoven symphonies, and he wrote an influential book on their interpretation, though it hardly bears comparison with Wagner's great monograph *On Conducting*.

extraordinarily primitive. These questions of interpretation are of course inseparable from the problem of the conductor, and in order to be at all clear about the whole development of conducting in terms of reproductive music-making in recent times, we must reach back rather further. Since western music has existed as an art, and particularly since the liberation of music from worship in the seventeenth century, every age has been formed, altered and led by the *productive* geniuses that it has brought forth. In earlier times this was expressed in the fact that 'productive' and 'reproductive' were barely separable. Bach and Handel were famous as organists, and as far as Beethoven, and even Mendelssohn and Liszt, were concerned, free fantasy was one of their most important means of expression. The creative genius formed, consciously and unconsciously, the style of reproduction of the age. Handel's oratorios, Haydn's string quartets, Mozart's operas, Beethoven's symphonies – each represents a world of its own, and through each the feeling and playing of one or even several generations was influenced and given form. Chopin's piano music, Brahms' chamber works, Verdi's song, Wagner's and later Strauss' orchestra – to name only a few – these creators shaped the style of their times, and the army of reproductive musicians, of pianists, instrumentalists, singers, conductors, could only follow them, make their intentions reality and be guided by them. For these generations, the past existed only in as far as it was connected to the present which, as everything shared one and the same continuous development, was naturally the case. Today, when that is no longer so, when the present chiefly throws down the gauntlet to the past – neither in its own nor in the general interest – now that the new music has been invented where previously there was only good and bad music, the matter is different. However highly we may esteem the attempts of today's producers to attain self-expression, however necessary their often thankless task may be in comparison with former times: it is still an unquestionable fact that, with their style of playing, they no longer control and shape today's style. No amount of encouragement from the conscience of the public can compensate for the basic lack of interest on the part of the audience; the most important phenomena of the past are given increasing power. The emergence of the historical sense can be seen equally as a weakness of the organic and productive and a strength and extension of vision and horizon. But the consequence is that the mass of reproductive artists is no longer led and guided by the productive as it was before. And this is happening precisely at a time when the task of the reproductive artists has been extended and made more difficult by the increased importance of the past. This fully explains the growing importance which is therefore attached to the reproductive artist, and the conductor in particular. He carries on his shoulders a greater burden of responsibility than ever before; for it is no longer the great creator who shapes the style of the age, but the conductor who must shape the style of the individual works from within themselves, from within these alien works. He is not carried by the age, rather he must generally help to carry the age. This creates a whole series of new problems. This situation adequately explains how important the conductor is, and also how rare he is today. Indeed these two things are necessarily connected. It also explains the malformations: the boundless vanity, the innumerable desperate attempts to create effects through charlatanism. But much else is also explained. Where production ceases to be reflected unambiguously and compellingly as the focus of the musical life of the age, otherwise unimportant things take on significance. Here, then, is the source of today's ridiculous personality cult, of conductors of 'genius', who turn up as supermen of the conductor's desk, either 'obsessed' or 'suggestive' or objective, either as animal-tamers and trainers or as male cocottes, who in any case appear infinitely important to themselves and the audience. This is also the source of the cult of the orchestra in the American style, the cult of the instrument itself in its material being, as it corresponds to today's technical attitude. If the 'instrument' no longer exists for the sake of the music, the music immediately comes to exist for the sake of the 'instrument'. Here the proverb also applies: either be a hammer or an anvil. And as a result the whole relationship is reversed. And now we see the emergence of that ideal of technically 'correct' playing which is presented to us as a model by America. In orchestral playing, this takes the form of an even and well-groomed beauty of tone, which never oversteps certain boundaries and represents a kind of objective ideal of the instrument's beauty of tone as such. But whether it is the composer's intention to sound so 'beautiful' . . . Now it becomes apparent, on the contrary, that relentless rhythmic power as well as Beethoven's modesty of tone is basically distorted by an orchestra and conductors such as these, in fact the whole of Beethoven's art, like that of Mozart and Haydn, becomes completely redundant. It survives, like so much today, only in the fossilized opinions of the pedant, as a classical bugbear. From the conductor comes the demand for the most uniform transparency and clarity possible. This leads to the same 'painstaking' detailed work being extended to pieces of the most diverse styles, which call for it to very different degrees. To use an image, the black and white of a Rembrandt, the broad painterly scope of a Rubens are subjected to Dürer's subtle treatment of detail as much as works in the style of Dürer, producing a completely false impression.

It must be stressed that it is always the public which suffers as a result of this. The conductor, the orchestra, etc. benefit from the falsification, for every piece – the image of Rembrandt and Dürer used above may best explain this – works best in its own style. If conductors today declare that their function is to uncover the different layers of the work, that is a ridiculous presumption on their part. It is actually a task which demands extreme productive power in order to do justice to the demands of a work such as a Beethoven symphony.

In music in Germany, we have the greatest concert tradition to defend that ever a people possessed. We have more important things to do than take part in ridiculous sports competitions.

On Bach and the interpretation of early music in general

The less Bach is known, the less naturally evolved the relationship to Bach's music, the more is written about him. Pieces of helpful advice on how to help along the composer and his works, their performance, etc., proliferate like mushrooms.

About the actual 'problem' that lurks within this, that today he is indeed – as is also already the case with Beethoven – infinitely more of an authoritative power than a vital force. For it is clear that not so much would be thought and written about him if the things that relate to his name, to him as a figure, were not somehow a reality in our life today. While it is just as clear on the other hand that a natural, uninterrupted and *real* relationship with Bach is not the general possession of a period that writes and thinks so much nonsense about him, which reproduces him so inadequately in an excessive proportion of its performances, etc. As far as the question of performance is concerned, the naïveté, indeed the primitiveness of everything that our contemporaries have to say on the matter is particularly striking. There is the old argument about the number of performers. It does not yet seem to be apparent that the question of whether one should have sixteen or four first violins, a choir of thirty or 300 people, is simply a matter of the space in which the performance takes place, the question of whether it is being performed as chamber music or not. That the acoustics of the Thomaskirche, as in any church, are different from those of the Philharmonie, and that therefore not only the size of the orchestra must be different, but that the dynamics must be handled differently. It does not seem to be known that the church, with its particular acoustics designed much more for *linear* effects, copes much less well with dynamic variation, and consequently with variation within the individual performance, than the concert hall, which reveals tone with merciless clarity, although it must be known that Bach specifically intended his *Passions*, etc. for practical performance in the Thomaskirche. And it should also be noted, in relation to the question of categorization – and this applies particularly to those who claim that the performer should only execute those expression marks which Bach has set out in the score, and must otherwise completely avoid any emotion or active comment – firstly, all the expression marks, *f, p,* symbols, are indications. An indication of the fact that Germany and France are both states tells us no more about the nature of the difference between Germans and Frenchmen, than the fact that every piece contains the marks *f* and *p* tells us about those *f*s and *p*s. Rather, in each case they are always different, of a different order. But going beyond this it is true that we achieve least from those things which are natural to us. To conclude, from the fact that Bach's music contains no expression marks, that all personal interpretation is to be avoided, is therefore the most misguided thing that we can do. Because it was *taken for granted* that individual performances occurred in an infinitely more free and productive manner than those of our own times, Bach refrained from providing special indications. And the idea that Bach, because he did not dictate it, provides no *espressivo*, attains such a level of naïveté that it could only have been thought up by an intellectual unacquainted with art. They discuss the romanticization of Bach, expressing all their loathing of Romanticism, which they believe must be overcome. But if, instead of coming out with partisan phrases, more concern were shown about these matters, it might be seen that it is not a question of lumping together Romanticism and *espressivo* – whatever one might mean by it. One should be aware of what the characteristic traits of so-called Romanticism actually are, what new things it introduced into the world. This consists of two elements: first the sensuous aspect, beginning with Weber and Schubert and virtually given a sensual stress by Wagner, which is fulfilled to a greater or lesser degree by all Romantic music. Then the personal, the nervous which, strictly speaking, only enters music after Beethoven.

Contrasting rhythms had not yet come into their own. Apart from those thoroughly natural closing *ritardandi* which proceed from the structure of the whole, nuances of tempo are inadmissible. But first and foremost, his music is an expressive music just as much as any other music worthy of the name. That is, the expressive and the musical are in accordance with each other, condition each other, fulfil each other. That is why some call it the most objective music, others the most subjective (which, in a work such as the *Passion*, is completely accurate). Lazy theories on the part of lazy listeners from lazy times, such as today's ludic theory, are ridiculous. Art has never been anything but expression and game at the same time . . . Thus, for example, in a performance of the *Passion*, justice must be done to both. This is only as difficult as it is because – in performance just as much as in creation itself – only the sharpest and brightest of musicians can turn everything expressive into music without allowing anything else to intervene, and, to the same extent, only the very fullest character gifted with the most vital strength of mind can manage to give music its appropriate expression in every case. The medium with which our age is so especially and unflaggingly concerned, to find the sole satisfactory style of performance, but in a form which will be universally comprehensible and valid – so that one can have it black and white, so to speak – has not yet been found. Nor will it be found as long as art remains a living thing; for while that is the case it will not be possible to eliminate reproduction as a productive factor. That may be regrettable, but it is nevertheless the case; life is not to be messed around with, and the conciliatory and universally human mildness of Bach cannot, any more than the tragic and heroic greatness of Beethoven, be affected or faked even by the person who is only concerned with the reproduction of their works. Whoever does not have it within himself to start out with will not be capable of reflecting it, despite all his musicianship.

The fate that befell Romanticism was that its expressive tendencies outgrew its formal capabilities. The fate of our own time – or rather the tendency of our own time as a reaction against Romanticism, which in fact, in a changed and hidden form, is at the root of everything even today – is the fact that the formal aspect has become overgrown. We are not aware that the whole problem, of form on the one hand, content on the other, is only the expression of the impotence of the age. Expression and form can create the most various and wonderful connections – as they actually have in the past – in innumerable variations, but without ever causing one another problems in their necessary mutual relation. When that happens, the worm of destruction is already in the woodwork.

Our other illness is Romanticism as formal inadequacy, or rather: the

Romanticism which we want to overcome is one manifestation of formal inadequacy; the other is ludic formalism, which loses nothing by armouring itself with theories to cover its nudity.

Essay: The role of great art.

We have the greatest geniuses of musical history. We have – through a set of remarkable relationships – brought about a situation whereby we have to defend the existence of these geniuses. The lack of intelligence, the triviality of our intellectual standards has, entirely without our noticing it, grown over time to an unparalleled size. Everything revolves around the issue of whether it [is] still possible for man to be the centre of everything. As a result everything has turned into political chatter of the most stupid and lowest kind. The seed of impotence over the last few years is now springing up. We watched and listened together, we were amazed, as Beethoven's symphonies, Schiller's dramas were preposterously sentimentalized. Nor were we spared the consequences. Complete confusion, absolutely hopeless chaos has fallen upon us.

The reproduction of old works – by this I do not mean the reproduction of those works which no longer affect us and have only historical value, but those which, although far removed from the present, still belong to us. As the present is incapable of great creations, this applies to all *great* works. Therefore the question of how we keep them alive for ourselves is *crucial* for our musical life.

The modern orchestra – a contemporary problem

Germany's first concert orchestras do not make their appearance until the beginning of the twentieth century. The main concert institutions, the Gürzenich,* the Gewandhaus, †, etc., still work with theatre orchestras. The contrast between concert and theatre playing had not yet been invented, or rather the whole question lay, as it did, after all, throughout the whole nineteenth century, in the beneficent obscurity of the unconscious. Only the last few decades, here as elsewhere, have brought about that great development – as it at first appears, in any case

* The Gürzenich Orchestra was for a long time the principal orchestra of Cologne, of which Gürzenich is a suburb.

† See footnote † on p. 21.

– that sudden leap into the light of consciousness. The reason was the waning of the power of those unconscious connections which governed all playing until the age of the younger Strauss. Suddenly, and from all directions, we are seeing the appearance of problems which had not been seen before because – without our knowledge – they had all been mastered.

Production led reproduction along by the hand like a younger sister. Reproduction was shown the way. This dependence was always more or less unconscious, but no less strong for that. The age had a style from which it saw and grasped the styles of the past, and this style was, as it was universally human and had man as its centre, even at the time of Wagner, and despite all the limitations and weaknesses of Romanticism, still capable of finding and embracing the essence of other styles with the certainty of the somnambulist. The invention of the conductor, i.e. the first *conscious* instance of emphasis on reproduction, means the waning of this strength. Historically speaking, the decline of the art of reproduction can be dated to the arrival of the conductor. That does not mean, however, that the conductor is dispensable. On the contrary, his arrival demonstrated his necessity; and it was only in the nature of things that he could carry out his task only in exceptional cases. One cannot argue away a necessity through imagined postulates, etc . . .

Technique

Previously, technique something positive, because it only ran parallel to what it had to express. Since it has become an end in itself, since it has become learnable, something – mind you – which was not the case before, since then it has moved further and further away from its meaning. In this, Hindemith continues on from Strauss. The real problem of our time is therefore how to reunite it with content. Brahms pioneering in this. And now it becomes apparent that there is yet another technique of which today's world is no longer aware, which is infinitely more difficult. The difference between these two concepts of technique contains everything of any importance that today's world should and does not know.

The decline in hero-worship in general and in all ways is bound up with the end of the common goals of love, the decay of the mass soul, nation, etc. One is *always a hero for* something, even if that something is only courage and noble ideas which, for their part, create a higher community.

Two parallel tendencies, which only make up a reality in combination: 1) the increase in calculated effects in word and deed, the calculation of audience effect while relying on 'subjectivity' of perception, the individual desire for effect, 2) the same thing from an 'objective' point of view, namely simplification and concentration. Only in a completely complex state (Bach) where complication and simplicity are everywhere coexistent and where nothing needs to be simplified, do uncontrived effect and individual reality coexist. But all *development* and abstraction demand concentration, simplification. This produces Beethoven.

Essay! 1928

1) The modern orchestra – a contemporary problem.
2) The modern conductor – a contemporary problem.

Reproduction has freed itself from the guidance of production. Hindemith and Strauss certainly have their own performing styles, but translating this to other works, as happens from a certain tendentious point of view, reveals nothing but the fact that they no longer occupy the central position of their predecessors. The change lies in the conditions of the age itself. The past has become more important than before. We are in search of *authenticity*. It would take us too far from the subject at hand to examine the consequences of this. The crucial thing is that the productive artist is no longer (unconsciously) in control, and hence the growth of the importance of the reproductive artist. From the point of view of the music, both conductor and orchestra are overrated – and yet the basic instinct is correct. The thing that is overrated is technique . . . The orchestra as an expression of the soul should never be ignored – but the standards are thrown into complete disarray by an instinctless public, by sensation, desire for effect, etc.

In short: the development of the orchestra up to the American luxury orchestras, which in any case correspond to the American self-image by being the most expensive. The advantages – the disadvantages: different nationalities (e.g. the Viennese sound). Where they are not given a character by the hand of the conductor, they all have something of the beauty contest about them. The question only remains: are all works designed to be played by such beautiful-sounding orchestras? The decline of Beethoven, etc. is bound up with this (relentless rhythm). Sensuous brilliance is not always appropriate. This could all be compensated for by the conductors, but instead it is intensified, because they too tend in the same direction as the orchestras; then: is studying necessary (five rehearsals weekly), what are its intellectual consequences? Nothing can be said against precision, but it practically eliminates the most important thing about playing, the intuition of the moment. This too could be compensated for by the conductors, but instead it is intensified. In Germany we must – and we are the only ones who can speak on the subject of concert-music, since all symphonic music is German – we must be aware of where the centre of the music lies. We have more responsible things to do than to take the old argument of which is better, the Boston or the Philadelphia Orchestra, more seriously than it deserves to be taken.

There were two major forces behind the birth of the modern concert orchestra: reproduction, freed from the control of production and turned into an end in itself, and learnable technique in the 'modern' sense.

But the same thing is true of both orchestras and conductors: by recognizing that they are overrated, by identifying their redundancy and indeed the damage they do to music in this sense, we do nothing to improve matters. It is a question of turning them into what they could be, of avoiding the American temptations. People today are still not aware of this, and on the contrary fall straight into the trap.

It is not primarily a question of becoming acquainted with the difference of the various styles. For that can also be done – apparently – from outside.

The only orchestra that can be compared, in terms of its method, with what is being performed by today's American luxury orchestras, is the Concertgebouw Orchestra in Amsterdam. The other orchestras, in Germany and France, in Italy and England, were working orchestras. They did not exist for their own sake, but on the one hand for the sake of the past, to which these countries have various internal attachments – how different are the roles of Bach, Mozart and Beethoven in Germany and America – and on the other hand for the sake of the artists. It was Strauss and Hindemith, Debussy and Stravinsky who described the curve of musical events here, and not orchestras and virtuosos. Completely preoccupied with their own issues, the Germans did not understand what was happening in America, and are now seeing with astonishment that there, as in Holland, etc., they now have orchestras the like of which we do not possess. (Only the Berlin Philharmonic

Orchestra, the most outstanding of Germany's pure concert orchestras, can be to some extent compared with the Americans in its working conditions, and even then only in the concerts which I conduct, as it is otherwise nothing but a hired orchestra with completely different requirements.) And however little we may be inclined, from our own point of view, to assign a decisive value to the orchestra as such – or to reproduction in general as such – just as little can we ignore the athletic perfection of these newly created instruments. This is a part of the whole character of the age. The passion for seeing things from the point of view of sport, and evaluating them according to the standard of the technical perfection to which their functions have developed – for their own sake – has taken hold of Germany, along with its standards of world records and tournaments. In America the question of whether or not a performance of a Beethoven symphony, say, is good, is entirely secondary compared with the question of whether the Philadelphia or the Boston Orchestra is better (precisely because this is a matter of taste). We have not yet reached that point; in the meantime we cannot and will not close our minds to the special merit that is nevertheless created by this; indeed, as things stand, how German musical life will solve this problem is still a crucial question.

The ways and extent to which the American method is superior to our own became immediately clear to me when I visited America as conductor of the New York Philharmonic Orchestra. There, thanks to the money behind it (and that is always privately raised), it is possible to assemble the best forces from the whole world. So, for example, the violinists are mainly chosen from Austria and Bohemia, the woodwind-players from France, the brass-players from Germany,,, etc. The technical virtuosity, lightness, elegance and natural beauty of tone of such an orchestra are extraordinary.

For this apparatus, which as basic material is already the best in the world that money can buy, the best conductors are employed (or those who are seen as such) as the most judicious and shrewdest experts who could manage such a precious apparatus, take it to the peak of its ability and keep it there. For the fact that this is not achieved by the individual musician, for all the enormous – relative – importance that he has, but that orchestral art is much more of an ensemble art, is something of which they are much more aware over there than we are. Conductors therefore have an amount of time at their disposal, which, in our own musical industry, would be completely beyond the realms of possibility. Thus the conditions for the very best performances are established; the American public is aware of this, and not without a degree of pride.

The more fully we seek to acknowledge the justice of this pride, the more we must also recognize the major drawbacks of these priorities. All the more so when one bears in mind that people who are actually in America, because their field of vision is narrowed down by the whole attitude, are unable, and naturally unable, to do this.

First of all there is the composition of the orchestras, made up of players of many nationalities. Certainly the French woodwind-players are incomparable, certainly the Austrian violinists are warmer than those from other nations, the German brass-players more self-assured, more majestic. But how do they fit together? This puts one in mind of the artist who, in order to create a Venus, assembled, from various models, the most beautiful nose, the most beautiful eyes, arms, legs, etc., in the opinion that he could thus not fail to assemble the most beautiful figure. Perhaps to create a synthetic stone that catches the eye of the non-expert; but can a real diamond be made in this way?

But even more important than the character of tone which I have mentioned are the different ways in which the various nations feel. An Italian, a French, a German orchestra not only have their own particular sound, but also their own particular kind of instinctive, living way of playing, in which the feeling of the individual vibrates sympathetically with the feeling of the mass, as if of its own accord. This common feeling is of the greatest importance in the performance of every melody, every bar, and even a decisive conductor can only ever compensate for it to a certain degree. It is an imponderable question precisely with regard to those most delicate vibrations of the performance which, because they are spontaneous, can necessarily not be achieved by rehearsals and drill, however much time is put into them, and which are inseparable from a living performance. An orchestra with this uniform tonal character in all its sections, with a naturally unified way of feeling, with such roundedness and homogeneity of tone in the *tutti* passages, produced of its own accord and not by being externally and artificially smoothed off, like that of the Vienna Philharmonic, cannot be found in America.

It is easy to recognize the diversity of these ways of feeling if one plays a Brahms symphony with an Italian, the *Meistersinger* with a French, and *Trovatore* with a German orchestra. Of course one might think that these differences could and should be compensated for by the conductors – indeed that this should perhaps be one of the conductor's chief tasks. Elsewhere I shall explain why this does not happen, why, on the contrary, it is the public, or rather the music itself, that has to pay the price for this unsatisfactory condition.

The most disastrous consequence of the lack of unified feeling is the constriction and limitation of the improvisatory element of playing in general. The smaller the independent and homogeneous part played by the individual musician, the more the conductor's intended agogic, dynamic nuances, etc. are either left out altogether or carried out in more or less mechanical ways, that is, through numerous rehearsals, through endless drilling. But the most important and the best thing, namely that imperceptible variability of tempo and colour, can in no way be achieved mechanically by means of rehearsals. In the end the conductor is often faced with the decision of either having to exaggerate or of completely neglecting his intentions in this regard. Either without a natural structure in the beat, or with studied intentional 'nuances' – a situation, then, which also to a high degree corresponds to contemporary reality.

Often this great expenditure of time on rehearsal work because of the composition of the orchestra [is] much more of a crucial necessity than it is in an orchestra which has a natural uniformity of feeling; so when it is exaggerated, when there are too many rehearsals, there is a danger of completely killing off the improvisatory element, a danger which is at least as disastrous for the conductor as it is for the orchestra. The possibility of rehearsing *ad infinitum*, which is sometimes portrayed as a special privilege, necessarily diminishes the sensitivity and consequently the quality of the conductor's technique – about which more remains to be said elsewhere – as well as the psychological sensitivity of the orchestra, which becomes used to typical, uninspired, craftsmanlike work. Even certain qualities described as 'technical', such as good sight-reading, etc., are more or less forfeited by a lack of practice. The higher level of technical correctness and control achieved does not make up for the lack of inspiration, but instead has the most disastrous consequences for the playing as a whole. Excessive technical control, that is, an evenly-accomplished perfection in all the details of a piece, which are thus turned into something quite different from what their creators intended – that they should be a part of the whole – prevents the intellectual cohesion of these details into a whole, and the natural and productive way in which details are seen and interpreted via the whole is reversed. Improvisation is lost as both essence and idea. Improvisation, which does not represent a mere accident, an attribute which one may or may not have, but rather simply the source of all great, creative, necessary playing.

The sense of the orchestra as an artistic medium is that this body, consisting of 90–100 different people, different heads and hands, becomes one instrument through which a soul, a feeling, an intuition is communicated to the listener in its tiniest details. The more it achieves this, the more it loses the vanity of wanting to be something itself, the more it becomes the mediator, the communicator, the vessel and point of entry of the divine, speaking through the great masters.

Here the apparently quite special question of modern orchestral art comes into contact with the question of the most general or marked foundations of our playing as a whole. And the decision will depend precisely on the final stance taken by Germany. For Germany – this statement is purely historical and objective and has nothing to do with nationalism of any kind – is the actual creator of pure instrumental music in the grand style; a true symphony has never been written by non-Germans. (Half-symphonists, such as Berlioz, César Franck, Tchaikovsky, are in all essentials completely under the influence of Germany.)

A bored, hedonistic society that keeps orchestras as one keeps prize dogs, as a sport – we have not yet reached that point. We still have a past which we value, we still have a fighting present. We can only take a stance of orchestral *l'art pour l'art* if the past is dead as a really vital force, if the present has ceased to fight.

The conductor

And only then will the conductor fully occupy the position that he – does not deserve. The importance of, and the search for, the major conductor has increased enormously, particularly in most recent times, marked as they are by hugely heightened communications and the corresponding growth in the influence of the press and of capital cities. The smaller towns have developed an almost obligatory dependence on opinions invented in the big cities, often very much at the cost of true relations, as people in the smaller towns are unaware just to what extent developments in the capital cities are influenced by all kinds of factions and opinion-makers. Personality cults in the worst sense are established, and that which could be learned and achieved through a diversity of conductors and their abilities, through the development of one's own ear and judgement, is practically prevented by this over-nurtured, uncritical belief in authority. The conductor is given a crucial importance which he does not, in fact, generally have. This is bound up with the fact that externals are hugely overrated – the important thing is seen as being not what it sounds like, but how the conductor clears his throat, how he spits, how he stands, what he does with his hands. What is observed and noticed is not how he realizes the immanent sense of a piece, how he awakens the life within it to communal experience, but how he interprets it, with the result that it is the variety of intepretations that is seen as interesting, while their degree of power and truthfulness is treated as a side-issue. The whole basis of the conductor's occupation, as well as his name and his fame is, as one can see, largely fragile and inauthentic, and it is no wonder that illegitimate celebrities, really dazzling charlatans, can cover their expenses quite nicely in this profession.

Of course it would be a mistake to make the profession as such responsible for this state of affairs, to throw the baby out with the bathwater and claim from now on that the conductor is unimportant and irrelevant. In this matter the popular instinct is right, that the conductor in a performance is the needle on the scales; that he and he alone has it within his power to let a piece appear in all its inherent brilliance, or to ruin it from its very foundations.

1930

Sketches

The expression of intention – here, say, like the draught on . . . about . . . to take the work, or all-too-irresponsible outbursts of temper. I am of the opinion that I do not know Beethoven from his life, of which we know nothing, or even from his handwriting, but more from his works.

The interruption of tradition in composition first of all isolated fact. In time it becomes clear that a change in playing was and had to be the result of this. The capacity for interpreting the past was lost. Experiments.

Literal rendering

Literal rendering – in as far as a performance cannot deviate from the master's intention as laid down in the score – is actually a self-evident prescription, so self-evident that any further discussion is superfluous. The interesting thing is not this concept, which in itself cannot even be called a concept, but the fact that it could become a programme. This can only be understood historically, as a reaction to a type of performance which was usual at the end of the nineteenth century, and which was already described by Weingartner as 'robot conducting'. The truly interesting question is why the robot conductor and the robot pianist (incidentally more prevalent as an irritation today than the conductor) did not appear until the end of the nineteenth century, and not, say, in Beethoven's or Chopin's time, although the demands of the music of that time differed in no way, in terms of the freedom of performance, from their status in 1901. It becomes apparent that what we mean by the concept of the robot conductor makes its appearance in an age in which music was slowly becoming incapable of producing an independent performing style, in which the style of the age was gradually turning into the age's sensitivity to style, in which performance and music are moving apart and, as a result, performance is on the one hand becoming a problem, and on the other a 'task' in its own right. Now it had to bear a responsibility that had previously been borne by the composer. As a result a burden has been placed on its shoulders, which it cannot bear because not all interpreters are geniuses and because now genius was suddenly being demanded from interpreters. Not by the public, say, but quite instinctively by the audience, since everything I have mentioned occurred as an unconscious process.

Essays:

1) Orchestras.

2) Conductors.

3) Crisis in musical life and musical experience (i.e.: no time and no concentration, no opportunity to experience form).

4) Style and life.

Previously style defined life, now it would constrain it. A Catholic of 1500 is different from a contemporary renegade. Today it is true that we have the least style if we put on a style. Style is a uniform, not a costume.

5) Complication, simplicity, comprehensibility in music, ferments of progress.

Toscanini in Germany

An article on the true situation of German music-making in 1930
As a conductor in Germany, the land of orchestras and conductors, Toscanini had a success enjoyed by barely any other foreign artist. It is worth exploring the reasons for this success, and testing it for its authenticity, durability and significance.

The unanimity of his success in the press was striking, for within the music press in Germany – as in other areas – political differences have been greatly intensified, and unanimity about purely artistic phenomena is therefore encountered much more rarely today. Of course there is also the relative predominance of non-objective viewpoints. Without wishing to characterize or belittle Toscanini's success by saying this, it must be said that he has the advantage, with the left-wing press, of not being a German – something which has a very particular effect in the Berlin press. But on the other hand he is not a Jew, which again recommends him to the other side in Munich. Otherwise, the fact that foreignness has always played an excessive part particularly in German musical life is something that even the most convinced internationalist must admit. At the time when Rossini came to Vienna, Germany was not only at the zenith of a truly great, solid musical culture, but there were also people like Beethoven, Schubert, Weber, etc. walking about. They ceased to exist for the Germans when the Italian master appeared.

And this was true not only for an easily inflamed, easily influenced superficial audience, but also for the best people in the country, such as Goethe, Schopenhauer, etc. – in so far as they knew nothing about music. Might this case not be compared with that of Toscanini? But this is all by the way, as it really has nothing to do with the matter which exclusively concerns us here. What are Toscanini's real qualities? The only thing left to us is a precise analysis of the facts. It was understandable that such an analysis should have been so terribly rare in the German press. First of all it is not so easy, even for the most experienced critic, to weigh up the real qualities of a conductor straight away, particularly not if he comes with a foreign orchestra. And then in the case of Toscanini prejudice and expectation also play a large part. In fact it was always possible to read what one knew already: the very great precision of the orchestra, although in truth this was in no way the strength of Toscanini's Berlin concerts – the literal rendering, although in Germany we have had much more literal rendering of the *Eroica* (which is, in my opinion, not to say anything against Toscanini, as literal rendering, the true ideal of the pedant, is actually neither new nor an ideal).

I myself have heard Toscanini in Milan and Zurich, in New York and Berlin, and not only once or twice, but at numerous rehearsals as well, and have therefore had opportunities to judge him such as a German critic can only have to judge German conductors whom he sees many times.

I shall base my discussions only on a precise description of the two Berlin concerts, for which I must naturally appeal to the memory of the audience.

The first began with Haydn's *Clock* Symphony.* The introductory *Adagio* immediately arouses tension: the tempo, unusually restful for Haydn, the stiff execution, the extended *crescendi* gave the whole a certain seriousness that seemed to edge into the sphere of Beethoven – still, it was something. Certainly, psychological coherence and stylistic unity had to be abandoned with the subsequent *allegro*, but one could still accept that the brash, almost violent interpretation of the first *tutti* was an attempt to produce this stylistic unity, and place the grandeur of the introduction alongside an *allegro* interpreted with a bias towards grandeur. It certainly became clear that this was an error, for even during the *allegro* it became clear – something repeated over and over

---

* Haydn's 'Clock' Symphony is number 101.

again later on – that the *tutti* is precisely the usual Toscanini *tutti*, on which the sonata form relies, and that evidently not the slightest attempt is made to turn it into a real musical and psychological connection of contrasts. The *tutti* in itself was certainly given a very elastic rhythmical character, which has nothing to do with precision but which the average listener calls precision and accuracy. It is a certain militaristically exact spirit of playing, which is incidentally not something exclusive to Toscanini, but which is the fashion in America today, as is evident in the instrumentalists who come from there, even the greatest among them. Significantly more impressive, more than the *tuttis* at any rate, were the more tender *cantabile* passages in the first movement of the Haydn symphony, which, despite the rather slower tempo and the resultant, still rather deliberate-sounding treatment, most beautifully brought out a major quality of Toscanini's orchestral sound, its floating slenderness and sweet lightness in all the *cantabile* passages. If the first movement was a mixture of the beautiful and the less beautiful, I must say that as the *andante* progressed my interest waned considerably. The carrying of the melody in the violins in no way corresponded to the introductory bars, delightfully played by the orchestra's wonderful bassoonist, which have given the symphony its nickname. Over the basis of the mechanically hammering rhythm of the accompanying figure, a freely breathing, floating melody should be made to blossom, an immortal inspiration of Haydn's, in its particularly precious loveliness. Far from it: over this too, the iron rhythm forges ahead with steely determination, the whole thing has a stiff and soulless effect (incidentally, the symphony is also available on record, so that anyone may easily check this up). I should like to hear a passage like this done by Bruno Walter, for example.

I will spare the reader any further progress through the symphony, as the characteristic features had already become apparent in the above, and were repeated in the course of the other movements. The impression of the whole was therefore divided, because the essence of Haydn's music and its style, that inimitable mixture of cheerful sweetness and tautened energy which makes Haydn one of the greatest masters ever to have created anything, was not forthcoming, so that the individually apparent qualities of the performance hampered each other rather than complementing and mutually supporting one another.

Expectations of Debussy's *La Mer* were more eager from the outset; one might have expected that here the Italian would be particularly understanding in assisting the Frenchman with his delivery, as one Latin to another. The people who know *La Mer* either very little or not at all –

in contrast to New York, it is very seldom played in Berlin – might still be of this opinion after the performance and attribute the work's lack of effect to the composer. In fact the disappointment was greater than in almost any other piece performed by Toscanini. His even, primitive and unintellectual manner so consistently, and with such a naïve lack of awareness, ignored Debussy's sensitive tonal language, that one could only wonder why he had performed the work at all, and one completely understood its comparatively slight resonance in France. I shall refrain from going into the details of this work which will in any case be unknown to the majority of readers, and treat the course of the rest of the evening in a more summary fashion. The second part included a piece by Donizetti, at which one could only wonder that Toscanini, as an Italian, should have chosen this unusually feeble work – even by Italian standards – by the otherwise outstanding composer to present to the people of Berlin. The subsequent scherzo from *Midsummer Night's Dream*, always one of the orchestra's famous *pièces de resistance*, revealed a particularly striking quality in the strings' excellent *spiccato* technique, which, played like this in Germany, would have at best a barely subsidiary role. It also showed up certain inadequacies in the passages where everyone played together, which we shall go into later in a different context. The overture to *Leonora*,* which concluded the concert, presented Toscanini, for the first time, with a thoroughly weighty task in the German sense. Here his failure struck even those people whose prejudices had stifled the beginnings of any criticism. Here too I only want to bring out the few characteristic elements, which were repeated everywhere in the course of the performance, and which must therefore be seen as characteristic features of his interpretation. That such a characteristic curve as the modulation to E-flat major in the ninth bar of the introduction to the Florestan theme remained thoroughly unimpressive, because '*streng im Tempo*' was passed over without the slightest awareness of its existence, is only by the way. The functional meaning of the modulations in the long term, which in absolute music such as Beethoven's play such a different role, seems to be completely unknown to his naïve feeling for opera music. But beyond this too, there is not the slightest attempt to transmute purely musical forms into a spiritual and psychological insight. Particularly illuminating in this respect was the introduction of the *allegro* theme. Instead of letting it, as Beethoven intended and imagined, grow out of the held B-flat in

---

* The overture to *Leonora* which Toscanini performed was no. 3.

the introduction, in its volume – B[eethoven] indicates *pp* – as much as in the tempo and identity of the theme, which must stay in proportion throughout, he begins, suddenly and without any motivation, in a cheerful *mf*, liberally fast, as if it were the *allegro* of a Haydn symphony. But neither does he make up for this slap in the face, dealt out to the feeling and knowledgeable listener, when he noticeably holds back, in a disagreeable operatic manner, at the peak of the *crescendo* of the *ff* repetition of the theme – where did Beethoven suggest that? – while later at:

etc. he seems completely unaware of the specifically Beethovenian attitude and the tense stillness which hovers over the entire passage, and helps himself through it with a sudden, completely unmotivated acceleration, etc. I shall refrain from drawing any further attention to the number of misunderstandings which followed one another in quick succession within the piece. The final word about his Beethoven interpretation cannot be said without also including the *Eroica* played the next day.

Of the *Eroica* it must be said that it is among the works of Beethoven's extrovert youthful period, which does not yet bring opposites crashing together and exploit them as the later Beethoven does, but rather lets everything unfold in a more epic manner, in a broad succession. If it is played in more or less reasonable tempi, that is not too quickly, simply and without special effects, this is still present to a certain degree – just as it can also still be heard in the work of many conductors who find the much more difficult Fifth or even the Ninth Symphony impossible.

Toscanini's impetuous nature, which (forms the true key to his world-wide success and) is characteristic of him, here enters a synthesis with certain similar traits in Beethoven, which find their expression precisely in the *Eroica*, for example in its first movement. The audience doubtless feels this, and an impression is formed which cannot be devalued by the fact that its relation to art as such is a very tenuous one. But we cannot let this prevent us from giving priority to the demands of the art-work as such. Toscanini rises to this with much less success. Precisely here, in the press, which is so easily suggestible, much has been said about literal rendering. But that is exactly what Toscanini's performance was not. It is said that the extreme *ritardando* of the song-theme of the second movement goes back to a tradition handed down by Beethoven's friend Wegeler. Without a doubt, Toscanini broadens much too much, for which he gets his come-uppance in the conclusion. For in the bars 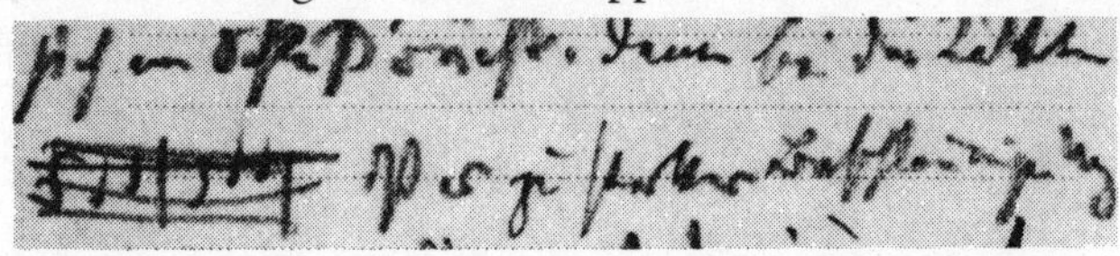

he is forced into a strong *accelerando*, which on the one hand completely fails to recognize the still restrained, tense character of the passage, but on the other hand completely disregards and destroys the origin of this figure, which, in the preceding bars, is the accompanying figure to the wind melody. Doubtless he has never understood the origin of this passage. But as a result – and that is the reason for our probing deeper into this point, which can serve us as one example for many, for the same process, indeed the same misunderstanding, recurred many times during the symphony – he reveals his lack of acquaintance with and his naïve ignorance of one of the main demands of properly symphonic music, the demand for organic development, the living and organic growth of every melodic, rhythmic, harmonic formation out of what has gone before. What was striking once more in the first movement of the Eroica was the noisy, undifferentiated, elastic and energetic *tuttis* which quite suddenly appeared alongside the *cantabile* passages, played with a degree of embarrassment and a hint of sentimentality. Apart from these two contrasts, however, there was . . . nothing. All those things that make up the actual content of Beethoven's music, namely that which is *organic*, in the way it passes from one thing to the next, etc., fail to exist for Toscanini. There are technical reasons for this too, as we shall see later. But we now recall that until quite an advanced age he was never anything but an Italian *Kapellmeister*, who always thinks in the forms of Italian opera music, for which the *tutti* on the one hand and the purely homophonic aria on the other remain the basic musical concepts. We also recall that Italian music – however highly we may esteem it – has only produced one composer of absolute musical form since Scarlatti, and that incomprehension in the face of the essence and meaning of the sonata – which in all its major examples is a German creation – is almost its chief characteristic. How can one demand that the Italian opera-conductor should deny his own self? And there we also have the meaning of his treatment of the *Eroica*. Either *tutti*s or arias – the entire infinitely rich scope of Beethoven's music is broken down into these two elements. Truly a royally primitive process. The exaggeratedly sluggish tempo of the death-march – what about literalness? – could also be explained by peculiar needs. The march-like aspect was completely unrecognizable even in the realistic first bars, and Beethoven's gloomy, tearless and wordless mourning is dissolved into beautiful-sounding sentimentality. Particularly typical of this is the exaggerated, sentimentally extended treatment, which practically slips into the realm of tastelessness – something of which, incidentally, Toscanini cannot otherwise be accused – of the fairly long violin phrase finally continued on the flute shortly before the conclusion. I will not go into further details, of which many could be added from the course of the last two movements as well as the Brahms *Variations* which followed the symphony. That Brahms is not exactly Toscanini's domain was only to be expected, and it was probably more an obeisance before the *genius loci* that led him to play Brahms here in Germany. Here too, the Italian operatic *Kapellmeister* did not deny his own self. The fast variations, conceived as special effects rather in the sense of Verdi's mocking choruses, played much too fast and thus completely losing their sense as parts of a strongly-executed work of variations, revealed this just as much as the highly over-extended, sentimental 6/8 *grazioso* variation.

For *Tod und Verklärung*, that inspired piece of 'theatre' by the young Strauss, the theatrical *Kapellmeister*'s sense of effect was an advantage. Admittedly the first part was very uneven. Toscanini's completely homophonic feeling does not allow the melodic line in the basses, the many lively middle voices, etc. to emerge according to Strauss' wishes. The death itself has been heard both more realistically and more impressively. The beginning of the transfiguration was lacking in any tonal imagination, in a stiff and slow tempo, and created an extremely boring effect. But the conclusion saved the day, as they say. And rightly; the relentless, emphatic strength and breadth with which Toscanini constructed and executed the closing build-up and the finale were simply correct, great and admirable. Thus the great and authentic final effect of the concert as a whole was placed beyond any doubt, and I do not wish to belittle the merit of the others by saying that, with this piece and at this point, such an effect would perhaps not be all that terribly hard to achieve. It still remains a real effect, and these are still rare in the concert hall.

We have attempted a brief characterization of the interpreter of the works. A word about the orchestral conductor still needs to be said from the technical point of view. Here one might apply Keyserling's saying to Toscanini: Make a virtue out of necessity. In contrast to, say, Nikisch, he has no innate manual talent, and what he does have has been fought for and worked upon. But cerain striking shortcomings have remained;

above all the enormous waste of space in the *forte*. The size of his beat in the *f* is such that it makes any differentiation impossible. As a result, these *tuttis* are all the same, they sound noisy and are always at the same volume, and the conductor's ability to bring out differences within the *forte*, in the lower or middle range or even in important major parts, is quite minimal.

I do not hold with taking the conductor all too seriously as a person. It is of no consequence whether or not he is disciplined, whether or not he looks good. But I must acknowledge his importance, not because he is playing such a role today, but because the lives of many masterpieces absolutely depend on him.

Toscanini believes what he says, that he plays, as far as possible, literally and in a disciplined manner – not superior and not rational – but still himself and the orchestra.

His greatness lies in his character. This helps him in the eyes of the world, but it does not, unfortunately, help art. One can say with certainty that if he were a greater artist, if he had deeper insights, a livelier imagination, greater warmth and devotion to the work, he would not have become so disciplined. And this is why his success is disastrous.

Those of us who hold great music close to our hearts can never replace true artists with prima donnas and others who are just as disciplined, even if they appear in the sheep's clothing of literal rendering. The view, previously held unconsciously in Germany, that inspiration and understanding in art are more important than discipline and autocratic behaviour, is still correct.

The 'literal' rendering of classical music
A crucial musical question

Literal rendering plays a major role in the practice and reception of music today. If one is to believe the eulogies, it is the morality, the ethos of a whole new generation of musicians. Fidelity to the work. Placing the creator above the private person is naturally quite self-evident, something with which every schoolboy is familiar and must be familiar, and in spite of this it is today given the value of a demagogic slogan, a watchword.

It is worth examining the deeper reasons for this state of affairs, as it is very instructive for the analysis of today's intellectual situation.

First of all the concept of literal rendering itself: of course it is an act of almost infantile naïveté – and today's public is not lacking in traits of this – to propagate literal rendering as such as an 'ideal'. If it is an ideal, it is at best a pedantic one. Fidelity to the letter as against fidelity to the sense, formalism as against life – everything that is dead, decayed, already outgrown or yet to be outgrown, is present in the concept of literal rendering, as soon as this is taken to be a true ideal, and therefore a goal to be striven for and the final point of desire. If it is not this, however, but only a precondition for it – then it would, as I have said, be something self-evident, which would not merit discussion.

There are two reasons for its being discussed so much in spite of this. First of all it is a manifestation of reaction. We have behind us – and to an extent we are still living in the midst of it – the age of the excesses of interpreters who want to let their own light shine forth, who use the works of the great composers to satisfy their little virtuoso vanities. Our age – and especially the most recent past – can be seen as the heyday of this phenomenon.

But then – and this is even more important! – the art of interpretation has lost the control of the creative person, so that it has become an end in itself. This control – of which one was not previously aware, but which nevertheless had an inevitable and beneficial effect – was much stronger than was generally imagined. Indeed, it is not the so-called interpreters who create the interpretative style of an age, but the creators – apart from a few productive interpreters such as Liszt and Rubinstein. Under the compulsion of the creators, unnoticed yet having a profound effect, there emerged an art of interpretation which, taking the whole, the creative, as its starting-point, as it were inherited the structuring relation to detail – the alpha and omega of all reproduction. This natural hegemony of creativity has been destroyed today. Since the age of Strauss, Pfitzner,* Debussy, and even the most recent works of Stravinsky, it is no longer possible to see a unified line in the

* Hans Pfitzner (1869–1949) was the leading conservative German composer of his time, continuing to write in the tradition of the early German Romantics, especially Weber, Mendelssohn and Schumann. His finest work is the magnificent opera, or 'musical legend' as he called it, *Palestrina* (first performed in Munich, 1917). But he also wrote other operas, some of them highly successful, a good deal of orchestral music, and much chamber music. He was a prolific and vitriolic polemicist, notorious especially for his attacks on Busoni and Berg. Though he was fiercely nationalistic and anti-Semitic, he quarrelled with the Nazis and, like Furtwängler, narrowly escaped ending up in a concentration camp. Furtwängler's frequent references to him suggest that he found his attitudes sympathetic, but most of his music – much of which he premièred – disappointing.

development of creativity, and one can see the beginning of those specific and partial phenomena which are no longer responsible for musical development as a whole, and which therefore feel they are not a continuation of the past but are rather in opposition to it. In this way they also lose their external relation to this past, from which they wish to be quite separate, and also, as a result, the ability to interpret it directly and correctly. The interpreters – at least in so far as they are concerned with this past – are thrown back on themselves. It is this that gives rise to the massive insecurity, the proliferation of theories and opinions, the vanity of trivial men, self-importance, the abuse of the great organic art-works . . . effects. The lessons of the few creative artists among us, of the Strausses and Pfitzners, are neither understood nor followed (and this is all the more true the further one is from the centre of creative events, something which could best be judged by those who knew what was on offer in America). Something else as well: late Romanticism, Impressionism and the successors of Wagner placed an exaggerated stress on colour and expression over and above construction. This specialization itself, which was a sign of the times – the particularly German tendency to formlessness and the exaggeration of the expressive side – had severely weakened the relationship to great, that is, complete music, in which expression and form are in balance with one another. This insecurity finally opened the floodgates to empty capriciousness. The theory came about that tempi, dynamics, in fact all questions of interpretation, were matters of taste. More or less ridiculously, interpreters became more prominent than creators, as true . . . drawing their strength from the creators and usually ending up by ruining them. It was the onset of chaos; and the consideration of the score, of what the authour wanted, the demand for fidelity to the work, was a natural reaction to this, a deliverance. In the face of this professed capriciousness – whether sailing under the colours of the desire to make art contemporary, or of the theory of individual taste as the one true faith – consideration of the original, 'literal' rendering is thoroughly understandable. And one could draw some comfort from this if music were a matter of museum knowledge, of education. But it is not; it is a matter of life, and the moment it loses its authentic, necessary relation to life, it becomes, more than any other art, superfluous.

Now it also becomes apparent, however, that both tendencies, apparently so mutually contradictory, towards unlimited freedom of interpretation on the one hand and literal rendering on the other, flow from the same source. Both stem from the deep insecurity of the age when faced with the great art of the past, the complete lack of any instinctively assured direction. Out of a fear of chaos, one adheres slavishly to the letter rather than the sense; there is also a certain real experience at work here. It was noticed that a so-called subjective interpretation had a better rather than a worse effect on the great works. With 'literal' rendering, the effect – which is then, throwing the baby out with the bathwater, enthusiastically decried for all classical works – is more or less ignored, and one is satisfied with the good conscience of having realized the composer's intention [with] that which one produces, of having allowed his character to emerge from behind the work, or whichever of those pseudonyms for dead and didactic styles of playing – so popular today – one chooses. Of course there are very unexpected consequences to this. The theory will suddenly arise, say, that the works of Beethoven – not to mention Brahms and other 'bourgeois' composers – are out of date and no longer affect us – nothing but a consequence of these performances. Or it may even be declared that concert life as a whole is dead, that music is finished.

All these theories, unimportant as they are in reality, are relatively justified today when applied to our way of making music; this is undeniable.

If the personality is overestimated in the individualistic model, in the literal model it is eliminated as far as possible. More or less unconsciously, one has the feeling that interpretation is something that must be learnable. In the search for a solution one happens upon other social tendencies of the age, and America is especially important in this. For in America – without the burden of an overly responsible relationship to the content of the music – not only has the individualistic model been given freest rein, but it has also been taken furthest as a mechanical and technical control of playing. This was combined with the idea of literal rendering as something which, like everything mechanical, it was possible to learn. They want to have something down in black and white.

1931

Rendering and performance of old music

When, with R. Strauss and the young Stravinsky, an end was seen to the flow of production which had had a compelling effect on the whole of Europe, old music began to take on a new meaning. This had been prepared a long time previously, as had the end of production. The relations between the old and the new music began to be revised.

There are people who include under the heading of old music everything that is not directly a part of contemporary production. For these people, then, old music and old iron are more or less the same thing. It is one of those cheap generalizations which are customary today and which have no bearing on reality. The fact is that since the uninterrupted direct development of musical production began to flag, since modern music ceased to be the immediate and exhaustive expression of the modern audience, of modern man – in the last 10–20 years, say – older music, the music of the recent and distant past, has been given a new and unexpected importance. It is attracting some of the lively interest that was previously reserved for contemporary production; one's relationship to it becomes a problem, a duty. That does not mean that it has already become historical, that it no longer concerns us. On the contrary, if that were so, it could not be a problem. According to the level of importance that one sees old music as having for contemporary man, its performance also receives a different stress. Or the other way round; whether the performance is good or bad, inadequate and exhausting or unsatisfactory and schematic, depends very considerably on the way one sees old music, how much of a vital force it is for contemporary man – in a word, *how seriously it is taken*. It is in accordance with the ideology of the late nineteenth century and therefore the theory of the average which still prevails today – which can be notably combined with certain 'revolutionary' efforts – to see and understand the music of the past and, if possible, all music up until our own time, in an historical way. The relativism of art-history, which has had music appreciation following close on its heels like a frightened little sister, has also created a situation whereby the Parthenon find and certain Indian sculptures are given the same historical importance, whereby we successfully seek to stand aside from the whole drama, where possible, as uninvolved and objective observers, and pride ourselves on the fact without realizing just how much we are sawing off the branch on which we are sitting.

1932*

Some of what you mentioned in your speech on the occasion of the fifty-year Jubilee of the Philharmonic Orchestra provoked violent opposition. Were you aware of this while you were speaking? No – this opposition came as a surprise. It is based almost entirely on a misunderstanding of what I said, and I only realized later that it was a mistake to touch at all on such delicate and vulnerable points as the place of contemporary music within musical practice. I should have had to be much more thorough and detailed to be properly understood. Otherwise it would be better to remain silent!

What are these misunderstandings that you mention? First and foremost I have not spoken of opinions – not even my opinions – but only of practical experiences of which, having been in active musical life for more than twenty years, I can certainly say a thing or two. In this case, opinions, theories are of little interest to me – above all I have not, as many understood me to have done, spoken against, but rather in favour of modern production, and so it was far from being my intention to use a cheap oppostion of modern and familiar classical music to speak in the defence of pleasurable and thoughtless comfort, and to make life even harder for contemporary production, which is already in a difficult position. On the contrary, I have emphatically spoken in its best interest, which can of course only be fair if one looks the facts in the face. And it is a fact that of the production of the last twenty years – in comparison with earlier times – horribly little has remained in the concert hall. And if I say that contemporary music cannot replace Mozart and Beethoven in the eyes of the audience that is simply an empirical fact. An empirical fact that cannot be taken seriously if one does not take the public seriously. An empirical fact seen from the lofty standpoint of the last twenty years. It has only a very particular relationship to the audience; the immediate reactions of the audience to new works are very often thoroughly wrong; its reaction in the longer term is always right. This is the only explanation for the fact that anything of any importance wins

* It hasn't been possible to determine for whom this sort of a letter was intended.

through in the end. And it is a dangerous undertaking for composers or groups of composers to escape the correctly understood and healthy control of the public. In the end one is left high and dry. And particularly today, when concert-life is seriously threatened, it is unforgivably short-sighted.

It is said that in saying what you did about modern music you had in mind a particular group, I might say the left wing, and did not sufficiently take into account the fact that perhaps the bulk of contemporary production presents an entirely different aspect. It might also depend on the attitude with which music is written!

I cannot agree with that; it is not attitude, but only capability, not desire but ability and execution that creates the living art-work. And to take this specific angle: who can fail to have the highest respect for Hindemith's simple and authentic attitude to work, or the consistency, bordering on self-mortification and despair, of Schönberg? From the point of view of its attitude, this left wing – certainly only a part within the whole of contemporary creation, but the most characteristic and the most significant in terms of historical development – has a large amount, the largest amount of justification on its side, and one might be inclined to say that it relies too much on its attitude alone. For it is not their intention, but only the realization of what they want that makes Bach and Beethoven great. And in the true sense there is, in the world of art just as in that of reality, of empirical facts, no morality of the attitude, but only one of strength, of life, of accomplishment.

You still claim not to be speaking for reaction? What is reaction? Even that is an attitude, a tendency. They tried, in those days, to use the attitude as a means of finishing off Brahms with Liszt, Liszt with Brahms. With a few minor exceptions, Liszt's works belong to the past, while the effectiveness of Brahms, despite all the efforts to the contrary, continues to grow. As a representative of progress, Liszt had the full protection of the press. What press does not want to be 'progressive'? Brahms, since his emergence, has been underrated, trivialized, presented as being of no importance, without suffering any damage whatsoever. He is damaged – and often disastrously – by bad performances. When I was young I once read in a major Berlin newspaper about Brahms' *Tragic Overture*: There was nothing tragic in it except its composer's lack of ideas. The same things can still be read today, with his centenary fast approaching. There is nothing tragic about all this except the inability of the author in question to listen properly. The living effectiveness of the music of Brahms – in Germany, Scandinavia and the Anglo-Saxon world today one of the most-played composers in the concert hall – is suddenly a fact, reality.

And there is nothing I can do about it, these facts interest me more than so many well-meant theories, analyses, attitudes, if the latter do not do justice to the world of facts. And the world of these facts does include the quiet vitality of Brahms' music, which is certainly bound up with Germany and the past, but organically alive and therefore entirely unshakeable within itself.

Within today's musical life, it is really no longer the time for entertaining ourselves with theories and opinions to while away the hours. Here, as elsewhere in the world, we want *reality*. This is the only thing that is still of real importance in our time of need.

Today we are in a position to be able to see the characteristics, the advantages and disadvantages of radio. Its great benefits cannot be ignored: the previously unimagined possibility presented by mechanical reproduction for the popularization of music. Alongside this, the boundaries clearly emerge once more (here, particularly since the association of Philharmonic with the radio, I can speak in some detail from my own experience). Extremes of pitch and levels of volume are reproduced very partially and often not at all; in the case of larger ensembles, particularly orchestras and choirs; a self-contained and uniform sound cannot be accomplished simply by setting up various recording devices. As a result of all this the most important aspect in creating the artistic impression, the interrelation of the individual factors and consequently the correct impression of the whole, is distorted, twisted, indeed in most cases practically a forgery.

1933

Staatsoper

Our first and final duty is the nurturing and preservation of the great masterpieces. This care is more apparent qualitatively than quantitatively. One sole Wagner opera truly performed in a manner true to its sense is of more value than a whole Wagner cycle. But this can – and let us not deceive ourselves on the matter – only be brought about through the intervention of the artistic personality, through time and concentration on the task. The general public is not sufficiently geared towards a just evaluation of these efforts. It wants programmes that look impressive. The only programme in this sense is the cycle organized for Strauss' seventieth birthday, which is spread out over the year, and the work of this great living musician . . .

Also the other great living composers. Pfitzner – *Palestrina*, his greatest work.

The nurturing of contemporary art is the duty of the Berlin Staatsoper. It should of course be pointed out that because a one-sided, overly-intellectual art has held public sway over the last few years, it does not mean that all of those who have lived in the shadows and stepped into the background as a result have to be great artists. Here too, as before, there are some who benefit from the current trend. Great art-works, or even those which are to a degree individual, have always been rare. Treatments and examinations of modern works are under way.

On the other hand, the German programme for the representative German institution should be made more prominent. That will have to be expressed in the commitment of human resources to its individual character just as much as in the programme itself. Wagner can naturally take his place within the programme only if he is performed with love. The same is even more true for Mozart, Weber up to Lortzing, etc. The least worry is caused by Latin and particularly Italian opera, indispensable for the maintenance of a daily programme, and for which the Staatsoper was previously best equipped from the point of view of its artistic personnel, etc.

Hitler

As posts are now available, all sorts of disreputable people are rushing in. So dangerous in music because people are on holiday and there is no control. The 'attitude' brings a false tone to artistic judgement. It can only be understood as a defence; beauty is the only criterion!

Question: To what extent is fear of one's own party doctrine necessary and real?

One must put the attitude of the intellectuals down to German objectivity. One must therefore not damage one's sense of fairness!

Without the reawakening of an awareness of the great masters no revitalization of music. Everything – both colleges and concerts – must serve this end.

The only way I could have any effect was with actions. But the Jews thoroughly understood that from the beginning.

The important thing is to see German music as 'European'. It always has been and must remain so. The nationalization of music, which has incidentally begun everywhere, is leading to decline in every case.

I receive another request to write the article about music in the projected book *Germany Speaks*.* At the moment that creates personal difficulties for me: Because of preparation for and acceptance of the post of opera director, because of artistic and other claims I have not recently even been in a position to write articles! And at the moment the doctor has – in order to effect a real recovery – forbidden me to engage in intellectual work. Also at the present moment it is not easy to write about music in contemporary Germany, as everything is either in transition or only in its initial stages. I should therefore like first of all to take the option of dropping the article about music in this book. Whatever it was like, it would, in terms of the present situation – if written by me – necessarily come across somewhat sceptically and hypothetically, and would only badly fulfil the propagandist purpose which it is indeed intended to fulfil. W.F.

Today if ever we are obliged to ask whether that which has been striven

* Furtwängler is here declining to contribute to a volume of Nazi propaganda entitled *Germany Speaks*. He was often to resort to medical certificates to avoid exploitation by the Nazis for propaganda purposes.

for can actually be achieved and realized in what results, whether the means used are actually helping music to root itself among the people, whether a new blossoming is in preparation. Not only in publicly visible musical life, but in the whole place that music occupies in the life of the nation *per se* – even internally – world war means a significant intervention. That is apparent first of all in the sudden breakdown and drying-up of production. The creations that followed on from this period, where they have nothing to do with the older generation, Strauss, Pfitzner, etc., have with few exceptions remained insignificant. That does not mean, say, that talents were less considerable. Neither does it mean that the public's receptive capacity has in any way dwindled. On the contrary, the search for contemporary production, etc. is more or less a characteristic feature of the age . . . Never has the 'new' been so yearned for, sought-after, cultivated and pampered.

Competition for the praise of work. It is not work in itself that stimulates the artist. Art cannot be placed at the *service* of public life. It must be left as it is, its materials are the great primal forces: religious content, the fatherland, love. Where these do not somehow show through, no art can develop. To look the facts in the face: If one wants art, then one must leave it the way it is. In art, content is always taken for granted as natural. If this content is a part of the age, art will deal with it. If it is not a part of the age, there is nothing to be done – it can never be treated in a living and artistic way, and one would do better to abandon any involvement with art.

Genius and people, the individual and the mass

The question of the relationship of genius and people, of the individual and the mass within art, has gradually become the question of central concern to the present day. That it could become so, that it has become an open question, a problem, is already typical of our time. And questions are there to be answered. Let there be no illusions on this matter: if problems arise, it means that they are emerging from the womb of the unconscious into the light of consciousness. And the wound that results can only be healed with the spear that opened it. The wounds of consciousness, the greatest and most fatal wounds, the real wounds of our time, can only be healed by consciousness, by *knowledge*, not by desire, organization, tendencies, feelings. And what depends on this question? Does not *everything* depend on the way in which it is answered? Not only the central question of how the creative musician should work and for whom, but also of the functions of the receptive mass, the audience, the people, what sort of share it must have, how the external and internal forms of musical life develop as a whole. As long as we are unclear about these questions – and that is by no means the case – we have no protection against making new mistakes with every further step we take.

The question has not always been a problem, rather it has been one only for a relatively very short time, namely since around the death of Wagner. It first made itself felt at the most sensitive and central point of all artistic life, among the creators. The relationship of creative artists to the audience became problematic, while outwardly, all around, an apparently comprehensive and intense concert and musical life flourished, even seeming to reach its height. This was seen particularly in the fact that the creators – and often not the worst among them – increasingly began to reject the control of the audience. The judgement of the audience was no longer acknowledged to be the final jurisdiction. That had not happened before. Apart from great individuals, the power of what they had to say to the world, what they created not so much in opposition to the audience as without direct contact with it, in all its innovations, and especially the so-called progressive music of Liszt, Berlioz, Wagner, involved the audience to a high degree. In fact the triumph of Liszt and Wagner was built on the involvement of the audience. Even Brahms quietly respected the laws of the listener, of the audience in the ideal sense, as showing the way, although he wrote a great deal from within the abstract essence of the piece. And how much more true this was of contemporary foreigners, of Verdi, Puccini, Tchaikovsky. But then, first of all with Bruckner – who remained an individual case, however – later with Pfitzner, Mahler, Reger and finally in our own times with Schönberg and the new or atonal music, the break is quite apparent. The individual places himself, sometimes as an individual, sometimes in groups, in conscious opposition to the 'audience'. He does not suffer as a result as he did in earlier times, but is even proud of it. The audience is no longer the ideal forum before which battles are to be fought out, it is the simple numerical accumulation of stupid people, who are never in short supply and who will fall for anything. Of course early music was flourishing at the same time; however this music too, which was written for a real audience and still had one, was made increasingly suspect to the audience – by a press which consciously or unconsciously served the interest of creative artists, partly out of social conscience, partly out of a community of interest, partly also in good faith of being closer to the centres of real productive music – and it was made more suspect the more immediate its effects. In this way the effects created by Wagner and Beethoven were nipped in the bud, people's opinions were led astray. These efforts passed right into the theory of performance; this was supposed to be objective, that is, structured in such a way, if possible, that a Beethoven symphony affected and concerned the audience as little as a modern, abstract work.

And this – not sport, not so much the radio and the gramophone – was the *crisis* of musical life, which has made its presence felt very clearly over the last few years. The split between heart and head, the lack of trust in one's own feelings was what finally made the sense of all playing and listening impossible, for the individual as well as the community. The end of music – really the end of a particular type of playing whose existence was only possible on the back of the other, 'usual' type, as a protest against it, which has now finally succeeded in doing what it always unconsciously wanted to do, namely reducing itself *ad absurdum* – and also a literature of the most unprecedented masterpieces, a source of power and illumination for today's humanity, which no other art comes close to possessing . . .

All this follows on from the troubled relationship between the individual and the mass, as it has become apparent for the first and only time in the recent past. Previously, say before 1850, the question did not yet exist as a conscious problem. Why was that so? How does our age differ so radically from all previous eras of artistic life?

If we consider the Greek visual arts, say, the first artistic era which we know individually and precisely, we are struck by the minor importance of the individual artist. Sometimes the names have been handed down, sometimes not even that; if one wishes to appraise the works, however, a consideration of the epoch from which they come is always much more important than the consideration of the person who created them. This is a phenomenon which also recurs later on, particularly in the early stages of every artistic development. But what is most particularly visible in Greece, but also elsewhere (Early Renaissance), is the small variation in quality between both individual works and artists. But this means that the level of artistic activity as a whole was *incomparably* higher than in later eras, let alone in our own time. The various reasons for this are: For one thing the artistic vocation in those days brought no advantages beyond itself. It brought no kind of civil honours, there was no artistic industry, nobody was interested in it apart from those who were directly involved in it. In Greece it was even seen as manual labour, despised. This is how the youthful and magnificent development of Greek sculpture occurred, thus standing more or less alone in world history, with the exclusion of the public, so to speak; hence its long and healthy organic development. How different was the case of Greek tragedy, which was finished after three generations, destroyed, talked out. The secret actually lies in the relative unconsciousness of the whole process; the only person to become an artist was the one who had an inner calling, who had to be one. (What a contrast to our own music industry, where almost the exact opposite seems to be the case.) A further factor was the uniformity of the Greek cultural and religious world.

The decisive thing is that we now think only in terms of *eras*! The classical age as well as the Middle Ages – eras of trust and faith – plotted their chart of values directly against the things themselves. For us there are no longer any unconditional values at all, and so we can no longer approach things directly. This and this alone is our tragedy!

The danger is always the same: the rigidification of forms of thought which one has created oneself. This form of thought in today's Germany is that of thinking in terms of eras. The superiority of Goethe's thought lies in its independence from this. Thinking in terms of eras is a drug which blinds one to things and which is responsible for the idea of upheaval, of breakdown, of the 'end' of a development. All of these things are true for superficial, relatively unimportant phenomena; not for truly productive life. The profound lack of interest in our intellectual life today is the reason for its constant analysis of this. Today we really believe in the basic difference between cultivated music and folk music, as if every really great work of art did not have to be both, as if every 'folk' wanted nothing but itself and was not merely always sought after and yearned for by the educated classes. Everyone wants to become himself, but not his contingent conditions, rather his true being. Everything else is demagogy – in which case it still has a practical sense – or 'literature'.

We no longer know what a great work of art is, but only what period it belongs to, which influences – it is nauseating –

1934

The importance and the weight of youth keeps becoming greater. It is not happy to adopt the ready-made feelings that already exist in any age, it is consciously unhistorical, it lacks more than ever the rigour, strength and the form to shape its feelings. Hence the contrast: On this side youth, that is, a demanding chaos, on the other side formal ability without responsibility, that which is enormously 'clever'. The feeling that form must express something has been lost just as much as the feeling that something that is expressed must have form. So little in the way of great art is to be expected from 'youth' alone, however important it may be in politics, with its blind and instinctive essence that constantly pushes forward. The concept of the 'youthful work' is a creation of the historians. It is actually astonishing how unyouthful and consummate were the works of the great (Beethoven, Brahms, Michelangelo) at the beginning of their careers. The artist is made by the ability to form, not by youth or age.

False concept of individuality! Hence also the faith in demands made on the 'younger generation'. Intellectualism to believe that one could use external means, social demands, etc. to reproduce productive periods (Early Renaissance, etc.). Also the great make the average impossible. Conservation of craft (*Meistersinger*) and conservation of the great works is the task of average talents, and nothing more. It is false historicism to turn them into today's 'generation'.

Centralization is the reason for corruption. Its drawbacks have revealed themselves to be much greater than its advantages.

Impairment of my job and authority by interference in my private sphere, or the Hindemith affair.

Sehr verehrter Herr Kollege,

After serious consideration I should like to ask you to amend the programme of the second Opernhaus concert to replace the planned work by Alban Berg, *Suite from the Opera Lulu*, by another piece, and to play it in the Philharmonic instead. From what I hear, a demonstration against the work – because of the text alone – is certainly to be expected. Such an event, however, is not desirable for the Opernhaus under present conditions, and could mean automatic damage being done to other and greater artistic interests.

In this way the Berlin public will still have the opportunity of dealing with the piece. But for your part, you yourself have the opportunity to take on the responsibility for the performance in all its magnitude, while if the work were performed at the Opera, a large amount, if not the majority of this responsibility would be borne by the institution. At the present moment this would be in no way desirable.

You yourself know that these concerts, which previously played a major role in Berlin's musical life – you conducted them for seven years – have seen steadily dwindling attendance figures, to such an extent that last year, at the beginning of my period of employment at the Opera, the question of whether they should not be abandoned was under discussion. If they are to be rebuilt on a new foundations this is at least a beginning, which must not be disturbed by demonstrations which, at a time of high political tension, would necessarily take on a political character and, as a result, have unimaginable consequences for the institution.

I hope that, out of concern for the Opernhaus, of which you have been a member for many years, and whose success must also concern you, you will agree to my request, the more so in that, as I have said, it is not a question of abandoning the performance of a work – with which I am unacquainted, but of whose importance you are so convinced – but only of transferring it from one auditorium to another.

Dear Kleiber,

I am sending you this letter in such an 'official' form on purpose, so that it can, if necessary, be published for information abroad.

But, as I have said, I also hope that, as a colleague, you will appreciate my reasons and observe my request.

Yours W.F.

1934–5

Riezler's Beethoven*

The inability of the Romantics to see him as he really was, was nevertheless linked to a deep instinct for his actual essence. Today, this instinct has unfortunately been lost to a great extent; perhaps, then, our greater knowledge and awareness of the real Beethoven could be useful in winning back that lost image of his essence. It will be argued that this has not been lost; without realizing that arguing the point is the best way of proving it.

This book is a first step; the life has never been so accurately presented.

Any artistic style can only be understood as an aspect of the whole. Wagner, who had to master the vast surfaces of the *Ring*, could only be sparing with lyrical and self-sufficient melodies. Bach's concept of the whole is different from that of Beethoven, for the former it is style, i.e. floating, for the latter it is pattern, i.e. becoming. When the postulate of the one is transferred to the other, the result is false judgement and all the other awful things that follow.

The judging which is nowadays so customary in our circles – that is, condemnation, criticism of one's neighbour – is almost always the sign of an unproductive person. It is a product of one's own vanity, of self-defence, the urge for self-preservation. It often does a great deal to impoverish collective life.

(Ernst Jünger.)† There is a recurring tendency to give a deeper necessity

---

* Walter Riezler (1878–1926) was a teacher and friend of Furtwängler who wrote an Introduction to Riezler's book, *Beethoven*, which can also be found in the English translation.

† Ernst Jünger (1895–), a German writer and soldier, who in his many books glorified the military life, giving it a kind of mystical glamour. The Nazis dismissed him from the army in 1944.

to the simple needs of practical life, of self-preservation – especially in our philosophical Germany, this is vain and impoverishes life. No power of persuasion in the world will be able to give *technique* a deeper religious significance, however much those who live by it might like to hear this. Its needs and consequences are those of self-preservation (along with global over-population), nothing more; this is also the source of closer contact with pain and heroism. True heroism consists in mercilessly recognizing and naming this. Modern war is fatal necessity, nothing more. It calls for the readiness to die, fine; but one does not die for war or for the state, or the race, etc., but for something completely different that stands *far* above it – the sacred life of the nation that is established in God.

All attempts to glorify technique are foreground attempts, *journalism* and nothing more.

Goethe himself truly saw the actual state of things. Confronted with technique there is only one thing to do: one must distance oneself, that is, stay constantly aware that it is only a device and must remain such.

The more an art strives for regularity and that which is universally compelling, the more it approaches 'convention'. But only apparently. Regularity is not at all the same as convention, even if it has more in common with it than it does with boundless individualism. But the similarity in the latter case is just as misleading as the dissimilarity in the former. For convention and individualism are two sides of the same coin, while convention and deeper inherent laws are basically deadly enemies.

1935

The '*Diener am Werk* [servants of the work]' nonsense (Toscanini). A self-evident truth is held up as a major breakthrough. It is really a barrier, the self-restraint of a society of 'literati' which has got out of control, against its own licentiousness. In a more profound sense the problem is not 'servants of the work' but how the work is to be understood. Even Pfitzner's polemic is, because it is aimed merely at a phenomenon of the age, merely conditioned by the age. The real problem is, however, not mathematically resolvable (as even Pfitzner liked to believe), but depends on the power and plenitude of one's own nature. '*Was man nicht ist, kann man nicht machen* [One cannot do what one is not].' This phrase of Goethe's is also – unfortunately – true of interpreters. The popularity of certain conductors (Bülow, Mahler, Toscanini) comes from two different, completely divergent sources. On the one hand the purely artistic and interpretative qualities (more productive but still problematic in Mahler's case, in the case of Bülow and Toscanini more passive and pedagogic). But then there is the myth of the ruler, of the animal-tamer. The latter quality is based on the slave instinct of the so-called audience and – let there be no illusions about this – was also in many ways the determining factor in the greatest cases mentioned above. So it is not the experience of art, but the experience of the ruler. The dullness of this source, the subjective, all-too-human aspect of this quality, when compared with the true greatness of art, does not merit discussion.

It is incidentally no coincidence that the 'servants of the work' theory was not invented for the conductors R. Wagner or Mahler, say, or the pianists Liszt and Rubinstein, etc., but for people such as Bülow, Toscanini, etc.

Otherwise it is difficult to discuss the matter here, as conductors seem long ago to have become political symbols – not to the advantage of art.

England interview

Why the great classical works? Admittedly they are the most frequently performed. But it is not a question of that, but rather of how well a work is performed. In fact they are the most inadequately and inaccurately performed, so I feel obliged . . .

It is understandable that a part of the press should make its demands from its jaded position – but it does not carry any authority. My task is greater than this; I am a conductor not for literati and connoisseurs, not for a trend, a state, a government, whatever it may be, but for the people.

If I am giving an account of myself to you at all, it is because I believe that much of what I say has never been said before. What I say is not thought out and logically deduced, but only simple, direct experience. May it also be evaluated as such. I am an artist and not a writer.*

Morality of the public

Take contemporary criticism, which thinks it must reject Beethoven in the name of 'good' taste; Naturally everyone means something different by 'good taste'; the highly educated, important Spohr will mean something different from some newcomer, but the general concept remains. On the subject of which we rightly ask where good taste might be found if not in Beethoven, i.e. in the manner of saying something clearly, simply and exhaustively. Later 'good taste', the 'conservative slogan', was replaced by the fanfare of progress, which has only abdicated its position relatively recently. 'Good taste', where it had existed, had completely disappeared in the meantime.

How does one achieve 'authenticity'. In the absence of the collective platform of the audience, that is the new question that is being asked over and over again. All I can do is say yet again: one should say what one has to say simply and directly. The rest should be left to fate. That is the course taken by Goethe, Beethoven and many others, recently by the straightforward Brahms. The creation of a solemn vocabulary, as in Ferdinand Bruckner,† Stefan George,** makes many things easier at first, creating an artificial platform. Later, when this breaks down, unfortunately most of the work breaks down with it.

---

* 'England Interview' is a note prepared by Furtwängler in connection with his first appearance at Covent Garden in 1935, conducting *Tristan*.

† Ferdinand Bruckner (1891–1958), poet, novelist and playwright. He was fashionable in the last years of the Weimar Republic, but emigrated in 1933.

** Stefan George (1868–1933), poet of a highly hermetic variety, and also spiritual leader of a hand-picked collection of beautiful young men.

George. Vanity of the intellectual, based in the essence of the intellect. Music naturally amenable to 'form' as much or as little as any other art. The way all general theories of music, whether for (Schopenhauer) or against (Nietzsche), have nothing to do with the actual music, but only with its effect on literati and philosophers. See also the attitude – instinctively so much more correct – of Goethe, unblessed with a direct musical sense.

The refertilization and revitalization of art would require – much more than the establishment of practical organizations, etc. – a purification and overhaul of our aesthetic concepts and value judgements. Over time these become clogged up by people who do not make their judgements on the basis of the subject itself, or in the interest of the subject, but who have subsidiary intentions quite apart from the music. Schopenhauer, Wagner, Nietzsche, George, progress, 'development', beautiful form, Expressionism, etc.

It is not politics, not 'reaction' or atonalism or anything that threatens music, but the fact of its being turned into *literature*.

If someone declares that Praxiteles is decadence, if someone 'loves' Bach and Mozart, and turns up his nose at Beethoven, he is generally taking a stance not on the works, but on the development as a whole. Historians in particular make their judgements in this way, and it is they who represent the morality of art history, not of art. They forget that at any time the individual can break through the level of the spirit of age, that the person who contemplates himself can always be close to God.

I should like to distinguish the authentic artist or poet, who lives and vibrates within himself, from the artist who works by willing and wanting. One like Goethe, the other like Schiller, to take typical examples. In music, as an art which is very close to nature, this distinction is less easily seen. Nevertheless, Wagner, and Strauss even more (not Beethoven), would be placed on the side of Schiller. It is characteristic that this distinction is particularly unclear to the 'political' people.

The term 'literal rendering' has become a slogan. At the same time it has taken on a political meaning. Like all of these slogans it has a moral character and is designed, in the eyes of the public, to erect a barrier against the distortions of virtuoso interpretation. It represents one of the most concise concepts of the morality of today's public, which cannot be at all aware of the bad condition in which it must be if, in all seriousness, it can take this primitive platitude as its final and highest goal. 'Literal rendering' like the whole related complex of the 'servant of the work', etc. is an obvious *precondition* for all serious performance. Those who believe they have found the philosopher's stone in this term are unaware of the extent to which they are moving in the realm of simple literature, simple opinion-making, far removed from any reality. Confronted with the smallest real example, the concept immediately collapses completely. For it is quite clear that the expression marks, whether they are sparse and schematic, as in Bach, or abundant and realistically minute as with many of our contemporaries, are not the slightest use if the sense and spirit of the music are not captured.

They can protect one against bad mistakes the first time they are encountered, nothing more. For one can never simply deduce the sense of the music from them. Rather they presuppose the knowledge of this sense, and vice versa.

Anyone actually satisfied with the 'notes' knows nothing of the *secret* of the great works. This is often the case in many ways in countries not naturally involved in this great music – it should be remembered that music written in the sonata form is almost exclusively German. Here the danger of arbitrariness is also intensified by the lack of a natural counterbalance.

How do things really stand? The public can do absolutely nothing but put the private person above the art. It repeats this every day, because it is by and large no longer capable of grasping art. It believes – all of these processes are played out in the sphere of the unconscious, and the morality of the public forms an interesting and instructive chapter in this – that if it applies the concept of the 'servant of the work' to a person, it will be relieved of the duty of having any new artistic experiences, and calls anyone who really serves only art, who lets the art speak for itself, a subjectivist – because he confronts them with the problem of *reality*.

Good intentions aren't enough – if they were, any conservatoire student could be a servant of the work – but the intellectual preconditions suffice. Not ability, or desire – but being. That must be stated quite clearly. The productive artists, the composers, are fully involved in this, for their works speak for them and finally win through in the face of the regular errors of their contemporaries. Does anyone believe that these errors on the part of contemporaries – most so-called expert criticism has failed at the beginning when dealing with any great new work or new artist – are less substantial than those of the so-called reproductive artists? But the latter are, throughout their lives, exposed to every forgery, every critical dilettantism – not to speak of the tiresome politics that run through everything these days – and subjected to them again and again. And not only the reproductive artists, but also – and this is more important – the works which they represent. If, today, this or that pianist or conductor is famous as an interpreter of Beethoven, while he is really only producing distorted images of Beethoven's works – and if someone else is ostracized in the most preposterous way because he carries the true models within himself – who is actually damaged by this? Beethoven, Beethoven and the misguided audience, which ends up really thinking that Beethoven is a more or less 'out-of-date affair'.

This is all based first and foremost on boundless insecurity in the judgement of great works of art. It is expressed in the exaggerated historicist view, and every available aid is anxiously clutched as a means of avoiding having to deal with the works themselves. So the basic conviction is that one's conception of a work, indeed its ultimate worth, is a question of taste varying from individual to individual. This conviction is the real reason for using any foothold which, like literal reproduction, provides even only the appearance of something secure, incontestable. Chaos as such is *proven* – to play the psychologist for a moment – *by the* fear of one's own chaos, and nothing more.

On closer inspection, it becomes apparent that this insecurity, as one might incidentally expect, is not so apparent in dramatic music, where the human voice, the situation, the words offer footholds of all kinds, as it is particularly in so-called absolute music. And, indeed, the more absolute it is; particularly in the case of the symphony. Or rather, of all music written in the sonata form, which specifically includes the majority of German classical music. And that is to a large extent true because completely incorrect ideas – or rather no precise ideas at all – prevail about this sonata form, and indeed about the meaning of form in general.

This is the core of the whole problem. It must be remembered – this sonata (and fugue) form is a purely German development. It is the Germans' real contribution to world music, indeed to world art, its true original contribution. In other countries – even in Italy, almost as musically gifted – the precondition for the understanding of the sonata, as Verdi so rightly saw, never naturally existed as it would have needed to. Now, however, composition and performance are highly interdependent.

Literal rendering is the business of those who see music as the product of someone else, and not as their own most private concern.

To examine the matter more closely let us first of all ask ourselves where or when the theory of literal rendering first made its appearance – in other words: when did the general artistic situation come about and exist which produced or demanded such a theory?

Which is creative, the individual or the people?

27.1.36

Today this question is drawn into the sphere of political discussions, with which it has nothing to do; for nothing involved in the liveliest and also the most sensitive area of human life and work, creativity, can be considered patiently, humbly and objectively enough.

Properly considered, history can be our best teacher here.

Greek sculpture – anonymous – folk art, individual only gradually. Likewise Early Renaissance – even minor artists, the most trivial, can create delightful things.

This lasts only a short time, and is related to a certain naïveté in the general level. Here too great and greater individuals begin to emerge, But the flow also carries the minor artists. Despite this a decidedly youthful situation. We like to consider it, to empathize with its intentions and views, and imagine ourselves into a youth which we no longer possess and which would also not suit us. That is Romanticism, or rather, bad Romanticism.

In any case it is unmistakably true that during these periods everything is pushing towards the arrival of synthesizing personalities, who then actually appear and, generally overnight and with only a handful of works, render most of their colleagues superfluous. For their own world, certainly, but also in a certain sense for us, their successors. For if we wish to enjoy the charming plenitude, the varied richness of the early periods for their own sake, we cannot – if we are living people who can perceive things in their entirety – escape the fact that the simplification, concentration, to an extent monumentalization that so-called classical art brought with it, represents an improvement. It is not without reason that it has provided the standards through the ages – an unarguable *historical* fact. And as a result it has, in the true sense, penetrated through to the *people*.

Here lies the contradiction: the truest 'folk art' essentially only the work or individuals. The reason for this contradiction is not difficult to discern. The people itself is too divided into professional and economic branches, into ranks and classes, parties and visions of the world, as is the case in all historical periods. Only the individual genius was able to fight his way through this; he found his way to the heart of the people, made this heart beat and brought the people to an awareness of itself.

This apparent contradiction goes still further: Beethoven, the *solitary* man, creates an art of community as no one else does. What blindness it is to equate external social attributes with the internal social attitude, disturbing the profound internal relationships between individual and community by means of an external over-emphasis on collective thought, to weaken the productive possibilities of the people by depriving productive artists of the space, the time, the opportunity to be themselves, by believing, as in Soviet Russia, that this can be realized through a concept of popular community seen from the outside, merely intellectually, that is with only a 'political' intent rather than the sense of the person as a whole.

So the opposition between individual and community, which sustains the politics of the day, vanishes to nothing when faced with living reality, i.e. when faced with the *great man*. The individual is the one who actually creates the community in the true sense. And it is not a 'star' system if Beethoven and Wagner repeatedly . . . Neither is it a star system if the best of the reproductive artists . . . Any more than it will be a service to the community to encourage a hundred superfluous composers, spoil modern music for the public with them and, if possible, to regiment, trivialize and suppress the one or the few real creators in the name of the many, etc.

The concept of community which has permeated art appreciation (even before the war), has created a situation whereby a 'class' was able to sustain itself on the back of an audience that did not want it at all, as is the case for example, with the new, i.e. atonal music.

But the feeling of social responsibility in today's public, which blindly seeks to *encourage* instead of examining, which does not know that it is only possible to 'encourage' by means of authenticity, by the application of stubbornly maintained standards, by means of *surveying*, is completely misguided.

Why is it that the recent early periods, which are inherently the closest to the 'people', have not discovered the most simple, the most folkloric things? The most recent great example of simplicity, e.g. Beethoven, is at the same time a *simplification*, not a product of chance, as naïve temperaments believe, but absolute simplicity and the complete exhaustion of a subject. And remarkably – this ‘simplicity’ is what goes most directly to the heart!

Currently, when *Brüder, überm Sternenzelt* and *Seid umschlungen, Millionen* by the Germans Schiller and Beethoven are being rejected from the *racial standpoint*, it is the very *best* of Germanness that is being rejected.

Art is truthfulness, what we have now is the opposite.

1936

A vision of the world that is merely talked about, i.e. one to which lip-service is paid, which is at best *known*, rather than one which is lived and active, is the signature of our contemporary conditions.

Book

For decades the essence of our age has been the dismissal of the consequences of intellectualization, etc. That will occur of its own accord, and in my life I have wasted a great deal of time on it. Here I am concerned only with what is accessible in the realm of the individual, that is his constructive will –

Extreme artistic trends (atonality), for example the rejection of comprehensibility, are examples of overblown individualism, the rejection of community. The artistic and the natural community (Christianity) –

Art is always a particular, finite and limited synthesis, hence *reality*. Science an historically unlimited idea, hence *unreality*, a working method for the disposal and abandonment of reality. An understanding of the relationship between the two is the crucial task of the future. Only the 'classical' work can effectively put an end to the cancerous excrescences of science, which are followed by those of art. With the devaluation of the word, indifference to truth is unfortunately growing. –

Precisely because superficial reactions occur more quickly today, deeper development is not only more hidden but also slower. –

Development of the historical attitude: At first people tried to rediscover themselves in some historical epoch (Jacob Burckhardt).* Then they began to understand the naïve ages. Then, increasingly, historical consciousness begins to overwhelm *all* expression, and the gradual relativization of values sets in. And as a result the unexpected

---

* Jacob Burckhardt (1818–97), great historian, whose most famous work, *The Civilization of the Renaissance in Italy* is not so much a work of scholarship as an attempt to establish the permanent relevance of the age with which it deals for understanding the possibility of human greatness.

thing occurs and suddenly exists. All at once we were standing aside, no longer living, only observing. This has never happened before; it is immoral and lacking in life.

In art, what is meant by 'close to us'? Bach is not modern, neither is Mozart, because they lived in natural and healthy times, because the *threat to life* does not yet correspond to our own. That only becomes the case with Beethoven.

The historian always attempts to decipher from the music itself what it is, to read into it his own concepts, which he has brought from elsewhere, because he cannot hear its language.

The most dangerous falsifications of reality, something about which we are not at all clear, particularly in Germany, a country overburdened with scientific perspectives and synopses, are the 'eras', the connections, etc. of science. In general these are basically working hypotheses, or too broadly conceived to express anything precise. As soon as someone great appears, they use him to kill off the future. That is what happened to Brahms, and what happened to Strauss.

The attempts at creating artificial contexts and periods are legion.

Today's art appreciation does not take the work as its starting-point, not the unique organism – today's generation is in no way trained to comprehend this – but rather the material and the method. Technique is discussed as if there were a 'technique' in the true work of art which could be of any interest to anyone not 'part of the trade'. Historical influences are discussed – as if they had ever been the crucial thing in a real work of art. Harmony, rhythm are discussed. Nothing but *general* concepts which have only a distant and abstract connection to the work. (The discussions of aestheticians on the matter are very often completely wrong.) That is all *intellectualism*, the attempt to use a general orientation, which is all too easy, to *avoid* direct confrontation with the work.

What is the situation? The essential thing that separates us from earlier ages is the fact that we have to deal with a completely different mass of artistic material. But like the human stomach, the human mind can only cope with a limited amount. And since actual production came to an end, at the end of the nineteenth century, and attachment to the contemporary finished along with it, the new problem has emerged. Fear of the past is driving contemporary music – this started with Wagner – into an attitude that is increasingly hostile to tradition, which has finally finished it off.

Nietzsche was the first to validate the view of the literati, which no longer analyses art but rather exploits it. This stance is comfortable, seductive and iniquitous. The other way of getting rid of art is the historical one which, guided by the academic study of art, which is some decade's more advanced, has now taken hold of the study of music as well. It may also be finished *already*. We must now grasp certain facts: that we are the way we are. That is why we can have only *our* beauty, *our* standards. Standing by and watching is not an attitude finally appropriate to art. This is the reply to the historians.

Art is the expression of strength and beauty, the symbol of community. A work of art is a king, one must wait to be addressed by it. One must take trouble over it, one must take time. It does not want to be considered, tasted, felt, but taken in its entirety, by the whole person. That requires strength and time. The problem of art is a problem not of artists but of the audience, the consumers. This must be finally understood.

The importance of the conductor depends on his talent for balancing the rhythmic and melodic lines. The one seems to exclude the other in principle. This is the start of the problem. The composer lacks the conductor's knowledge. He finds it trivial, chiefly dealing as it does with details. It is actually the case, however, that mind is to be translated into reality, whereby not always, but very often, the tiniest detail can disturb or even destroy the whole process.

Borderline case e.g. *Pastoral* 2nd movement. Rhythmically inhibited conductors beat 12/8, which can never let the sound develop freely.

The over-assiduous fight against a lack of fidelity to the work, led even by a mind of the rank of Pfitzner, is out of date. Now it should be: a fight against literal belief, on behalf of real fidelity to the work, true to its sense. But of course this is only a matter of competence, of ability, not a mass slogan.

We understand today that everything in every case depends on limitation and restriction, e.g. the harmonic sequence in Beethoven, with the definite feeling of its organic arrangement, and in Schubert and later Bruckner as an end in itself. How much richer and more sensitive is Beethoven's concept of form.

The real struggle is the one against half-education. This is generally intellectual, unaware of the mysteries of existence (faith in the machine and faith in organization), is boundlessly presumptuous without being aware of the fact, and lacks the one decisive thing, the feeling for values.

Morality of the warrior class – fine, but only for itself, for that kind of people.

The characteristic feature of all intellectualism: treating everything the same way, e.g. Riemann* – beginnings in music.

Pfitzner if the only one to have upheld the primacy of the spirit in music (for example in chamber music). He is not afraid to drop his guard. He is more open to attack, more vulnerable than anyone else; but he is, as the others are not, authentic. And as a result he is – not compared with his predecessors, but compared with his environment – great.

Is there any point in writing? I do it at random. The world has not come up to my expectations. It does not see art and reality with the eyes of a fifty-year-old. But this, the assembling age, should be in charge. If our culture and its artefacts are to continue to have any meaning, they must be seen in this way – for their own sake, and also organized from within.

Constantly approaching other works distracts from one's own fate and makes one's existential crises unrecognizable.

For many years I saw the fight against intellectualism as the most important thing. Today, I no longer do so, I have no more time for it. I see that others do it. Intellectualism takes care of itself, lives its own life; it is currently the destiny of the world, and must be lived through.

Goethe: As soon as tradition becomes too much for one, one either becomes apathetic and yet pushy or yields too easily to the temptation of throwing everything overboard. Now tradition has become too much for us, radically and completely.

Concept of the unity of life, a helpful concept. Exaggeration would risk devaluing life.

---

* Hugo Riemann (1849–1919), musicologist whose influence, once very strong, is now forgotten.

Faith in the greatness of the masters is faith in human greatness itself. Faith in development is faith in the material itself.

With faith in human greatness the soul is once more placed at the forefront, where it belongs.

Crucial to remember: The majority of human emotions exist not in man but between men.

Life today, more than ever, is a question of courage.

Authentic passion: built on wealth, goodness (Wagner). False passion: based on the impotence of negation (Nietzsche). Hate more inauthentic but more irreparable than goodness.

Crucial: staying away from hatred.

Sorrow – not hatred.

It must be said openly, and is my personal conviction: every real productive movement that becomes organized loses its backbone in the process.

Youth and beauty anticipate the greatness of maturity in its classical inevitability.

I now realize how curious was my passionate youthful attitude to the late Beethoven (also seen in Wagner in later life), and to late Goethe – an apprehension of my true nature.

Problem of beating time: for example the figure which one beats destroys the feeling for the flowing melody.

The fundamental moral attitude indicates the source and hence the quality of the music itself (Schenker).*

One's level of cosmopolitanism has its limits if one is to be oneself – and

---

* Heinrich Schenker (1867–1935), Austrian musical theorist who had a profound influence on Furtwängler, who visited him frequently in Vienna to discuss the works he conducted. Schenker believed in a fundamental musical idea underlying the structure of any great musical work, which gives it its unity, and traced such 'ideas' in many specific pieces, with the help of elaborate multi-coloured charts. His influence is greater now than it has ever been, and lies behind the whole contemporary movement of 'music analysis'.

everyone must be that. Keyserling* overstepped this limit a long time ago, he is a virtuoso. Hence the opposition to him despite the evidence of his great accomplishments. Above all, that sincere and idyllic inner life so beloved of German people, is misunderstood by worldly minds such as these. They should realize what would be left of their cosmopolitanism if the whole world was nothing but urbane, if it were, like themselves, devoid of substance.

Introduction: What music is *not*.
Not Keyserling,
not Nietzsche,
not science,
not art in its usual meaning,
not Stefan George,
not nationalistically German.

The German experiences more in imaginative forays into the past than he does from the immediate present. As a result he does not understand that contemporary music is not anything of the sort.

The artistic importance of individual works is as independent of the evaluations of art history as religious truth is of historical criticism and textual exegesis, i.e. entirely independent.

Movements of the spirit, art, love, understood as a part of hygiene or sexuality: the last word of semi-education, which has fallen upon the people of Europe like a frost.

It is curious that the strict classical work, for anyone who has ever truly experienced it, becomes more important than all Slavic and Romance works, which are superficially much more colourful and lively. Hence the mysterious, defiant effect of Brahms: the effect of the profundity of the living context.

Schweitzer says that Goethe's view of the world was incomplete. Goethe says he knows nothing about philosophy. The truth is that Goethe understood something about something: the relation between

* Hermann Count Keyserling (1880–1946), philosopher, polymath and indefatigable traveller. His anti-rational philosophy was once very popular. He knew everybody.

word and deed. He knew only a fulfilled, a lived vision of the world, not one which simply existed in words. He stood at the beginning of mankind's age of intellectual awareness and saw in this the greatest danger to it, to which it later irrevocably succumbed. Ever since man has been able to think, this has been the problem that recurred in many different forms. Which is why the right books (Keyserling) are of so little help.

I have often wondered whether the concept of 'great art', as I champion it, is far too highly charged and therefore unnatural to most people. It touches the genesis of genius itself. Whether this is necessary – since, as such, it has been absent from many eras, particularly the most productive! The contemporary will to manage without it is the best proof that this is impossible.

Art in the usual sense is an expression of life. 'Great art' is an 'orientation' of life.

Art and 'literature' are the deepest and most irreconcilable enemies. The former is real, only working in and through itself, in its being and its self-preservation, the other the exact opposite. In terms of their power today, 'literature' not only has the upper hand, but appears to be solely in control. Art only exists in secret, and intellectualists, who do not understand the deeper layers of the world, believe it dead. But it cannot die, even if its outward effectiveness, as our own times have already shown, can dwindle dramatically. 'Literature' and world-view – two enemies, actually the same thing. Schiller himself wrote to Goethe about how infinitely more difficult it is to produce art than to make philosophy, Goethe, the artistic man *par excellence*, distinguishes most sharply between fulfilment and conservation, between wanting and promising. It is typical, indeed crucial, for the born man of letters, that he does not see these distinctions, that he cannot and will not see them.

A sense of connections and symphonic consonance for Wagner too, e.g. *Tristan*, Act III, joy motif.* Why did he not end it with what now forms the close of *Siegfried*?

---

* '*Tristan*, Act III, joy motif.' Furtwängler is referring here to the fact that the fugato theme which now ends *Siegfried* was originally intended by Wagner as the theme the shepherd plays when he finally sights Isolde's ship, but then abandoned as unsuitable.

In art it is always thus: the tendency of the age is to become aware of previously unconscious processes, to have a conscious understanding of reality. But that can only happen in individual parts: in Wagner they see only the harmonist, or the master of form, or the artist connected to the people, or . . . But his true value depends on his being all these things and more simultaneously, in one. This is generally the case: individual things are seen correctly and sharply, but too many conclusions are drawn too quickly, and a sense of the whole is lost. In this the past, which was generally dedicated to the whole, was incomparably more correct, although it cannot be reconstructed. We must pass through this period of transition, we must fight for total awareness and hence the new vision as a complete unity, the new naïveté, if everything is not to collapse. Is the all-too limited human intellect capable of doing this?

All reproductive playing *spoils the character*. It is authentic at first but must then necessarily become false if it is to become an end in itself, as *experiences* cannot be repeated at will in a routine fashion. All truly great people have other resources with which to renew their reproductive power.

The process of awareness, the general process of the age, extends both to the music itself and to its performance. But it is impossible without dedication to the whole; consequently, modern efforts have had a particularly devastating effect. Love – that love that is forever being seized and shaken by the work – can never ever be replaced; love alone creates the preconditions for the visionary and correct understanding of the whole in the work of art, for this whole – even if it is a great work whose effect is long-lasting – is nothing but love. Each individual part can be more or less understood intellectually, but the whole can only ever be grasped by the living feeling of love. It is the only thing which is appropriate and fitting to the whole work of art as an image of the active and living world. Everything else, however skilful it may be, is limited, and therefore profoundly boring to me. Nowadays one has to spend half of one's life *defending oneself against* the quick-witted, the overly clever piecemeal thinkers. And one wonders whether the end of this intoxication of thought, which sees itself as mastering the world, of the desire to make everything conscious can ever lead to anything but general exhaustion, indifference, barbarism? If everything becomes a problem, one might just as well do away with the problems. (Germany!)

In fact, intellect is *not strong enough* for all this. We are not up to the task of consciousness with which we have been presented. Our intellect is not generally deep enough to recognize its own limits and hence the true composition of the world.

Wagner as musician

The leading lights of my early youth were: Haydn, Mozart, Beethoven. I only came to know Wagner later on; the more I came to know him – in my way, as a musician – the more I began to admire him and to love him. This period includes an experience which I found curious. My father gave me tickets for all four performances of the *Ring of the Nibelungen* in the then Munich Hoftheater. These performances, conducted by the famous Wagner conductor Franz Fischer* with the best singers of the Munich stage, were certainly no better or worse than many others. And yet they thoroughly destroyed my illusion and love of Wagner for years afterwards. What I . . . suddenly appeared as theatre. The most wonderful melodic curves were trivialized, made banal by the movements of the singers and their style of singing. At once I understood Nietzsche and all the others who reject Wagner, and in their rejection, whatever their reasons might be, the weight of true pathos was unmistakable. Theatre, nothing but theatre . . .

This sobering process was repeated several times. It was always connected to the experience of performances of works by Wagner. Only later, in fact only after I began to conduct the works myself, did I understand the entire range of their greatness, and rediscovered my initial relation to it.

I am no Wagnerian, in so far as I see Wagner as a genius who provides us with norms and a sense of direction. He is and remains an exceptional case as a musician. But he is one of the most productive geniuses that the world has ever seen, a creator of almost colossal dimensions, for whom any standard is inadequate. He must be taken as he is.

Why is this? Why is it that Wagner, the most powerful and effective of all musicians, has also remained the most hotly debated, why is it that resistance to him is continually revived?

Why was that? Back then I was not sure, today I know: it was the way in which it was performed. In this performance – as always in unexceptional performances – Wagner was performed not as a poet, not as a musician, but as a man of the theatre.

---

* Franz Fischer (1849–1918), famous as a conductor in his lifetime, but without an enduring reputation.

Now, as I have said, it was not a bad performance, but merely one which paid tribute to the main things, a routine, average performance, as all these performances are. And the problem of performing Wagner opens out from here.

We can understand why the performances of Wagner's work were so important to him. The difficulty in the performance of a work by Wagner lies in the essence of these works, in the essence of the music drama itself. In Wagner's work these difficulties are greater then in other works of art. A Beethoven symphony can also be badly performed, and even generally is; then it seems boring, academic, outdated, it ceases to affect us. But it is not performed, as Wagner's works so often are, falsely and mendaciously.

There is a generally prevalent idea that our operatic performances are better now than those of Wagner's time, which he spent his whole life attacking. We probably believe that because in those days the conductor did not carry so much weight as he does today, and the director was seen as barely worth mentioning. I believe that this is a mistake, and that, if Wagner were alive today, he would have just as much to complain about, whatever the works of great art under discussion (as is well known, throughout his life he dedicated nine tenths of all his writings to the problem of the performance of his own and other great works). But to some extent the shortcomings are different today. The problem is no longer one of sloppiness, of singers left to their own devices (and there are often worse things than this), of trivial performances left to chance. But whether the artificially-produced performances by ambitious directors and conductors (Pfitzner) are better, is a major question. One thing has remained: theatrical routine, emphasis on craft, which is where the main damage is done. And it cannot be otherwise, because routine must be repeatedly attacked in all ages and by every individual. It is the great enemy of all artistic life. And it and all its attendant dangers have grown today along with the growth of the industry itself! In fact, both now and in the past, it is in the largest cities, in the largest institutions that one finds the worst performances, that is those with the most frozen routines, the least appropriate to the *works*.

The passive act of immersing oneself in a work – it is particularly lacking here. This – more female – function of the conductor, from which rebirth follows of its own accord, experiences, through comparisons, excessive awarenss, coldness, worldliness, routine, etc. – the most diverse kinds of inhibition.

Conducting by heart has another great advantage. It demands that the interpreter deal with the work intensely and for a long time, which is *always* the necessary presupposition. And always treated differently!

Modern conducting: originating in the audience's instinct for actors and virtuosos, but above all its slave instinct. The authority of a Toscanini, say, could be contrasted with the truly natural authority of the piece! Truthfulness can only be attained through the soul. And one might say: truthfulness is the first and the most beautiful sign of noble humanity.

Fidelity to the work clearly means today: playing in time! Toscanini's *Fidelio*. A large proportion of absolute music – from Haydn onwards – consists of concentrations: the content becomes more dense, more intense, and then dissolves once more (*Eroica*, development, first movement). Playing in time throughout is not 'true to the work', but the opposite. Italian music does not have these concentrations. Neither does Gluck.

Meaning and soul, which in art are one and the same – that is why it is art – have a different sort of conciseness from intelligence; so different that intelligence is often unable to see where a sensual and spiritual accomplishment and *form* are present and where they are not.

Between the good and the better, between the better and the even better in art, there is a massive gulf. Our own age tends to choose not to see this gulf. This means the end of art. For it is only the very best, the artistic geniuses, that draw the true audience to art, because they alone speak to it. Everything else is sham, mediocrity and insufficiency.

Let it be understood: this refers not to solid and authentic playing on a small scale, but the routine of the cities.

I demand: living tradition, not aesthetics. What is left within the history of our music? And why? We must ruthlessly ask ourselves this question. Let us also, in intellectual matters, finally be as ruthless and realistic as we need to be. For: reality has escaped us!

The things which people feel the need to fight against are characteristic of the present age. It relates to our awareness that absolute concepts, particularly that of 'progress', were conceptual errors!

1936

Progress would have been finished off a long time ago if something equally literary and effective could have been put in its place. Properly understood, this could be the people; this is in fact not the case, however, since the people is always interpreted politically. We must say quite openly: an effective slogan such as this, i.e. any kind of 'slogan' in this sense is contrary to the essence of art. It is a violation of reality.

I have made the observation great thinkers (Klages,* Keyserling) tend towards violence, hasty dismissal, resentment, etc.

A thinker who has never really gone through life – and of how many is this true, particularly of late, with our premature specialization – finds it hard to come to terms with life.

The audience, properly understood, leads the artist to simplicity which becomes increasingly deep. This is the ultimate direction of the greatest art.

The will to power is not only typical and revealing for Nietzsche personally, but at the root of *thought* as such. To destroy the diversity of reality with an *imagined* ideal and therefore – will to power. Ideal *instead* of realization, the presupposition of all literature. This is the tragedy of 'thought'!

---

* Ludwig Klages (1872–1956), a once celebrated philosopher much influenced by Nietzsche.

1937

Today there is a political prejudice that individuals owe more to the community than it does to them. The two are mutually dependent, equal partners.

Impressionism is based on the premise of the fragmentation of sensuousness, therefore transient. Another consequence is its separation from the public.

The most refined technique cannot only be united with the innocence of feeling, but is needed in order to accentuate it. As soon as refinement invades *feeling* itself, the germ of death, self-awareness, sentimentality, etc., invades with it; this starts with Liszt, even to an extent with Romanticism.

Brahms

Not only for modern concert audiences aiming in a particular direction, but for man in general. This man is certainly different from those of fifty or 100 years ago. But he is still a man. This is his core, the source of his being and his strength. It is not contemporary jargon – which enables the members of a secret society to recognize one another, but distances everyone else all the more – that makes him familiar and comprehensible. He stands, a real Titan of the deed, against the whole world, against his time, and is now the composer who is played the most.

Hindemith is writing a work about harmony which is, in his opinion, exhaustive. In conversation he explained to me that the laws of 'form' did indeed exist – they will certainly be discovered and analysed as such at some point – but had previously been completely unexamined. In fact, harmony is explained by form, the part from the whole (millipede legend). As a result Hindemith's theoretical efforts are characterized as those of an age which has forgotten how to find its origin in spiritual unity as a whole. Instead, it seeks a kind of balance between the demands of form – as a whole – which is sustained by a limited tonality on a small scale and at the same time by certain devices of rhythm and motif and the demands of harmonic detail, controlled to a very large extent by the analysing intellect. This floating balance, which may also be observed in Hindemith's compositions, is of vital importance to the composing generation, but not to contemporary people, as it is not rooted in the centre of spirituality, but in the contemporary state of the material. The content and tensions which may be realized on the paths chosen by Hindemith are too thin and insubstantial to be taken seriously as an expression of the age. Hindemith's music, Hindemith's harmony, is modern from a specialist musical point of view, but not at all modern as an expression of mankind today. Rather it represents a working hypothesis for composers. That is certainly something; one might only wonder whether it is particularly desirable to seek, find or possess such a hypothesis. Is all art that needs working hypotheses to function not, in the end, stillborn?

The importance of tonality is to be found only in the possibility of *complete* form. Complete form, which can also be called '*große Form* [extended form]', is the creation of something truly organic, and consequently something that we organic beings are presented with as a symbol of ourselves – all art is a symbol of ourselves. Without complete form there is no truly organic form and therefore no truly compelling, expressive art. This deeper sense of tonality must be understood. The 'language of the age' is polytonal or atonal. A child could speak it, and it does not take courage to employ it today (especially since the intention of using it to mask any other lack of content is almost always successful). Courage, a great deal of courage is needed – and a greater amount the more exposed one's position today – if one wishes to be consistently tonal today, and, for the sake of a living and modern *content*, to leave oneself open to accusations of speaking the 'language' of the nineteenth century.

The art of various peoples and ages is related, even to an extent identical, in that the same motifs are inevitably always repeated, precisely because they are universally human. Everywhere and always, nature is in some way the same.

How do trends come about? How did spare homophony come about? Romanticism? The 'new music'? Wagner? Contemporary asceticism? Always *reactions*. Never against authenticity, but against manner. There is a danger of mistaking manner for essence and thus of seeing the reaction as part of this essence. Neither is correct.

Scribes and Pharisees!! Art and morality

I am not a moralist. In a certain sense, however, art is concerned with morality. Namely 'placing oneself within the work', an action on the part of the audience, a demand on the part of the artist. It presupposes concentration and dedication; real art – like real love – demands the whole person. But this is what is refused, and this is the beginning of the tragedy of art itself. I might call the spirit of non-dedication 'journalistic' . . . It is the sampling of details, comparison, the whole overemphasis on historical thinking that has gradually, particulary in *Germany*, its country of origin, become the most considerable enemy of all real art.

If I am dedicated I know, or my subconscious knows, what sort of dedication this is, whether or not it is lasting and of value. But it is dedication, fate, that I am taking on. If I am not dedicated I remain outside, in judgement, I stand above it, I am proud and just, but I am not alive. I belong to the scribes and the Pharisees. They believe that to have a complete view, to be able to judge, one must not be dedicated. This is not only an error, it is a sign of human limitation and weakness. First of all and at the same time, it is always a sign of human envy and the unwillingness to deal with anything new. The Pharisees and all the clever people actually represent limitation and stupidity. And they suffocated art. From the desire to do justice to so-called reality, we cease to be just to ourselves. We cheat ourselves out of our own lives, we cease to be who we are in order to be many-sided, to be all-sided. We cannot see the ridiculousness of this undertaking; we cannot see that in fact – as is actually the case – only the empty shell remains.

About the meaning of all 'comparisons'. One can never make direct comparisons; something in Bach has a different meaning from the same thing in Beethoven (Halm). The same thing is true of Beethoven and Wagner (Lorenz).* Either people are in love with one of these and unjust, or they are not in love at all and even more unjust, for the feigned justice that results really is feigned.

* Alfred Lorenz (1868–1939), musicologist who wrote a four-volume work entitled *The Secret of Form in Richard Wagner*, in which he attempts to show the rigorous musical shaping of Wagner's mature works, relating them to early German musical forms. The work is a fascinating failure on a very grand scale.

1937

There are two kinds of good performance. Those where the good performance as such jumps out at one. Those are the performances of the most famous of my colleagues. And those where the performance is not discussed at all, but the *work* alone makes an impression. A performance where the work in question as such has made an impression on me, in which I have heard the composer's voice, is always good. And in my opinion this is our real duty. Many people can carry out a precise, virtuoso, brilliant performance; but to give voice to the soul of Beethoven, Wagner, etc! There is nothing one can do about this, for one cannot do what one is not. Anyone who does not have a piece of Beethoven, Wagner, etc. in him, who is not in some way 'ccngenial', will never really be able to interpret them. Notven the greatest sincerity – loyalty, effort – no virtuoso abilities can replace that. Who will doubt that Beethoven and Wagner were extraordinary spirits! But among our own artists – however much may be said in their favour – are there all that many extraordinary souls?

One can say of interpretative artists what Pericles says in his famous speech about women to the Athenians: The more they are what they must be, the less said about them the better.

Today, of course, it is the other way round.

Every tradition that has once been alive tends to rigidify into orthodoxy. This danger also naturally exists for Bayreuth, and all the more so since Wagner's *Gesamtkunstwerk* involves, for the achievement of its effect – which, as such, is in the end as simple and clear as the very greatest art – an unusually large number of subsidiary factors, factors which are only given their real significance as means to an end, in mutual co-operation, while individually always tending to take control and become ends in themselves.

The only possibility of countering this lies in repeatedly measuring everything that has become 'tradition' against the work itself. Every generation faces this task, every one of us throughout our lives. This and only this is truly service to the work.

The success of this does not so much depend on conscious efforts, but on congeniality and . . . a task which is also conferred upon the talents of each new generation.

Here, and only here does one see that 'service to the work', that acting – in terms of Bayreuth – for the sake of the thing itself, of which Richard Wagner speaks.

Man is made only to think about that which is immediate. If he is ill, he always thinks in the narrowest sense about defeating the illness. Hence our overemphasis on the 'biological', excluding the superstructure of religion.

Against 'literary' heroism. Real life is a mixture of the heroic and the idyllic. Heroism is 'imaginable' in a literary way because of the moral challenge contained within it. Not so the idyll. It prefers to be terroristic. But there is another difference between the heroic challenge and true heroism, which comes from greatness. Certainly heroism can be abused for other ends.

Clever people love cleverness all too much. They bask in it. They still believe in progress, because they believe in the progress of cleverness. They cannot see that cleverness, i.e. the observation, expression and recording of things – which has made great progress but which could be developed infinitely more – is not complete or even 'real' life. One can truly say: The 'word' can be given its true meaning only by someone who does not believe in the word, who sees through the relation of word and reality. That is wisdom, shared equally by the tree and the 'sage', but not by the educated European! That is why he has put the world out of joint.

Why is terrorism in art so disastrous? Because it eliminates stimuli and stimulations. That is the death of all art.

Opposition to classical 'beauty'. The Greeks, according to Plato, meant something quite different by beauty. It is the *image* of 'classical beauty' that has ruled the last two centuries, not the thing itself. The thing itself is unfortunately extinguished by the image. We must dethrone the image and rediscover it.

It is an error to believe that criticism exists in order to be right. It exists in order to discuss. Where discussion cannot take place, no opinion of any value can form.

Nietzsche

Nietzsche believes – and this distinguishes him from us contemporary people – in progress.* And as a result he believes in decline. He

* 'Nietzsche believes . . . in progress.' No he doesn't.

cultivates the heroism of solitude, which deeper and purer minds – Goethe – because they knew it, did not want to perceive or express. The shamelessness with which he speaks of this heroism of his is the shamelessness of the man who confuses literature and life.

Is it matters 'of principle' that make up greatness of thought? It seems to me that man's strength lies in the machine that he uses. I am tired of the matters 'of principle', of solutions based on principle. They are as cheap as their pathos. And they do not gain in value by being right. It is easy to *say* the right thing. It is difficult to do it. It is dangerous to believe that saying is the same as doing. It can mean temporary and practical power, and that is what it meant for the egoist Nietzsche, who was only interested in people in so far as he *influenced* them. Anyone who uses his own means, namely those of '*Entleerung* [emptying]', to recognize him for what he is, the great man of letters, today risks being exposed to that doubly most poisonous hostility, the hostility of the naïve, who are never in short supply and who mistake words for deeds and – worse than these – the people who, themselves involved, feel attacked, the literati themselves. The older I get, the better I understand hostility that is not only based on resentment and envy but also, as an adequate reason on its own, on the 'working hypothesis' which is to be upheld.

Above all faith in the word, in literature, which has passed down through the centuries, causing and creating religious wars in the past as well as today's poisoned campaigns, is not *truth*, as Nietzsche would have it. Nietzsche's 'truth' is a counter-position, a reaction against a reality – Christianity – which was no longer a reality, and *because* it was no longer a reality. In so far as Christian morality was a preached morality, the morality of the word, it was a slave-morality. Nietzsche was right in that. But in so far as it was lived, meaning humility before God's creation, a daily new beginning, it was the greatest and most severe master-morality there has ever been. The *pathos* of the moralist Nietzsche draws its strength from the fact that Christianity is dead. The pathos of the age is the belief that the ideas of history are more real than the people who bear them. It makes use of this force-field, like Mephisto's 'foot on learned stilts', his six horses or even his motor-car, his aeroplane. The morality of the weak man, the physically disadvantaged man that he was, who needs history to prove his own greatness to himself. His loneliness is certainly hard to bear; in so far as he speaks of it, he is not exaggerating. His weakness lies in speaking of it, in 'cultivating' it. This is where real heroism would begin. At one point Nietzsche speaks of an 'intellectual insomnia'. How accurately observed for one who can only see the world from the position of the critical moralist.

Nietzsche, who never understood Wagner because he never grasped him as a whole. As he succumbed to the sensuous charm of Wagner's music, he had to liberate himself from Wagner once more. Only a Wagnerian can end up despising Wagner. Let us ensure that we are not Wagnerians, but that we honour and love Wagner.

The 'lukewarm are spewed out'.* True justice is in fact very rare. The Brucknerians fight Brahms, the followers of Brahms pull Wagner to pieces, etc. And the just? Those who have a broader perspective and who are capable of seeing 'development', who . . . No, a thousand times no, I would much rather have all those people who are unjust because they *love*, a thousand times rather. The only person with a broad perspective is the one who has loved a great deal.

If I read art history nowadays (Buschor),† a clever and complete survey. We have come so far. And yet – we ourselves stand on the sidelines. But that is something I shall never comply with.

*Clemens Krauss***

Delightful technique. Repeatedly stimulated. But – prisoner of his own technique!

The active person and the critic – two fundamental positions. It depends which one believes oneself capable of. The active person is, in any case, the courageous one, the real one.

One must take an attitude to a work of art, i.e. it is a closed world, a world of its own. This attitude is called *love*. It is the opposite of appraisal, of comparison. It seems that which is beyond compare, unique. The outside world, the world of critical intelligence, never does justice to a single artwork. And this is the enormous deception of art

---

* 'The lukewarm are spewed out: So then because thou art lukewarm, and neither cold nor hot, I will spew thee out of my mouth' (Revelation, III, 16).

† Ernst Buschor (1886–1961), distinguished archaeologist.

** Clemens Krauss (1893–1954), Austrian conductor, especially of opera, who was a close associate of Richard Strauss. A brilliant careerist and schemer, he moved from Vienna to Berlin when most of Germany's top-ranking conductors left; he and Furtwängler were never on good terms.

history. This is what is so wrong about today's art education. If we hear old art, old music with the awareness that it is 'old' music, i.e. not entirely our own affair, that is a mistake. Faith in the most insane Dadaist things was still closer to true artistic receptivity than the scepticism of today's comparative art historians.

One can also write the whole of artistic development from the recipient's point of view. The change in reception; placing oneself less and less close to the work of art. Hence the striking eccentric effects, hence, in the end, the lack of soul. Where this disintegrates or is wasted amid cheap irony and superior attitudes, one is better advised not to appeal to it.

1938

Originality can be based on two things. On the novelty and originality of the sounds themselves, the immediate material – new harmonies, new rhythms, etc. – or on the *novelty of the contexts* in which the material, already familiar in itself, is seen. I might call the former sort speculative; it has been practised quite enough since Wagner, and has brought us to the abyss. The second presupposes real human and artistic power and also runs the risk of not being recognized. For it can only emerge in a congenial interpretation, and anyone accustomed to looking only at the material itself – like almost everyone today – is excluded from it. But precisely because of this it remains the only possible kind, because the possibilities for the development of the material itself are exhausted, but not the possibilities of development in art.

The crucial thing is always: is the art-work ornamental and decorative or does it grasp life, does it reflect the *whole* of life? In this case it needs space and will always need it.

The art of 'space' necessarily becomes tragic. It touches the edges of being, the world moves within it. All decorative art remains necessarily untragic, cheerful, at most slightly wistful. It never gives a decisive explanation of itself.

The style of every artist, every work of art, is always a *transition*. Its uniqueness and its greatness, even among the greatest – and particularly among them – consists in the level of this transition and its *balance* (of tonal and chromatic, of 'form' and expression, of dramatic and lyrical Verdi, etc.). Subsequent generations are too keen to see this as the 'progress' of one tendency, and feel the need to progress further, forgetting that this will disturb the balance and – today – render art practically impossible.

Bach, Beethoven, Schubert, Brahms, finally Bruckner, Wagner, Hugo Wolf, Richard Strauss, Pfitzner, etc. all adhere to the same laws – they form a world. Not the nineteenth century, not the eighteenth, not an 'historical' world, but a common concept of music. But then comes the break. Now they constantly try to hide this by making everything historical. But that takes us to the heart of the matter. We must have no illusions on this; anyone who makes atonal or 'tonally relaxed' music today is doing something quite different from his predecessors.

Many roads lead to Rome. One can take this or that one, but not two at the same time. One approaches the world as a philosopher or a poet, or as a politician, or as an historian. Each of these believes that he is the only one who exists. In any case the politician traces everything back to politics, the philosopher thinks he knows more about art than the artist, the historian in particular – well, he is familiar with everything, knows everything, organizes everything, but much in the same way as the aviator who knows the country he flies over, knowing less than anyone else about its essence from the perspective of his aeroplane. Of all travellers the aviator sees the least – the world has become small and poor since the invention of the aeroplane. In intellectual life we have also become used only to 'flying'. Here too the world has become oh! so small and poor.

It takes profound insight to know that there are various roads one can take which rule one another out.

The person who is simply 'nothing but an artist', if he is a real artist, may be the one most blessed with this insight, because art in the true sense is the most objective thing of all, the one most based on real achievement and the least on ambition and intention. The artist knows that he only has to carry out his work; that he does not have the task of taking a know-all attitude, of judging others. It would be a good thing if the philosopher, the politician or even the historian also thought this way – and if they at least understood that they basically know nothing about art while they still believe that they can evaluate the artist according to their own standards. I know of only two philosophers who 'organically' knew what art is: Goethe and Plato. Of course both of them were artists.

One can examine art from various points of view. I should like to examine it as a relationship of effect – the effect that passes between the artist and the public – like politics. It should be pointed out: true artistic effect is threatened by: 1) routine, 2) as a consequence of routine, the isolation and encapsulation of real life, finally impotence, 3) consequently, attempts to harness unreal devices to establish the relationship of cause and effect in its previous tensed strength, involving: expressive power that goes beyond the content of what is to be said, all the *conscious* means of stimulation, of colour, of rhythm. Then the intensification of the pathological to the point of distortion or, on the other hand, of sentimentality and finally conscious banality, secure in its effect.

In politics the end actually does justify the means. There it depends solely on the power of the effect achieved. But in art, in complete contrast, it depends solely on the authenticity of the effect. How this authenticity is to be recognized, how it is to be achieved and sustained is the content of all thought about art. Consequently, art is the great champion of authenticity in a world where it is threatened from its very foundations. Like the nourishment of the body, so the nourishment of the mind – art – is everywhere distorted.

The great all have their own kind of order. The capacity for order is the sign of greatness. For their successors it is easy to become caught up in one of these orders. If, as happens today, to avoid this, one avoids that higher order entirely, one is naturally casting out one devil with another.

For art as well as religion – and for everything related to that which is spiritually immediate – the state *of consciousness* of the age is of crucial importance. In music this chiefly applies to harmony, then secondarily to melody, structure and rhythm. In all great art, matters of knowledge and consciousness counterbalance one another. But there is a condition – present even in Strauss – in which consciousness has entered a stage of clarity, and consequently pushes feeling more and more into the background, finally, in the case of many contemporary compositions, practically extinguishing it. But as a result this music becomes superfluous *from within itself* – note: not 'bad', for in many ways it is even very clever. But it loses its inner necessity. This music and those who are used to it, however, are unaware of this. It needs to be said by other people; hence the brutal and negative action of National Socialism.

Programme music by its very nature represents a more transparent state of consciousness than absolute music. With true programme music, beginning with Liszt, the inner necessity of music in general comes to an end. Strauss' music-historical theory is – naïvely – based solely on this state of consciousness, just as Liszt says that writing sonatas is an impossible task. This is the point, the decisive point where the development of any sort of music becomes *separated* from the development of the state of consciousness which bears it. This is where the problem of today's music first arises.

Brahms is still attacked by contemporary critics. And how! Did the critics concerned, whose right to such criticism in individual cases is beyond dispute, know that they were actually not criticizing the creator but only the mediator, i.e. the conductor or instrumentalist in question? That all their bitter words apply *exclusively* to this, must apply to this?

With the end of atonality the way is free for a direct recognition of what is authentic and what is false. The final illusion, which continued to live on in us to a certain extent, is dead. Now we can no longer avoid tackling it. It will no longer be a question of describing works as outdated simply because they begin in D minor.

Why is it so irritating when real music is verbally reproduced as moods? Because a mood is something subjective, but real music is organism, and organism is something objective. That the organism is subjectively explicable, subjectively rooted, does nothing to alter its essence, which is different in principle. It is, it does not represent. To understand a Beethoven symphony verbally, as a mood, is as impossible as it is dishonest.

If one could only teach people that truth, reality and harmony, divine harmony, are not *opposites*.

1939

Case of Wagner

The theatre, then. The theatre is the artistic institution that can be most or least given over to 'art', that 'presents' the whole 'art' complex most clearly and visibly. In every organism there are higher and lower organs, some serving the centre of life, of growth, others the need for elimination, which is inseparably connected to all growth. And precisely these baser sides of all artistic work, which drag us down, are particularly well formed in the theatre by its very nature. Wagner bound to the theatre by destiny like no other great German artist. Therefore he spent his life turning against the 'theatre', against everything that was nothing but theatre. It is the greatest injustice to denounce him as a man of the theatre, as is commonly done. The theatre is, precisely by sharing its point of origin with him, his most untiring opponent. And it is a profound falsification to reduce the poet and musician Wagner to the 'man of the theatre', unless one understands the theatre as not destroying the poet, the musician, but allowing him to thrive – as he himself understood theatre. But this is where one finds the profound misunderstandings, for theatre itself does not see itself this way. It knows that it is theatre and does not claim to be anything else.

Eroica! Exaggeration of the early style, sometimes almost abstract (first movement). For all its greatness a unique work, i.e. a work of transition. Even the Fourth is freer and, consequently, greater. A sign that any style, even the most natural, can rigidify, indeed rigidifies immediately upon ceasing to be a completely natural expression. And it is always only this for one moment. The differences between Beethoven's early and middle styles, particulary in the transition periods, are not so tangible as that which we now call Beethoven's style. There is no 'development' of harmony or rhythm, but only of the soul, which makes use of the musical space to a higher degree than before. The soul expresses itself more freely; that is the whole thing.

The organic is the element that is unknown today. However much, or precisely because so much is said about it. Colour, nuance, detail are the characteristics of a sensitive century, but it takes organism to make art natural, and in doing so it brings it to itself.

Plato – Klages is certainly right when he refers to him as an attempt to foist an 'interpretation' on the plenitude of life as a whole, which, as interpretation, has a teleological character and is thereby narrowed down. That is due to the attempt at interpretation in itself. If Klages rejects this interpretation, that is because of his higher state of consciousness, his 'later' thought, not his deeper thought.

All true authentic art is simple and bears restraint within itself.

Restraint in the sense that a Haydn symphony is more mystical than a Bruckner symphony. The modesty of the connected form, the shape, beyond ideas, beyond will, effect, programmes. Art stops where effect begins.

Every attempt to play Bach and Beethoven off against one another – usually in favour of Bach – comes from modern man's habit of not hearing anything through to the end, but only registering its development, its flow. Otherwise none of the fundamental oppositions could have been constructed.

Art history – and cultural history – are called creative if they elaborate on individual, unconscious major developmental trends. At least that is the concept as it applies today. But it is just as indisputable that there are conditions and laws which remain the same for all periods. If in the past the general was naïvely spoken of where the particular was meant, now everything is seen as being related to the age, as 'relative' – something that is certainly all too true of our own period. There will come a time when, in the name of *reality as a whole*, the two tendencies will interpenetrate, and each of the two concepts will be validated in its own right. The style of breaking everything down into historical tendencies has become facile today, has been devalued. We need only seek a new Archimedean point, and immediately the matter looks different. (See Steding.* As if, say, the crucial thing for Bachofen† or Jacob Burckhardt

* Christoph Steding (1903–38), Nazi writer, vulgarizer of Spengler's views (Spengler thought National Socialism was a catastrophe).

† Johann Jakob Bachofen (1815–1887), Swiss historian of law and anthropologist.

had been their attitude to the Prussian German Empire! There are actually both feminine and masculine, both idyllic and commanding contents to life.)

I am not impressed by the broad perspectives that all spring from intellectual and synthesizing activity. I even prefer that orthodoxy which is aimed at one point and attached to one point. Its source is love, even if it has finally become ossified and rigid in its love. The purpose of a perspective is one of self-orientation. It is loveless, and, if it establishes values, it is fake. How much more there is involved in taking a stance on one individual phenomenon, one individual true art-work, than on the greatest historical constructions *à la* Spengler or Steding.

The 'interpretative' aspect of our thought. Our artistic and cultural psychologists are so happy when they have captured a style and been able to impale it like a butterfly on a pin. They will say something about Baroque and Rococo, and along with the architectural style, all the other expressions of life from the period in question have to be shoved in together. Instead of understanding that in any age the most diverse trends appear, but that some are particularly dominant because of external or internal developments. It is impossible to ignore the fact that in Bach there is simply no 'Baroque' but only Gothic. Even the strictness of his Preludes and Suites is more Gothic. Handel, on the other hand, is partly Baroque, but even this is only historical and external, while the inner life of his music is quite different. The true Baroque is Liszt, some of Wagner, and certain passages in Bruckner. But that is called Neo-Romantic. Why? We do not yet know to what extent the layers of the ages are interwoven – how much more important and instructive (if more difficult) it is to examine the works themselves than their age and milieu.

There is nothing to be done; all consideration of art which lays claim to some value must deal only with the works themselves; all aids and mnemonics, such as age, artistic period, race – these too are among the unreliable aids which obstruct one's view of the works – milieu, personal psychology, etc. are bad. They falsify the picture. Why are there so few people in the whole world who – directly – confront the things themselves?

It does not matter whether or not one experiences and sees the world in terms of oppositions. But it is not unimportant whether one acknowledges these oppositions, or whether one *lives for their unification.* For all real life is a union of the masculine synthesizing will and feminine individuating being.

The deepest significance of Steding's construction is psychological in kind, the awareness that the emphasis on transitions, the avoidance of values, comes from a total attitude to life, and that this total attitude in return has the effect that health in thought is related to health in life as something deed-inspired. This observation is unquestionably correct. It is also one of Goethe's. Everything that follows – Steding – i.e. the bulk of his individual interpretations – is made up of constructions, produced by his violent reduction of all content to the masculine and political. Here the thinker is revealed as a displaced politician – and the falsification of reality is revealed as well.

In Goethe's time and into the middle of the century they spoke of beauty and ugliness, strength and weakness, etc. Since then – particularly with Nietzsche – they have begun to talk of ascendancy and decline, of youth and age, of decadence and youthfulness as opposites, i.e. seeing things *in their development* rather than directly.

If the healthy person cannot naturally work productively, his thinking changes. Indeed this happens very quickly, much sooner than used to be thought. It does not take only external frailty to produce the finer shades of what is called resentment. Indeed, thought is, so to speak, the mirror of action, and in it, in its structure, one can immediately and accurately tell how far the person in question is actively and effectively fulfilled. If one considers Nietzsche in these terms, one will understand why he had to think the way he did. But one will also understand the small degree to which this thought is compelling for us.

In this way, however, one can also tell from a person's thought what the value of his actions may be. The truer, the stronger they are, the better and therefore more courageous and less anxious his thought. Take Nietzsche, the prime example of all the displaced negative instincts of a man really meant for action.

Stravinsky: the conciseness which music no longer produces from its inner tensions it receives externally, from the ballet. As a result it becomes what it was before, for thousands of years: utility music. And one might ask oneself: Has the dream of absolute, i.e. of real music, been dreamt away? —

I am a man of experience. If experience tells me that this is the case, I would not only admit it but also act accordingly. In this most vexed of questions, theories have no meaning.

In the history of the arts, an over-constructed and exaggerated complication is always followed by a new simplicity (German classicism, Empire).

Anyone capable of self-analysis is not a creator. The creator knows to what extent he is different from others. But if he could 'analyse' himself in a true sense he would have to live in that thin, one-sided intellectual world which may indeed enable one to perceive creative accomplishments, but which is itself incapable of producing them in their three-dimensionality. But these days everyone is capable of self-analysis.

R. Strauss put his failure on display the moment he deviated from absolute music. He was not 'up to it'. Wherever and whenever he achieved something special later on, it was always as an absolute musician.

If we attempt to discover the reaons for the modern composer's alienation from the audience, we will especially arrive at excessive complication, the loss of universal validity.

The tendency of the age, ever-greater complication. Until Schumann, Wagner, Bruckner, natural phenomena within complication. But this is the limit. The Reger and Strauss generation already past this. It was clear that there had to be a reaction. The full extent of this problem was first seen by Brahms, or even, perhaps, by Beethoven. Sketchbooks . . . The last great man to experience this recognition with all its implications, who had it as a Greek gift from birth, was Pfitzner. He repeatedly attempted – most strikingly in the last movement of his violin sonata – to write universally. How misunderstood was this side of his art.

It is said that the age of melody is past. The ever-changing popular song reveals the opposite.

The development of the thought of the last 100 years is connected above all to two fundamental things: 1) The fact that man is increasingly taking the role of being nothing but an observer; 2) Something that is partially responsible for this: the fact that thought has become increasingly aware of its own incompleteness, and more aware of the division between its own claims and reality, the greater these claims have become.

R. Strauss is the great musician who has best been able to cope with life, perhaps in all history. He is the true child of an age which puts the individual as well as whole peoples to a new and more acute test of their fitness for life.

Criticism

I know a lot of critics who can write very readable reviews in which everything is in its proper place. Only the review never corresponds to its subject. Some eulogy is written to a person devoid of sensibility; the frigid city-dweller is described as an ardent fanatic, etc. Such people write with absolute self-assurance . . .

It can be seen in the forms of art as well as in those of religion – they become impossible as soon as *faith* in them is lost. This is what the audience observes. The experience of the active person: that this missing faith cannot voluntarily be introduced. Which is why the experience of the audience is of no use either.

The development of music over the past decades is the development of the scientific age. It is the paths of science that are being trodden here, the paths of disintegration, of isolation. Rhythm, harmony, are being 'developed'! It has been forgotten until now that the fragmented, isolated person is not capable of life, of having any effect.

Instead of thinking about reality, even today composers basically indulge in a madness for progress – which is now historically finished once and for all – as in a secret vice, which, however much they would like to conceal it, marks all their works. They are incapable of acting on it; an ability that is rare because it always presupposes true productivity.

Form exists in order to capture, to grasp, and, as it were, chemically to dissolve expression. That is its function. Where it is present, expression is authentic, legitimate. Today's aesthetic, hostile to expression (voiced, among other ways, in the word and concept of the much-used terms '*musikantisch*' and even 'literal rendering'), is therefore not what it imagines itself to be. Its deeper foundation lies in its incapacity to deal with form. Because form is not mastered, expression – and rightly in this case – is feared. For there is every reason to fear it. The asceticism of the present with regard to expression is the asceticism of the alcoholic whom alcohol would destroy, the vegetarian who suffers from protein-poisoning. A morality born of necessity! What other reason could bring together 'mass' and morality.

Since the last generation of the nineteenth century there has been an atmosphere that is expressly hostile to art. That is what makes life and work so hard for the artist. Today's clever person does not want art. He has lost his childlike nature, his divine childlike nature to the point where he does not want to be reminded of this loss. And that is what art does. Lacking good intentions, however, he also increasingly loses the ability to encounter art, his organs of perception atrophy.

The fate of César Franck, Smetana, etc., Reger's wanderings. The judgement of today's publishers. They do not feel the originality of the *soul.* They see, and history repeatedly proves it, that all really great achievements (Mozart, Beethoven) come about through a natural and unaffected adoption of the given material, not through 'originality'. But today they do not recognize – what does not smell and taste of originality. They no longer have the organs for anything else. For, of course, in order to feel true originality, the originality of the soul, one must have a soul oneself.

Rolland's opinion that if it had not been for his deafness Beethoven would have become a second Rossini. How ridiculous in the face of the first sonatas.

The generation of Strauss, Reger, Mahler, of mammoth development. This was the great first illness that was naturally followed by reaction.

What is the meaning of Brahms and Bruckner for the 'people', in the face of today's addiction to folk-music? Why is there an irresponsible slide into the 'folkloric'? What makes Beethoven and Goethe so great, so compelling? The fact that they had *both*, the natural strength of the earth, breadth and stature, 'sublimation'. Both in such a proportion that the one was able to *grow* out of the other. The liberal world, the intellectuals, needs to be told repeatedly that sublimation alone is not enough, and our contemporaries need to be told that folk-art and breadth alone are not enough. Lehár has as little meaning for Germany as Schönberg. Both are parts of a whole, and Lehár certainly corresponds to a real, if primitive, need, and Schönberg embodies an idea, even if it exists only in the will and in protest. But in the end I think less of ideas that cannot be made flesh than of flesh that is not or cannot be made idea.

What is style?

A password for mutual recognition.

A working hypothesis!

A crutch that gives the power of walking to one unable to walk on his own.

A method that enables one to compose without inspiration.

A jargon that gives one the soothing feeling of having companions to protect one from the audience.

Style can be productive, that is, a part of production, if it serves the 'poetic' idea of the work. As in Wagner, as in Beethoven, in Bruckner, where it is the 'world' of the individual work. (The epic attitude of the *Eroica*, the drama of the Fifth, the idyll of the Sixth, the humanism of the Eighth Symphony). But the general thing, the style of the age, which the young Beethoven was given, for example, was the initial premise on which he built, something taken for granted rather than something meritorious. But one never attains major achievements when – as today – self-evident things have to be turned into virtues.

Music or playing!

It did not start with music alone. Many people believe that playing came first, although that is unimportant. But the contrast exists and is being reawakened by the present day. Playing is, so to speak, the chaos, the primal soup, out of which structured 'music' developed. Playing depends on people, and it is claimed that people are more important than music that has 'evolved'. But it is true: Playing depends on *musicians*, but music depends on people. The idea that the composer's profession is more important than the audience is something that only – a composer could believe.

Why should we unbelievers celebrate a believer for his belief? (And not persecute him!) Bruckner believes that the infinite only exists in the great, in the non-finite. Brahms knows that it can also be in the small, indeed the very smallest thing. Bruckner not entirely himself when he hurls boulders around. That is also a limitation; but who is as great as he, when he is great.

It is an error to believe that Bruckner is the less understood.

One does not become a sonata composer; either one is or one is not. Sonata – natural form – Chopin – Schumann —. After Beethoven and Schubert only two creators of sonatas: Bruckner and Brahms. Sonata the German form. The significant thing not the schema itself, but the fertility of the oppositions.

The science of history has taught us to know everyone else; it has not taught us to know ourselves. It deprives us of the limits, the boundaries that all human action needs for self-realization, and in the process it takes away our selves, our very souls. If it claims to be more than simply a means of orientation, it makes us unproductive in the real sense.

You call great art 'educational experience'. That is like the fox and the sour grapes. For me that is education, and nothing else. But for that reason you defend yourselves against everyone who wants to drag it out of this accursed educational atmosphere. An historical construction – that is, education, which also prevents things being seen without the haze of historical determinacy.

The historian files things away for the sake of an apparent intellectual superiority, just as the psychiatrist speaks of 'types' and imagines in so doing that he has expressed something significant about the various geniuses. If I write a type of music that only seems from a distance to have certain devices in common, it immediately becomes in example of 'late Romanticism', that is, of the past. Even the present is only understood, as such, as a 'style', never as what goes beyond the style. In consequence, however, only that which is conditioned by the age is seen and evaluated, and never the eternal, the universal. So we have an attitude to art which fails precisely where art affects people, and precisely here it avoids decisions where decisions are the only truly important and 'interesting' thing.

A truth which has no effect is not a truth. An effect that is not true is inauthentic. The tension between truth and effect is, in a thousand disguises, as it were, the content of world history, but of art history at the very least.

Passion

Seen from outside, the *St Matthew Passion* is full of problems for the performer. From within, examining the work itself, as with all great and decisive works, that ceases to be the case. And is there a work that is greater, more unified, less ambiguous? Certainly the difficulty lies precisely in the simultaneous existence in Bach of monumental presence and depth of feeling. This difficulty is intensified by our knowledge, or lack of knowledge, of how the *Passions* were performed in Bach's time, as this knowledge is still limited and incomplete. We know, for example, that Bach did not use the harpsichord, but rather several organs. We know that he had at his disposal a small choir, all boys. We know that the congregation joined in the chorales, and so on. There are people who would like to have all this literally repeated. By so doing, they are forcibly reducing one of the greatest and still most contemporary works to an 'historical' affair. They do not stop to consider that the contemporary performance of one of the *Passions* faces quite different demands from a performance in Bach's day. Instead of churches we rely on large concert halls. This necessarily gives rise to the large mass choir. Only a large number of people can produce the warmth and fullness of tone that the work demands, and which, in Bach's time, could have been produced even by a significantly smaller choir. If we are to be historically accurate, they say, we should limit ourselves to boys' voices for the soprano and alto parts. Who could take such demands seriously? Only the deeper reasons behind these demands should be taken seriously. These are – as always with literally held beliefs – a lack of imagination, inflexible self-righteousness and the fear of taking on the work, the music in one's own time, one's own audience, in short, reality . . .

Hearing this, we are led to conclude that the world of scribes and Pharisees cannot be far away. The only serious reason for advocating a small choir is that the polyphony of the vocal arrangement can be heard more clearly. But this must be the job of the conductor. It is his particular duty to ensure that warmth and power coexist with clarity; this task remains the same whether the choir is large or small.

Like the size of the choir, the treatment of the *continuo* is also a practical consideration, dependent on the given conditions of our concert halls. We do not have several organs, as in the Thomaskirche. Therefore, the extent to which the arias should be accompanied by a large organ is always a problem to be solved according to the particular concert hall. The harpsichord, the instrument of the period, carries less far in our concert halls and can therefore only be used under certain conditions. In any case, Bach himself probably did not use it, as we know (only today! Schering). It seems to me that the modern piano, if used with care, still provides the best accompaniment for the narrator. More important than these issues is the treatment of the chorales. In Bach's time the congregation joined in with them. This is where we see most clearly that the whole work, like so much other church music, was conceived liturgically, that the umbilical cord, here connecting art with its mother, religion, was not quite severed. (Whether and to what extent Bach's *Passion* could only have come about in this way is a separate question.) But here it must be said that when we discuss the questions of performances of the *Passions* today, we have around and within us a different reality from that of Bach, that we have a responsibility to this, our reality, and that it is the one we must bear in mind. The audience in our concert halls does not join in with the chorales; the chorales have detached themselves, become embedded in the work. They must therefore be performed. They are not pictorially symbolic like the choruses, or individually emotional, like the arias. They remain a mass sensation, although with every possible shading, from the most personal, the most profound and still humility to the broadest hymnic expansiveness. But because they are placed within the whole, because they have become a part of the work of art, the *St Matthew Passion*, because they are separated from the listeners, the audience, and are now presented to them, they must be performed along with it. The form of this performance derives from the placing of the individual chorale within the whole, from its text and its musical development. The congregation in Bach's time also sang the personal chorale, which sends each of us back to the very depths of our being through the contemplation of Christ's sacrifice, the chorale *Wenn ich einmal soll scheiden*, with quite different emotions and therefore, even involuntarily, with different expression to the *Was du tust, das ist wohlgetan*, for example – the differences in feeling that filled Bach's congregations when they sang must, in today's performances, become apparent externally, precisely because the chorales are performed, because the audience no longer joins in with them. That manner of singing the chorales in an even *forte*, or perhaps with over-emphasized *pauses* (which had a directly practical importance for the congregation when it joined in, while for those who are simply listening they have only a formal and structural meaning), does them an injustice. It is, as they say, 'neither fish nor fowl'. But one thing must not be ignored: it must never be forgotten that we are dealing here with the testimonies and feelings of the faithful, of the masses in the noblest sense of the word. Every hint of a theatrical effect, indeed any nuance consciously intended to produce such an effect, is most strictly to be avoided. Everything must be the natural, self-evident expression of inner feeling. Such expression cannot be 'produced' or learned by tradition; whoever does not feel it himself will not achieve it.

And with this we come to the most important thing: namely, what the work itself says to us, that which cannot be learned by tradition. This needs to be quite clearly stated in an age such as ours, which, in the unparalleled insecurity of its instincts, has, more than any other, a tendency to see everything in black and white. Who can claim to say whether and how the traditional closing *ritardando* is to be performed in a piece by Bach, be it an aria, a chorus of a chorale? Why does it sometimes have the uplifting effect of a release, of a poem, of something completed, and at other times sound like an outworn and dusty convention? And where does it begin to be possible for us to work out the dynamic variations, the *p* and *f*, in a piece by Bach?

Our historical knowledge can tell us nothing about these matters. For it is general, external, while these questions always ask something new, something particular about the individual work, about internal issues. And anyone who asks patiently, not from a sense of smug superiority or prejudice, but humbly, with all the warmth of his heart and as a musician – for this is a question of music and nothing else – will find the answer.

These prejudices include above all the idea that Bach must be played 'objectively', that is, without expression. This concept, particularly prevalent in our cities over the last twenty years, is actually a reaction against the period before, inaugurated under Wagner's influence, of an excessive overloading of expression in all areas of music. It is an affectation, a convention, just as the 'expressive' playing which preceded it was affectation and convention. Certainly Bach must be performed 'objectively', that is to say, as the work was intended. But who could fail to understand that the *Passion* – even in terms of its text in many parts the most emotional and profound imaginable – is and means something different from an objectively articulated Bach clavier fugue? No, real objectivity means nothing in itself, but rather – at least for the performer – the performance of each piece according to its nature. To speak of one of the *Passions* in terms of the 'objective' Bach is simply nonsense. In the whole of musical literature there is no creation more subjective, more personal, more completely released into emotion than

Bach's *Passions*. Bach is here the greatest 'Romantic' that ever was. Realizing this means true 'objectivity'.

And so it is by no means 'objectivity' if a work filled with warmth and unbounded religious devotion is performed 'objectively', 'functionally'. Rather, a performance is genuinely 'objective', that is, it is really in keeping with the work's essence, if it freshly communicates all the warmth and religious devotion in the work throughout its rendition. And that is only possible if – and let there be no doubt about this – the interpreter himself makes this warmth and devotion his own, if he is also possessed of it. Wanting to show off, sham or make theatrical gestures in this context is just as great an error as the display of 'reported', cool objectivity (in accordance with today's rational spirit); false or exaggerated nuances on the one hand, coldness and dryness on the other are the inevitable consequences in such a case. But neither is objective, that is, truthful and appropriate, or, if one prefers, faithful to the work's meaning. And this is precisely our task. We want neither the conception of an interpreter nor the dead, bare, printed notes of the work, but the work itself.

Doubtless the discussion of the performance of old music would not have taken on such dimensions if people were clear on what it really takes to let music sound. This 'sounding' might also be described by the word 'realization'. It is a case of an interval – to keep the subject as simple as possible – being not only played but experienced. For only if the performer experiences it will the audience be able to experience it. And like the interval, the melody made up of many intervals, and similarly the piece made up of many melodies in combination, must be experienced. Books could be written about what this experience actually is, despite its simplicity and reality. It can only be said here that it is just as alien to average playing as it is conceptually unknown to average thinking. But it was not unknown to the great masters, being rather the initial presupposition for everything they did. Whether a performance makes use of so many players, this or that device, is actually of no importance compared to the question of whether or not the music is realized as it is experienced.

Historical in terms of current knowledge, 'literal', etc . . . these are all superficial things that only touch in a secondary way upon the 'reality' of playing. (And this is no less true for Bach than it is for Verdi or Tchaikovsky or anyone else.)

Certain principles can certainly be established in the performance of

Bach which relate to the essence of his musical imagination, to the devices that it uses. Bach uses rhythmical contrasts only under particular conditions. In his music the rhythm is always flowing. It only becomes completely free – historically speaking – with Haydn. This means that he invents and feels *melodically*, and consequently in Bach one finds the longest melodies in musical history, all in one piece and without interruptions. This manner of invention and feeling, which finds expression no less in Bach's instrumental works than in his sung melodies, rules out certain performing devices such as large, consciously calculated symphonic *crescendi*. The broadly based symphonic *crescendo* is just as bound up with the many organically related forms within a piece as the romantic *rubato*, that is, a treatment of the tempo which is not non-agogic. Particularly the latter – which, despite all the lip-service paid to literal performance, is still the real malady of our age and which originated in the theatre – should strictly and radically be excluded from Bach. Nuances, *crescendi*, *diminuendi*, clearly appearing for their own sakes, so to speak, are impossible. I will grant myself a single exception in the *Matthew Passion*, which I do not wish to defend stylistically but which seems to me to portray the meaning of the text so incomparably that I should not like to do without it: the great *crescendo* and *decrescendo* at the words '*Wahrlich, dieser ist Gottes Sohn gewesen*'. I have adopted this from Karl Straube.*

On the theory that the interpreter's personality appears between the work and the audience. Behind this is the false 'objectivity' of the intellectual, which is really intellectualism, that is to say, not a force for those natural movements of the soul that form the basis of all art.

A work that is written involving the whole personality – and this is true of every work of art – naturally demands that the performer make use of his whole personality. It is not true to the sense, and therefore not objective, to perform a romantic and ardent work 'classically and boringly' or in a modern and intellectual way, or vice versa.

The reproductive artist must first of all understand and perform the individual phrase as a whole; then the melody to which the phrase belongs, then the piece of which the melody is a part. If the demands of

---

* Karl Straube (1873–1950), organist who according to this passage was responsible for Furtwängler's overpowering climax at the words 'Truly this was the Son of God.' But a comparable effect can be found in many other performances of the *St Matthew Passion*, e.g. Willem Mengelberg's – and he was not likely to have known Straube.

the individual part are in tune with the whole, and the whole with the individual part, then everything is in the balance. The prerequisite is that both, the individual part and the whole, should have passed through living emotion. There are some who can feel the individual phrase. Only a few who can feel the line of a longer melody; hardly anyone who can feel a true whole in its entirety, as the great masterpieces reveal. But today there is an overly practical and hence generally accepted way of coming to grips with nothing at all, but of simply reproducing everything in a 'reporting' style, without having passed through one's own emotions. This is not performance so much as reporting, not so much a work of art as mechanical photography. The sources of error here are minimized to a high degree, but the possibilities of real, compelling artistic effect are similarly reduced. A hundred times better an incorrect version than no version at all. But the performer of the incorrect version takes a particular stance on the work, the art, the audience. Anyone taking a purely 'literal' view behaves like the mediocre person who avoids all responsibility. This is not objectivity, but subjectivity of the worst kind.

For most people, the forms which have developed from tonality are means of supporting and organizing the content; for the born symphonist, however, they are means of achieving the inner momentum of the music.

Brahms is – in terms of the number of performances, the diffusion and popularity of his music – after Wagner and Verdi the third great world event in music in the second half of the nineteenth century. That is all the more remarkable for the fact that he did not write popular operas but strict absolute music and songs.

Brahms' aesthetic has not yet been written, any more than that of Beethoven. In practical terms both of them have that many more followers. Recognizing the natural and its requirements is the most difficult, the ultimate thing.

The sonata and the fugue are the forms which have depth of proportion. Something happens, something changes, something is demonstrated, the music is three-dimensional, not mood but event.

One can approach the 'material' of music from various angles, from opera, ballet, even film, from the illustrative lyrical song or from purely musical forms. One might only wonder where and how the deepest and most personal, superpersonal content is arrived at.

Great composers are seldom completely satisfactory performers (conductors, pianists), because they never wholly dedicate themselves, even to their own works. From composing, they are accustomed to making sure that they do not lose their heads, and to seeing that passion is given form, that it is captured. Their coolness, or mistrust, towards their own passion, which has often so ruined their concepts, so often betrayed them, gives them that suspicious coolness, that objectively stand-offish attitude that we can see in Strauss, Pfitzner, Reger, etc. Only Wagner, the epitome of the expressive person, seems to have been an exception here too.

What critics lack in general, particularly the famous ones, is courage. It sounds paradoxical at first, but it is the case: they lack the courage of their own opinions, expressed above all in the *changing* of these opinions. I performed one of my works twice in succession. A leading critic had thoroughly decided upon his dismissive judgement after the first evening as these gentlemen so often do (in reality, of course, a long time before the first note was played). Nothing could move him to hear a difficult new work, the score of which had not yet appeared, for a second time. Does he not need to do this? Is it to avoid any threat to his own judgement?

Total admiration of and adherence to past ages (Gothic, the pre-Bach period, etc.) by modern people is the same as an extreme individualist of our own time retreating into the womb of the Catholic Church; the need to extinguish the individual, which has become all too painful, and to lose it in a greater universality. But at the same time it means that the person in question needs to extinguish himself, that he *no longer exists as an individual*. It has come full circle.

Why did Goethe not love the French Revolution? Why was he not a revolutionary? Because he saw obligations as well as liberties, that is, *at the same time as liberties*. He had the complete view of the world before him and knew that obligations, law, came from liberty, liberty from law. And that this was true wherever *life* existed. Anyone who has made this complete view such a part of himself, and who turns to it in every case as much as Goethe did, is cured for ever of all revolution, all propaganda.

It is strange that it is always different people, a different kind of people, who admire things in the newspapers and who really feel and enjoy a concert. Their language is different. The critic who really expresses what the true and good audience feels is the rarest in the world. And yet that is precisely what his real task ought to be.

Responsibility to reality, or authenticity – or simply: responsibility – although this does not express it entirely – is a part of every honestly practised profession. Responsibility towards authenticity in itself brings the most powerful self-commitments. Goethe, the man of self-commitment, of self-restraint, the most moderate man who has ever lived.

Hugo Wolf: *Penthesilea*. New departure, that is, performance good. The second theme (Rose-festival) dated and banal. Direct feeling is the crucial thing. Pfitzner better here.

The conductor is greater the more he can fill a simple melody with meaning, that is, the simpler the melody which he is capable of dealing with. Here it is a case of: '*Hic Rhodos, hic salta*'. It is not a question here of 'expression', of temperament, nerves, warmth, sensuousness, etc., but quite simply the right 'expression'. And that is difficult!

Why do many people no longer know what religion is? The classical belief in fate corresponded to a humanity which saw itself as surrounded by invisible and intangible enemies. Later it was seen that these enemies did not exist, that they could be overcome instead by contemplation and thought, and that there is therefore no fate beyond one's own actions. Anyone who probes deeper will see that that is still not correct. Like the eternal heavens over the city, made and inhabited by men, is eternal fate over the intrigues and concerns of the individual. A correct grasp of this is the first step towards religion. If one only becomes aware that this eternity – as it applies to both fate and the heavens – is divine, one understands that religion is something real, just as real as the heavens themselves.

One can no more govern Berlin from Vienna than Vienna from Berlin.

The local authorities must be taken into consideration, as they know the public. The audience is important. The recreation of the audience, which only happens through its being given rights and duties, being given a role, is the most important task of all.

I am told that my concerts are at least full, as I wanted them to be. Well, they have been full since my twenty-fifth year. Neither would I object to working, where necessary, as a guest, as a sensation, as a box-office draw; but what is not satisfactory – and what is expected of me today – is that this occupation should *take the place* of one that is regular, constructive and tradition-forming. That is exploitation.

How does it happen that good, mediocre and quite miserable things by today's 'young people' are all lumped together rather indiscriminately by publishers and performers? The feeling of solidarity of today's 'young people' is responsible. This 'feeling of solidarity' is the greatest obstacle to the recognition of true goodness, which has always been rare.

It is the tendency of every artist to reach his equilibrium, between the spiritual and the material. If there exists an equilibrium in his sense (Hindemith, Reger), he calls it skill. To explain this he concludes that the world lays claim to the degree of warmth, soul, etc. that he, according to his talent, is capable of giving. But, precisely in the case of this kind of artist, this does not apply. They are able to bring 'skill' so much to the fore because the lack of dominant spiritual strength is so marked in them. In Mahler, Reger, Strauss and Debussy, technique begins to distance itself from experience, to become high-handed. The disappearance of substance, an aesthetic formed by the age and also the form of the audience, is characteristic.

(Grillparzer)*

Es gibt kein erkanntes Genie?
Zu unsrer Zeit zum wenigsten nie?
Betrachte dich selber, wenn's beliebt:
So lang's gepriesene Dummköpfe gibt,
Gibt's auch verkanntes Genie!

* Franz Grillparzer (1791–1872), distinguished playwright who knew Goethe, Beethoven and Schubert, and delivered the funeral orations of the latter two.

Nicht, als wär gar so hoch mein Sinn
Ist's, was uns trennt, unendlich;
Vielmehr nur, daß ich ehrlich bin,
Macht mich euch unverständlich.

Die Zeitideen werden sich da am vollsten drängen,
Wo keine eignen ihnen den Platz beengen.

[So there is no recognized genius, and in our own times less than ever? Consider yourself, then, if you please: as long as fools are lauded there will also be misunderstood genius!

It isn't any loftiness of spirit that keeps us forever separate; it is rather only my honesty, which makes me incomprehensible to you.

The ideas of the age cram into places where ideas of one's own do not cramp their space.]

Anyone who avoids tradition, who flees the great past for the sake of a small present, who does not truly bear this cross, is avoiding fate for the sake of a comfortable life.
Greatness without warmth is empty. Warmth, sincerity without greatness are slight; both are the fate of 'descendants'.

Liszt, the composer who represents limitless striving into the far distance, Brahms, the composer of collection and self-contemplation.

Bruckner is a particularly curious case. Bruckner's success in Germany is a sign that the country in which music is the nation's truest expression is not satisfied with skilful and superficial music. Rather the naïveté – which are quite apparent – and the originality of nature than all the skill in the world and everything at second hand.

The further one is from nature, the more intolerant one becomes. The more intellectual, the further from nature an artistic direction, the more one-sided and fanatical its followers, that is, the narrower, the more threatened an artist's productive basis, the more he is dependent upon it, the tighter he clings to it. That is why Spontini is so much more petty than Wagner, Stravinsky so much more blinkered than Strauss.

The preacher, like the politician, is a man of action. He only becomes whole when he is with his audience, his word has value in so far as it is communicated to the audience. The artist's word does not have this value; he is a sage, he is creative by himself and for himself. In Schiller (correspondence) it is plain to see how much harder is the lot of the artist, how much higher, creatively higher he stands. As a result he is capable of seeing and evaluating things in terms of their being, while the preacher (which includes the philosopher) can see everything, including the work of art, only in the context of his desire for influence. Hence the profound ignorance, even distaste of all philosophers towards the truly artistic.

The neo-classicism of Busoni and Stravinsky is nothing but the desire to write as freely and in as apparently unhampered a manner as the true 'classicists'. It is therefore completely trivial in itself. The true classicists did what was necessary, that is, in line with their rules, while the neo-classicists are only following a playful and historical instinct. Neo-classicism, like any kind of 'classicism', is always second-hand.

The playful trait in Strauss: not the playing of a child, which is actually in deadly earnest, but the conscious play of the irresponsible person, of the person devoid of content, the redundant person. As he never means it quite truly, quite warmly, quite seriously, he is never heard or felt quite truly, quite warmly, quite seriously. He is, of all of them, the one who 'can' do the most and who 'is' the least. (Incidentally, the two depend causally upon one another.)

If someone, as is often true of the 'philosophers', has more intelligence than perception and sensuousness, he can often be labelled as clear-headed. Clarity is said to be the attribute of a philosophical, mathematical mind. Are people aware of how deceptive this conclusion is? Do people know that cleverness in the mathematically limited as well as the purely philosophically finite sense has nothing in common with the clarity of the world at large, and is even in conflict with it? Clarity in one's response to the world comes from the correct balance of intelligence and sensuousness; in this sense Wagner, Brahms, Beethoven were among the clearest minds that have ever been.

Goethe was a poet because he did not want to be one in life. If only, as Grillparzer says, he had written more in later life, instead of continuing to study! There was nothing of the professional about him, like Leonardo. For him writing was an illness, which he feared and through which he became healthy. And one might say: Only where it affects one against one's will – as in love – is it real. In this sense writing is not a job, but a suffering, an endurance.

Interpreting means performing, discovering the law in each piece. Of course, where there is none, none can be found. Such works can be performed at random.

It is believed that liberalism, intellectualism, individualism, the lack of connections in art can be removed by an act of violence. That is all very well in politics; but in art there are no acts of violence, any more than there are in love. Each and every thing is a gift from heaven, even the connections into which we are born and which first make freedom possible. In art the only thing that counts is nature, innate substance. Intellectual hygiene, which also attempts to create connections through understanding – rather like sport in life – is impossible in art.

This repeated isolation of things by the semi-cultured: as if the 'artistic' were really (e.g. in art) possible without the religious.

Musical history is used to judging and evaluating musicians according to the new, according to freedoms. One could work the other way round and judge them according to their connections. Each freedom is made possible only by a *new* connection.

I reject all music that has no audience in principle. What sort of music is that? In all real music, any creation of the intelligence must be steeped in emotion, and on the other hand all emotion must be so charged with intelligence that it produces a shape, a form, a natural process. Chaotic emotion or intelligence alone are not compelling in art, do not flash across. But the epitome of such a union is: intuition.

Bruckner speech

A question – how important is intelligence in composing. Strauss – Pfitzner. The celebrated Strauss must know the answer. Apart from that it is so pleasant to know that others are no better and can do nothing better that one can oneself. In reality the matter is quite different, and indeed very simple. The role of intuition and intelligence is very different for different composers. For Strauss it is very important, and certainly no one can get by without artistic intelligence. But the characteristic of the great man is precisely that the spiritual and artistic intelligence interpenetrate to such an extent that nothing is left over . . .

In a real and eternal art-work there is not a single bar that lacks soul, and it would never be possible to say where intuition and intelligence begin.

But this state of affairs is not only revealed in the strength of connectedness, but also in the strength of intuition itself. And not only is the strength of intuition spoiled by an excess of artistic intelligence, but this also has an effect on the way this intuition works. It does not give it free rein, or permit it to fulfil all of its inspirational power – Particularly strong in Bruckner. This is already revealed by the gesture of Bruckner, that broad and relaxed sweep between happiness and transfiguration, fulfilment without sentimentality, entirely without desire.

The ultimate end of art is still its practical performance; the meaning of music still lies in playing.

Cultural gossips. Some of them know something about things, the others only talk. The broad perspective, the 'historical' contexts are more easily perceived the less the value and stress placed on details. This is practically an Eldorado for all kinds of intellectual game-playing. Art history by people who know a substantial amount and can say something about things themselves is in very short supply. Here, remaining with the things themselves, is even better. It demonstrates a love-relationship.

Earlier ages solved the problem of universality by always having (Homer, *Tristan, Nibelungenlied*, etc.) a large number of people writing on the same work. That does not effectively happen any more today, but in fact it is merely a naïve form of a real state of affairs which also still holds today. Beethoven speaks for thousands, for everyone, just as Homer did, and the amount of personal genius which is to be found in Homer is no less than that of Beethoven.

1940

Plan!

Wagner, the most important man of all, the most misunderstood, to the extent that one practically needs an entire programme in order to declare oneself for or against him. Never has an artist divided the world so much into love and hate. This has been true from his first appearance, and has remained so after his death.

This is not immediately a question of greatness. An artist has as broad an effect as he wishes. Late Beethoven only has an effect on enlightened people. But he is no less great in spite of this, but rather greater than everyone else. The world-wide popularity of certain works by Wagner is unparalleled, but it is at least approached by Bizet and Puccini. And yet we also feel that there is a difference here. (Even Nietzsche knew this, even if, as a biased advocate, he does not say as much.) Puccini meets the world halfway. Wagner makes demands. He demands more than any other operatic composer, apart from the German classicists, who for that very reason, however, remain in their classical heaven. But Wagner comes down to our earth. The great hater of theatre, he fell prey to it more than anyone else. So he became the greatest theatrical reformer – theatre, yet not only theatre.

Sensuousness of musical language, sequences, chromaticism, etc.; extreme obviousness, etc. is the foreground, part of the language which he speaks, but it is not the content. People who only know him from afar, who do not really deal with him, take this as being the important thing. Nietzsche does the same, but with a bad conscience.

All psychologizing (Nietzsche), like the significantly judgemental attitude in general, is run through with, or even borne by resentment. The judgemental attitude is like a bent and twisted posture of the body; like this, held for a long time, it results in deformity and malformation. One might even believe that art is made for this kind of person, and can even only . . . quite feeble people who are still impressed by the tricks and sayings of psychology.

If, nowadays, someone wears his waistcoat higher than the next man because of his build, the onlooker will conclude that he sees a new principle of fashion and write big fat books about it – music historians!!

All state 'patronage' produces only hothouse flowers.

Beethoven

The great B-flat major quartet contrasts with Beethoven's other quartets, seen as a whole, more a suite-like, free formation than a strict sonata. That is revealed by the larger number of individual movements, held together only by the great first movement and the colossal closing movement, the famous so-called *Große Fuge*. When the work was published, at the suggestion of friends, the publishers, etc., Beethoven replaced it, because of the excessive length of the whole, with a different, shorter closing movement – incidentally his last composition. That the monumental content of the *Große Fuge* works better in a full string orchestra than in a string quartet is something that experience has often shown.

If we try to put this *Große Fuge*, which entirely refuses to fit into any framework, into the context for which Beethoven had planned it, then this is even more justified because these other movements have a simple and incredible beauty and, nevertheless, the greatest monumental character.

It is also an attempt related to the particular character of these movements, and one which should therefore in no way replace performance in the original setting or even be extended to the other Beethoven string quartets.

The 'apparatus' is an idol. For the concert conductor it is still plain that the artist is more important than the apparatus, in the theatre the most recent history of the Berlin theatre has unequivocally proven the opposite for our own time.

The readiness to do penance, the readiness for Christian humility, for respect, the readiness to find mistakes in oneself, is the sign of the strong and noble soul. An attitude of the soul both with regard to itself and to God. Certainly not with regard to others. For it knows only too well that they are even worse than it is – Christianity arises as a relationship to one's own soul, to oneself and to God.

The problem of Romanticism! Previously, it was still wholeness, the unity of soul and body, even if, since the Renaissance, which meant a brutal severity towards oneself, aimed at *große Form*, there have been various crises. Only in Romanticism did the soul begin to discover its independence. The dislike with which Goethe, for example, looked on Hölderlin. It becomes apparent that he was right, *in general* at least. The banishment of Romanticism stems from this, and it is a mistake to see it as a salvation for the present, either in its naïve early form or in its wild late form. It started that cult of the soul, sensitivity, etc., which has now made way for a soulless cult of the body and material, even more deadly to the artist. No form develops from the soul. But form is the body of the work of art, without which it cannot live.

Artistic judgement has two sources, the thing itself, that is, the work of art, and 'personality'. The latter often has absolutely nothing to do with art and allows people to get away with all kinds of trickery.

A truly sympathetic work, a piece of absolute music is like a sea. There are big waves, smaller ones on these, even smaller on these. The first thing one sees, and the only thing that most people see throughout their lives, are the smallest waves. But to reproduce them adequately one needs to understand the largest just as much, indeed above all.

Dacqué* *Lost Paradise.* Too much time-wasting polemic against modern intellectualism, something I too must beware of. People with an acute feeling for deeper levels must – in their defence, for otherwise it is pointless – devote an unreasonable amount of strength and time to this matter.

Extreme feats of memory, particularly of a large number of details, in opera, say, or inorganic modern works, are the sign of an overspecialized type, of one who has already lost his soul, decadence.

Present-day intellectualism needs complements; its sense of reality understands that intelligence alone does not grasp all of reality. For example, Kunkel (fate), Dacqué (myth, etc.). In all of these modern essays, in fact, today's Socratic person learns that he knows nothing, and that is all. Here Goethe, the artist, is truly better. Art is access to the

---

* Edgar Dacqué (1878–1945), German paleontologist and Nature-philosopher who published *Lost Paradise* in Munich in 1938.

'myth' in one's own breast, through depiction. The only access to it today is this 'depiction of the self', unless it be in purely religious experience.

Has it ever occurred to anyone that the great 'earthly' artists of the nineteenth century, that Brahms, indeed Wagner and Verdi, were the *only* ones who were able to put truly religious content into music? The acid test is whether or not one is capable of this. Imagine R. Strauss or Stravinsky writing a 'Mass'!* Thus we can see what is wrong with them. Distanced from real content. But . . . virtuoso.

There is music which is planned within a large context, and music that lives only in the moment. Bach, Chopin and often Wagner connect the two most naturally. But even in Wagner the context is created by the drama itself. The contextual composers, Beethoven, Brahms, even Wagner, must be offered in context if they are to be clearly understood. But in an age when even the concept of real context is lost (Debussy, Stravinsky, Reger), this is sadly increasingly rare.

The many corrections in Beethoven, and more recently in Bruckner, have provoked astonishment. But this can be understood as the mark of the dramatist who has to reduce everything to the concept, to the lowest common denominator.

Modern man is not interested in warmth, power, grandeur, love, the well-grown, but in the *deviant*. Deviance as a principle.

Strauss' works: as the expression of a vital state of liberation they are matchless. But that which is liberated is not worth talking about. It pays the price of its freedom with banality, or rather the banality is what makes the freedom possible. In our time, that is since the Renaissance, where personality is also a part of art, this is always the case. Those who have both, like Beethoven and Michelangelo, are the true exceptions. The first of this kind on German soil was Schiller; Goethe admired this and could still never have written a single line like Schiller.

Today's artists, productive and reproductive, now that the press has

* 'Imagine . . . Stravinsky writing a "Mass"!' As I point out in the Introduction, in 1948 that is what he did.

been brought into line, are behaving like hares and deer when all their predators have been shot – they have degenerated. All of our artistic conditions degenerate as soon as the air of ruthless and authentic criticism ceases to flow.

My reply to the moderns

Universal things can only be said in a universal language. Because this language is universal, because the things to be said in it are meant to be universal, it does not follow that they must have appeared before. The mark of all truly great work, whether that of yesterday or tomorrow, is that it is both old and new, that it has never existed before and yet one has the feeling of having known it for ages. But everything else, everything that does not in its own way strive for universality, is subjectivism, and *only* this is subjectivism. Which is, today, as it always has been and always will be – superficial.

One might say that modern art differs from classical art (in music) in that it alone tends towards artificial originality, while the latter proclaims that which is, in the true sense, natural, evolved, organic above all else, as its basic value or, rather, as the precondition for all values. This is the attitude of the person in contact with his natural roots.

Bach, Mozart, Haydn fulfilled both themselves and the age they lived in. Beethoven was the first to separate off the individual work and create the exception. This became necessary . . . Since he did this, no amount of reflection has been able to recreate the former condition (Hindemith, Reger). The isolation of the individual work, the objectification of the artist. Precisely *not* subjective; Mozart is himself in all his works, always Mozart – Beethoven someone different in each.

The possibility of isolation is the greatest music-historical event of the age of Beethoven. Here the playfulness of the transition period is rejected once more, and the massive seriousness of the Germans appears as it does in Bach and later in Brahms, Wagner, Bruckner. Today it has been lost although it is still sought (Hessenberg)* and felt to be the most crying need. This seriousness is not simply a mood, but simply consciousness of reality, the realization of reality. It is true wholeness and the full vigour of life!

---

* Kurt Hessenburg (1908–), composer whose search for seriousness has left no enduring traces.

Essay

There is a two-fold art history to be written: that of material, the soul of the mass captured in material, and that of man, who needs art as a true expression of himself and thus creates himself. The two things fit together at first, but separate as soon as a routine sets in within the material. This is where that art emerges which, following the dictates of the material, increasingly relinquishes the soul (Strauss), and the art that subjects the material to dictates of the soul. This is where the titanic manifestations started by Beethoven come into being. This is where the sphere of the tragic begins, which is why it never lasts for long. That is wrongly called subjective. On the contrary, however, it is objective, in as far as it provides the spiritual with the necessary form, *inherent* within it and not imposed upon it by the material of the age. This is the beginning of the problem of art today. In music we have, more than in any other art, a direct barometer of the degree of *necessity* of an artistic practice. Let us try to read and understand it. And let us understand that the discarding of the soul from today's art is not, as historians who can only examine historical processes would have it, the expression of the present day but the increasing redundancy of art in general.

The great artists of the past are not great because they made the art of their time, fulfilling, so to speak, the timely demands of the material, but because they were also human beings and as such expressed themselves mythically and symbolically. And *only* for that reason. The fulfilment of the material is solely of interest to the age.

Art history, as practised today, is based on laws of development which are entirely drawn from reality. In its basic tenets it is not less of an 'exact' science than chemistry or physics, but simply, by its nature, more unstable in its results. The crucial thing now, however, is that these laws – just like, incidentally, the parallel laws of the 'exact' world – somehow fail to grasp the whole of reality. There is a 'gap' in them that is to be found precisely where – the living person appears. In fact it is gradually ceasing to be the time for devoting oneself body and soul to these laws which have, in the meantime, become common property.

Goethe was a properly organized mind who saw things as they must be seen from the point of view of mankind.

Jung writes a big book about the metamorphoses of the libido. He completely separates the value of the libido and its object, and in this manner he arrives at complete disillusion, a situation which would be akin to Buddhism if Buddhism did not turn his 'libido' into the idea of the independence produced by the overcoming of the world, Nirvana, etc. Jung, like psychoanalysts is general, as a real scientist, puts his own 'libido' into the process of illumination, of examination, in this case the razing of all the sensuous bases of of the human mind. The consequence, that is, how one is then to 'live' with one's results without completely falling apart is not something that he reveals. He does what the age has commissioned him to do, but is more clever than wise.

In art the difference between 'education' and true vocation becomes painfully clear. Pfitzner, despite everything, is still somehow an 'educated' musician, an 'epigon', hence the slight traits of dilettantism repeatedly found in his works. He grasps the spiritual without giving it full expression in a naturally musical way. That is the highest kind of epigon; the less considerable one is the person who stays close to the technique of his model and in this way finds it easy to write 'properly'. But standards and yardsticks only exist from the moment when the spiritual also comes into play.

There is a certain type of excessive cleverness. A man such as Keyserling sometimes says more clever things in one sentence than others do in whole books – and still writes fat books. And yet he lacks the power to dwell on a theme, the simple ability to relate to the individual thought that characterizes the truly great man.

An essay about the essence of originality, culture, intellectualism and mythical power.

It is characteristic that what an artist thinks he can be most proud of is most rarely precisely his main talent, his major skill. Generally it is even the other way around. Proof yet again that real talents are unconscious, that is gifts of fortune.

The artist's attitude and talent, which encourage and develop production and what is commonly called 'technical' ability, e.g. innate banality, phrasing, false pathos, mediocrity of feeling, bourgeois standards of normality. Is Strauss more skilled in counterpoint than Brahms, is Reger more productive than Beethoven? On the contrary. They are only less restrained. The latter because of his banality, the former because of his decadence. Reger, for example, does not 'stand by' his discoveries; his means of achieving this is polytonality (or rather the means of rising above this disagreeable necessity).

Artists who to a great extent 'stand by' their discoveries to the last are Smetana, César Franck. Smetana does not slip into banality as Dvořák does, he is the true classicist, the distinguished mind of his nation, although he cannot, of course, always exclude the curse of conventionality. Franck is, in his best works, an individual, one of the most spiritual composers that have ever been. They are both enormously 'capable', but this 'capability' is restrained and purified by the will to expression, the 'spiritual'. In Reger and Strauss this is only true to a very small extent and only under certain conditions. They are called great, but only in terms of musical history. What their value will be, apart from their 'material' importance, which is all today's generation is interested in, is another question.

The 'poet' type in Goethe is still seen today as the epitome of the poet. But the occasional poet, who draws the stimuli for his work from life, is the lyric poet. The dramatist is not capable of this. He must delve deeper into the unconscious of his own nature. And if his life fails to supply him with these 'stimuli'? Shakespeare is greater than Goethe – Goethe's opinion.

Two kinds of music are not recognized by their contemporaries: that which appears too 'new', and that which appears too 'old'. If, in the first half of the nineteenth century, the former predominated – since there was still an established musical culture – from the end of the century onwards (Smetana, Brahms), when the established concepts slowly broke down, this has increasingly changed. Today the 'new' is no longer attacked, but placed at the forefront in principle. Since Liszt and Wagner, particularly since Reger and Strauss, however, nobody has been misunderstood for being new, but they certainly have been for no longer seeming new enough.

The decisive criterion for the achievements of the reproductive artist, whether as conductor or instrumentalist, is very simply the following: is he capable of playing so that the music he plays really 'gives pleasure' to himself and others? Everything else is superfluous.

The case of Tchaikovsky or: the curse of education. The world recognizes him, but musicians, particularly contemporary Russian musicians, reject him as 'commonplace'. Even today it takes all the authority of a Stravinsky to rank him among 'notable' composers as far as some people are concerned. 'Curse' or 'limits' of education: *the* current theme of our over-educated Germany.

The work of the generations of Strauss, Reger, Mahler (only Pfitzner has remained outside it) consists primarily in reproducing the content of the preceding music 'stretched' – in mammoth forms and diluted accordingly. This kind of 'progress' is now entirely finished.

There are two mutually contradictory things: originality and naturalness. Anyone who does not have both, who is not and cannot be original and yet natural, natural and yet original and capable, should forget originality. For of the two – and let this be said to our age again and again – naturalness is the more important and the greater thing.

Nietzsche is a decadent. He makes no secret of his love for all kinds of decadence (Heine). Beethoven for him is not much more than a musical *Moral-Trompeter von Säckingen.** When writing to Wagner, he cannot follow Wagner's writing about Beethoven. He is not capable of confronting the great and productive eye to eye. Here he cannot, as Wagner can, enjoy the nuances. He does not notice that this is where a 'sacred place' begins for Wagner.

The historical view takes as its starting-point the idea that all periods are essentially of equal value. One need only empathize with them. And in this way new artistic areas are being opened up.

I would like to see someone perform a Beethoven sonata *correctly* on the piano, and still say that it is an outdated art.

Not only the means, the entire contents are also seen 'historically', and dismissed accordingly. In Mozart there was love, in Wagner lust and

---

* The narrative poem 'Der Trompeter von Säckingen' by J.V. von Scheffel was a popular sentimental-humorous work published in 1854. Nietzsche's gibe is actually aimed at Schiller, not at Beethoven – it can be found in *Twilight of the Idols*. His frequent references to Beethoven are nearly always favourable. No doubt Furtwängler's hostile attitude to Nietzsche contributed to his making this slip.

today – vitality. Anyone finding himself in the unfortunate situation of needing love must, whether he wishes to or not, run back to Mozart. Hand on heart – is love today really, as someone once told me, finished once and for all? And all the other emotions . . . humility, modesty, harmony, but also pride, strength, greatness, etc., none of that is present in this world of modern music. Only vitality, always the same vitality. What impoverishment! What – let us say it clearly – what a lie!

I have always given a great deal of thought to the word 'vital'. It is a word of intellectuals for intellectuals – where would it ever be used by anyone who really depended on it, such as a soldier, or how ridiculous it would sound in the mouth of such a person. So Mozart and Beethoven are not vital either, but simply beautiful, great, good, what they want to be.

What highly praised modern art expresses: vitality. What it does not express: humility, warmth, real, straightforward simplicity, greatness, etc. And that is supposed to be in tune with the age. What an unhappy age that would be.

Composers!

A leading contemporary composer once said to me: We are only ever performed once. How do we get played many times, like the old works? The very question contained the whole problem.

Hauer* gave the world the discovery that Beethoven [. . .] only cadences – yes, but what cadences!

Dr Goebbels is churning out undisguised foreign-culture propaganda aimed simply at the lowest common party denominator, bound up with the unbounded liberation and preference of mediocrity.

And also an attack on all healthy tradition.

Never was art as necessary to people as it is today, when they imagine they can best and most easily do without it.

Music developed until Brahms, Bruckner, Wagner. After this, what subsequently looked like further external development was inflation

* Joseph Matthias Hauer (1883–1959), Austrian composer who developed his own twelve-tone technique at the same time as Schoenberg, but apparently quite independently.

(Strauss, Reger, Mahler). It emerged on the one hand under the terrorism of the historical view which always holds development in high regard and feels justified in doing so, as it has in the past, and on the other hand from the spiritual feebleness of the age. Pfitzner, also Debussy, Ravel, even some of Stravinsky, are different in this, while of course Hindemith, again, tends all too much towards inflation.

Anyone who does not have the courage to reduce what he has to say to the simplest formula should avoid saying anything at all.

There are artists who work from within, from the self: lyrical artists. There are those who approach from the outside and depict: epic artists. Those who move the external from within and the internal from without, are the rarest: the true dramatic artists.

If I say that man depends upon the divine, I mean: as much as a man with and of the community, as a natural being with and of nature, the cosmos. These two factors define the 'concept' of the divine. But the latter is like the universe surrounding the earth, more comprehensive, more primary. Every person who relates to the cosmos in a religious way is at once *eo ipso* a community being, even if he is a stylite, but not every communal man is religious as simply as that. Communal fanaticism can, as is shown by all manifestations of race hatred, etc., all too easily spring from the flat, negative and unproductive realms of the soul.

Criticism exists for art, but not the other way around. Which is incidentally equally true of artists. The two work together, are in the same boat, pull together. They are said to be enemies. Seen from a higher point of view, that is incorrect. The only enemy of the good artist is the bad critic, and that of the bad artist, the good critic. Those who are capable of doing something are also found here, as they are everywhere, and it is high time that they saw this and involved themselves in the construction of new German musical life.

They complain about the 'personality cult'. They demand objectivity from the artist, a self-expression of which only a few are capable. And can they do it themselves?

Musical life must be *musical life*, that is, close to the audience.

I know from the start that there is no point in my saying this. Even so . . . In one sense the critic's job is disproportionately more difficult than that of the artist, in the sense of *character*!

If they discuss State Musical Director X in just the same way as they discuss Sabata,* say, they are doing no harm to Sabata. But they are betraying and damaging art and confusing the public. If they overrate material qualities such as technique of conducting from memory, they are prizing hard work instead of artistic practice. They are aligning themselves with the stupid people who never seem to be in short supply, and who feel nostalgic for the circus when they are in the concert-hall.

The contemporary European's basic attitude to life is – as soon as it ceases to be simply a question of practical reality – that of the researcher, the person seeking to trace the very roots of the laws of this life, to understand the course of life and tear its 'mysteries' from it. Every German today has something of the explorer in him, if he does not deal only with practical reality. Even the way in which one considers music, in which one enjoys it today, is based in a desire for historical understanding.

The researcher's means of dealing with art is that of comparison. Using comparisons he believes that he can trace the development and distinctive features of whole eras just as much as the essence of the individual work of art.

On the other hand, the artist has the duty – today more than ever – of repeatedly stressing that comparison is not an adequate means of dealing with art. One can use it to deal with art history, which, however, differs from real art as a map drawn on paper differs from the land which it represents. No true work of art has ever been traced to its roots by means of 'comparisons'. Anyone who does not confront the work of art himself, as a person, should avoid dealing with it at all. He will never meet it by taking the easy route of comparison.

It is not for no reason that symphonies are no longer being written today. There is only ever any point in writing a symphony if, as was after all still the case in Bruckner, in a free manner, the form as a whole is tonally felt from beginning to end, that is that everything has its architectural-tonal place. This has long been abandoned by modern music, whatever else its attitude to tonality may be.

The basic premise of art is that the work of art can be a self-sufficient world, a microcosm. Only then can it bring salvation. History has

* Vittorio de Sabata (1892–1967), Italian conductor and composer.

discovered that this is not necessary, that those things which are lacking in the work are often replaced by the community which surrounds and contains the work. The moment that occurs, art is given a symbolic character, if not one of superfluous frivolity. It loses its true power over people, people become hard, the world consists only of action, it becomes insecure and godless. That is the end that we are faced with unless . . .

Sibelius is, along with Tchaikovsky, the only non-German who really works *symphonically*. Of the Germans, quite self-sufficiently, only Haydn, Beethoven, Bruckner and Brahms do so. Schubert is half, Schumann completely 'schooled in it'.

So why is the gift so terribly rare??? In Smetana, Dvořák, César Franck, Pfitzner, it only extends to chamber music. Liszt and Strauss come from the other side, and from the very start they find they have taken on too much!!

Title: Music history and how it is not taught.

An observation that is always timely: that which is really important, that which has true weight is viewed with a certain envy by the public world, although this world cannot escape the fact of its existence. See Brahms.

Resignation: always present, always necessary. Resignation: the lowest, the final limit, the most damaging, the most execrable and contemptible thing.

Mastery 'without an object'; the danger of the artist, particularly in maturity (Mahler, Busoni, Hindemith).

The healthy person needs a certain arrogance, nature has made sure of that. But it seems that the more a person becomes distanced from the sources of everything eternal, the more he oversteps the limit of 'natural' arrogance. It is an unconscious regulation on the part of nature. That stupid arrogance that so often characterizes the semi-cultured people of today, that real 'cultural arrogance' is an example of this.

Everything impressionist in art, everything that comes from outside, everything that is only based in material, etc., changes with the seasons and therefore ages quickly. Everything internally related, everything constructive, organic, self-sufficient, everything which believes in itself and 'is' itself scorns the epochs and lasts for ever.

All music that is not moved from outside, but moves by itself, either becomes a fugue and variation – if monothematic – or a sonata, if polythematic.

The case of Pfitzner

Pfitzner claims to be a 'genius', but also his own genius, likewise the superiority which it gives him, to enjoy like a normal person. As regards this one can only say: the more one can do and wants to do this, the less of a genius one is. Pfitzner peddles his 'genius' from door to door.

Pfitzner, the dualism of the Romantic, who confronts a rationalized world with hothouse genius, without even attempting a connection and an interpenetration of the two at a higher level. I cannot help it: Behind this there is – as, incidentally, there is in all Romantics – a profound *vanity*, a *desire* not to open oneself to the reality of the world. Pfitzner the composer is greater than Pfitzner the thinker; he has achieved more because he works more unconsciously, although the break is perceptible in him as well. It would be worth protecting the composer from the 'thinker'.

Any community which has created a real art, or rather, one from which art has sprung, has always been a community of love. Be it as it may in other ways – a community of compulsion, an economic community . . . as this alone it will never be artistically creative. All talk, intention, cultural affectation have nothing to do with real art, that is, with the community of love that lies at its base. And one can only tell whether or not such a community of love exists by examining whether or not a true art develops within it. That *this* community has nothing to do with political communities is revealed by the great age of German artistic development at the beginning of the nineteenth century, which was politically the most powerless. Nevertheless, the community of love of the German nation tangibly existed; a community of compulsion was not required, and any such community in the future will neither add anything nor take anything away from true artistic creation.

1941

The predominance of the onlooker stance is bound up with the fact that people have forgotten how to receive a work of art, how really to allow it to be effective. But bound up with this – and only with this – is the monstrous rise of mediocrity. People no longer know what music really is and is really capable of being; otherwise they would not allow so much to be presented to them as 'music'. The stance of the recorder, the onlooker, more or less demands mediocrity.

The natural person does not wish to acknowledge and reject, he does not wish to judge, rather he wishes to be enthusiastic. But he cannot do this with anything good, respectable, considerable, skilful or any of the other expressions for conspicuous mediocrity, but only with something extraordinary.

Nietzsche's success lies in the fact that, although profoundly unproductive himself, he became a companion in misfortune to all unproductive people. On the one hand he had the needs of the productive person, but on the other he had nothing to justify them, nothing with which he could escape himself and his age. So he was delivered up to the age like no other and had to suffer like no other. That is his greatness, his way of being great.

'*Wer immer strebend sich bemüht*', never does so in vain. He has set his gaze on what he *cannot* yet do. A certain degree of loneliness is necessary if one wishes to avoid vanity. One is more or less forced into this by the unreasonable demand of the mob, if one gives it too much room.

Not, like Rilke, or like the incomparably greater Hölderlin, to express content garrulously, broadly, so to speak, but to enclose it within the symbol of the 'form', and thus to restore to it its natural mystery. This is the true meaning of artistic form, which in our times is understood less and less.

Art cannot be understood, but only *experienced.* Clever minds can then seek to understand their own experience. But this calls for the availability of such an experience. A desire to understand *before* one has abandoned oneself to the work, before or during the 'experience', as is so often the case today, only leads to errors.

The musician's problem: how to achieve particularity of expression. What a piece of music gains in particularity it loses in infinity. Infinity in the particular, the particular in infinity – that is what characterizes the truly 'great', but not a gain in particularity at the expense of infinity as happened in 'naïve' Romanticism, or a gain in infinity at the expense of particularity, in accordance with our own intellectualized age.

The only person who has taken on definition of expression, even at the cost of breadth, is Hans Pfitzner. His work, however weak and fragile it may sometimes appear, has one thing at least: the intellect has regained its rightful place. Its importance in this respect will doubtless only be understood later on.

How does the intellectualization of musical perception manifest itself? Intelligence invades even *before* emotion has had time to take a stance. So intelligence demands immediate 'originality', related to the individual moment, while emotion calls for *authenticity* expressed in a context. But it is true that the two are unfortunately mutually exclusive to a large extent. This in itself would still not be catastrophic; we could tell ourselves that we live in an intellectual age, and must write music to satisfy the demands of the intellect. But this is unfortunately not the case. For the intellect, in its more far-reaching consequences, does not want or need art at all. It overpowers it, as it – the most power-crazed thing of all – strives to overpower all things.

Montesquieu says: A choice mind is less rarely found than a great soul. That also applies to creative artists, particularly today.

Anyone who cannot see true greatness in the past is also incapable of seeing it in the present. For the two belong together. And anyone incapable of seeing it in the present, cannot actually see it in the past either, however much and however loudly he may talk about it.

Certainly music cannot be created in the abstract, without any relation to the apparatus, the instrument for which it has been planned. The instrument is the soil in which it has its roots, through which it comes into its own. But just as little – and since Wagner and Strauss it has become twice as necessary to say this – can the instrument and its requirements be placed so much in the foreground that the interests of the music itself lose out. Take Strauss' attitude to the orchestral styles of Beethoven and Brahms, Beethoven's string quartets, etc.

Bruckner

They have found – it is said – setting copy. Haas* says this has changed nothing. The fact remains —. Violation of Bruckner by scholars. That could go a long way. One might sooner speak of a violation of the public by the Haas myth. The fact is that it was not the *Gesamt-Ausgabe* that made Bruckner famous, but the earlier edition. The question is even raised of whether the *Gesamt-Ausgabe* would have made him quite so famous. I am not concerned with the literal Bruckner, the Bruckner of the 'scribes and Pharisees', but with the authentic Bruckner. And I cannot call only the *Original-Ausgabe* authentic if another print from a later period is available. This is why Haas' violation myth is necessary, and it is not authentic. It even contradicts the psychology of all great men. Only unproductive minds can seriously believe that a great productive artist can 'be put under pressure' for the duration of a depression. Depression and productivity are essential opposites, the former only ever a reaction, nothing more. The falsification that is done here to the character of Bruckner – Bruckner as a fool – is much greater than [that done] by the essays of the first scholars, Löwe and Schalk . . .

On the matter itself it should be noted: the original editions vary. Only for the Fourth and Fifth Symphonies are there original manuscripts. They do not exist for the Second, Third, Seventh. In the Second and Third, Haas has reconstructed them. He is proceeding at random . . .

---

* Robert Haas (1886–1960), Austrian musicologist who was responsible for establishing sound texts of Bruckner's works, which had been extensively revised and mutilated by well-meaning but wholly misguided friends of the composer, especially the Schalk brothers and Ferdinand Löwe. It is interesting and surprising to see Furtwängler defending the corrupt texts here, and attacking Haas, since in 1941 he conducted the first performance of the original version of Bruckner's Fifth Symphony, and all his subsequent performances are in versions established by Haas, or only slightly modified. The only celebrated conductor to go on using the corrupt versions was Hans Knappertsbusch.

Original readings assembled in this way have no original value. The Fifth Symphony is a different matter —

Here the comparison works consistently in favour of the original version.

Although it is a part of the same case, the Fourth Symphony is different.

But now we come to a matter of aesthetics and principle: What is striking in the original version is style: stylistically unified, considered. Conclusion: Baroque master, choric instrumentation, etc. Contrast with Wagner's Romanticism, etc. Now the difference only actually exists on paper; a difference in practice. That this difference is emphasized to such an extent, and has found such serious advocates, has to do with the tendency of our age, which has formed the concept of style. Style, for the present age, is naturalness . . .

Vanity and confidence

The two sometimes look as alike as twins. And yet no two things could be more different. One is the necessary accompaniment of all great achievement, the other a burden.

The progress of any development depends on vanity, which always proceeds in a personal way, that is, at the expense of the matter itself, remaining within given boundaries.

Not true musical life, but rather the music industry, which imagines itself as representing the former, is an intersection of all vanities.

People who seriously and naïvely leave the peace of the family or the countryside for the metropolitan music industry, feel this strongly.

No objections could be raised against this, as the world never changes, but it is good to call it to mind, since, particularly in Germany, a great deal of morality is applied to the wrong area, and, as a result, the true manipulator – vanity – does not become apparent. The only important thing is: To what extent does it affect art in a directly and immediately damaging way? Does it do this at all?

Yes, to a large extent. Yes, to such an extent that it must virtually be seen as the true enemy of art.

All thought is nothing but defence. Defence in the form of clarification. Beyond this, thinking in itself has no value.

1942

The Baroque is basically an appeal to and inflation of power, later an exhibition of it. It always contains an idea of power as a guiding concept: in this sense everything Baroque has something intellectual within it. This is extremely curious. Brahms is free of any Baroque traits. Wagner is not.

In the announcements of a conservatoire I read: 'Masters of the Baroque: Joh. Seb. Bach, Buxtehude, Telemann,' etc. Bach is neither a Baroque master like the others, nor indeed a Baroque artist at all. What is achieved by this? Trivialization, levelling-out, distance from true greatness. And that is probably done in order that our own great figures may live. Only in the process the music becomes redundant. Or: the Bach family. Ph. Emanuel has much more of a promising future; but one must nevertheless accept Joh. Seb. Bach's *Goldberg Variations*, etc. What nonsense! It must finally be said: The devil take development and everything it implies. When will it once more be beautiful, authentic, great music that matters, and no longer music that is important for musical development!

The subjectivism of Nietzsche, the first to reverse the natural attitude to great works and great men, not adjusting himself to them but rather adjusting them according to himself, granting life to those who let him live. There is no more weariness of great works than there is 'weariness' of a ripe grape or pear. The only thing at work here is modern man's exhaustion.

The intoxication of progress might last a while, today we know that the ties must not be broken. Neither to the past nor the future; the present comes of its own accord, so to speak, for it has one great advantage: that of being contemporary. It exploits this advantage as much as it can. In music in a rather different way from the visual arts. It must, as the playing of music is always contemporary, assert itself against the good old things. This results in that previously unadmitted battle with the old works which, seen as a whole, is also a battle of the mediocre against the good. One will always see how much more tolerant *great* musicians are with regard to the past, how much more closely connected to it they are than minor musicians. Ask Strauss what is good about Mozart and Wagner, ask Stravinsky about Tchaikovsky. There are few in the past, but there are also few in the present. They fill the concert halls, in particular they fill the editorial offices. For the literary type in search of relevance, the only thing that exists is the present, the 'effect' of the present. The present exists; it is necessary, it is living. But it is only a transition. Like the peoples of the past, in every true art-work the future must coexist with the present.

It must be admitted that Wagner and Bruckner are greater in terms of their individual inspirations than the classics (who also include Brahms in this context). But the former are capable of inventing a larger sequence of related 'inspirations', which provide them with a stronger final effect. They are more organic, not so much aimed at originality.

Keyserling's merit lies in the fact that he – like no other – grasped life's complexity. This is, incidentally, a rare intellectual gift, which will always remain very rare. Its thinking is really too 'international' to be successful in the longer term. It is human *per se* and will always remain so, to judge from certain local prejudices which must at the present moment be called national. By which I do not mean that which is national is solely a prejudice.

The feeling of being able to form things organically – that is, as nature itself does – outweighs everything else by far. Failure, lifelong misunderstanding and exclusion, the bitterest thing: separation from people, it provides a replacement for all that. It provides ineffable independence from the age, ineffable peace in nature and in God. Of course, since Brahms, nobody has carried this out in music, only a few did before. This is my aim, an aim that is surely worth a few sacrifices.

In Brahms it is as if every movement said to the listener: 'It is all the same to me whether you like me or not, I am as I am, I live and enjoy my own life'. How different from Wagner, for example.

The good Germans – similarly: how they allowed the very greatest men – Wagner and Brahms – to be spoiled by literati, in the same way they are talked into seeing the apparently great, the unclear – Reger – as great.

For the reproductive artist

Every work carries within it its own 'distance', from which one must consider it. To discover this distance and act accordingly is the principal duty of the performer.

Is the job of today's composer not a 'neurotic' job? Is the condition of having to be a 'modern composer' – if one does not find one's satisfaction in pure playfulness as Hindemith does – not one great neurosis (with the exception of the few who are capable of organic creation), an illness?

About banality in Wagner and Strauss. In Wagner in the framework of poetic narrative, demanded by it, in Strauss a cleverly effective device applied by the skilful musician.

Reger – lack of atonality – lack of precise expression. We must get back to precise expression.

All historians exaggerate the differentiation of phenomena, and too seldom see connections. One must be productive to see these.

Philosophy is a decidedly masculine discipline. For this reason it overrates itself enormously. Precisely because it claims to interpret the meaning of life it is thoroughly incapable of doing so. It is and remains a matter for the 'great brain'.

Contemporaries find it difficult to define the limit of unnaturalness because it coincides with convention. It is hard to believe how much unnaturalness goes on being swallowed.

Even Wagner referred to it – music – must see . . . But on the other hand everything, particularly in the theatre, must have an external side. This is the task of the director, which often consists in not disturbing the music. Nowhere is independent action on the part of the director less appropriate than in *real* opera.

1943

Mind and body are divided in the new music. Strauss more body with little mind, Bruckner more mind with too little body (in a purely musical sense) (likewise Pfitzner). The last who had both was Brahms.

The *Matthew Passion* is the best example of modern man's embarrassment when faced with great art. The work that is strongest in feeling, stripped of all emotional affectation, and left only with the foolish concern for purity of style, the avoidance of all 'sentimentality'... what a farce.

Today we find 'closed form' too narrow. We admire Mozart for his elegance, but as a non-contemporary. We wrongly see Beethoven's form in the same way and fail to understand that here, in the form of Being, a constant Becoming is at work. This is modern man's basic error not only with regard to Beethoven, but with regard to all 'form' – expressed particularly in all reproduction. To experience Becoming in Being, and to let others experience it, to grasp the fleeting life of the moment in the solid form, that is real re-production. Everything else is hopeless stammering, schoolmasterish behaviour.

That which is called the 'spirit of the age' is really the level of consciousness of the age. Reactionaries go against this.

The state of poetic stimulation represented by a Rilke or a Hölderlin (sometimes even Nietzsche) must *precede* the creation of the image, the form. Today it is overrated in relation to the finished form, because mysticism, the meaning of the completely shaped form, is not understood (because there are too many clichés).

Never stop at historical impressions. Always, even with the art of the past, penetrate through to that which is universally and immediately human.

A conductor who is weak as an interpreter, that is, in terms of the factual and expressive content of the work, will always try to encourage success by drawing on other areas. Particularly by stressing the *Kapellmeister* situation, the only situation in art which makes the 'master' possible *coram publico*.

Everything to do with art is still, in an intellectual way, entirely enslaved by thought based on historical development. It is time that biological thought, which, in economics and medicine, takes the harmony of organic occurrence as its point of origin, finally spread to art as well.

Goethe says: Classical is that which is healthy, Romantic is that which is ill. I say: A Classicist is one who expresses something clearly and plainly, a Romantic one who does so unclearly, ditheringly and with far too many words. I love Classicists.

We agree that a closeness to the earth is the power of Eros, not only in the private sphere, but more or less *the* very thing that is missing from contemporary Germany, from modern Europe. One might only wonder how one is to compensate for this. Some people do not have it, but speak of it, while those who do possess it do not speak. I have never heard a truly 'vital' person speak of vitality.

Not so much Bruckner himself as the way in which he is cultivated and performed reveals a crucial weakness of organic form in our time.

The more of a technician someone is – Hindemith, also R. Strauss – the more he is interested in style, the less in the work. As he himself pays less attention to the work, he also notices it less in others. Strauss' rejection of Bruckner, etc.

The real effort of every mind is to escape 'destiny', to avoid committing oneself. So in all his barrenness and emptiness, the intellectual Busoni imagines himself as being far superior to Puccini, who simply does his life's work and, in return, is blessed with a living productivity which he can call his own.

Art is the language of the collective within us, art expresses what affects us as collective beings.

Short-circuited judgements – the mark of all intellectualism.

In Goethe's thought nothing is contrived; there is not a single sentence that has not been experienced. In Keyserling three-quarters of everything is contrived, if correctly contrived.

Pfitzner

In his old age Pfitzner is returning to his origins, here as well as there he is a simple musician, in the sense of the great German musicians of the past. He is not yet part of that tendency towards excessive scale, that peculiar inflation of musical expressive means which had its origin in his generation, the generation of Strauss and Reger. This is made plain particularly in the works of his old age, which have become known in the last few years. One can think what one will of their value – the old Pfitzner has the courage to make his music 'warts and all'. The importance of this only becomes clear if one considers that almost everyone else has lost this courage. In these works Pfitzner has restored justice to a category that has almost been forgotten today, the category of 'naturalness'. These works are 'natural' in the same sense as the great works of the past. Consequently they are presenting a demand, and placing themselves in stark contrast to what is being written today.

Or: They are presenting a demand which – however self-evident it may actually be – is universally avoided today, and consequently placing themselves in stark contrast to what is being written today.

The moral importance of this attitude on the part of the old Pfitzner is not easy to overestimate, even if, like all of Pfitzner's music, it is not well understood.

R. Wagner, in his later years, published a major essay on Beethoven which, even if much of it tells us more about Wagner than it does about Beethoven, is still the most important and clearsighted thing that has been written on Beethoven. We know today that Nietzsche rejected this essay, and that Wagner openly aknowledged that he could not understand his doing so. What Nietzsche is rejecting here, however, is not Wagner – their friendship was then at its height – but Beethoven. Nietzsche did not understand Beethoven, and so he also failed to understand why the demanding and fastidious Wagner should treat this particular naïve and unconventional composer with the quite unique and boundless admiration which caused him to write . . .

But many other people feel the same way as Nietzsche. Literature in particular took Nietzsche's side on behalf of the literati. Wagner's enthusiasm for Beethoven was casually dismissed as self-advertisement, and everything was thus comfortably put aside as all too personal.

But it is true: refinement, or even only what one might call heightened sensuous culture, is lacking in Beethoven. He has enough natural sensuousness, but in an elevated, masculine form. Self-indulgence is as far from his nature as feminine loss of control. What Wagner felt edified by and enthusiastic about in Beethoven was the massive 'grip', that directness and grandiose clarity of expression unsurpassed in the whole of music, that '*oratio directa*', as Wagner calls it, the expression of the most regal manliness. In terms of the power and clarity of the 'grip', Wagner became, in his way, a real descendant of Beethoven. But the other thing that he found in Beethoven, the other thing he admired him for, was something that he himself was not, something he was completely incapable of attaining, but which he was great enough to perceive, to recognize far above himself – the indescribable and completely ineffable – we cannot call it anything else – purity of heart, his innocence, the nobility of feeling that cannot be described, much less defined, but only experienced – and then only by someone with the faculty to perceive it. Nietzsche lacked that faculty. All men are not identical, and Nietzsche should not be reproached for this. He had other tasks to carry out. Nietzsche was also responsible for the Beethoven-Schiller comparison which has done so much damage intellectually. I do not mean to disparage Schiller, but Schiller and Beethoven are only similar at first glance, which is, indeed, where many people are content to leave the issue. Precisely those things which characterize Beethoven, the directness, simplicity and purity of feeling, are completely wanting in Schiller, for all the grandeur of his conception.

Music and metropolis
On the psychology of the city

Although I was aware from the start that my career as a conductor led me towards the city as the place where the widest range of choices, the greatest opportunities for comparison were to be found, and where real qualities could thus be first recognized, I nevertheless avoided actual cities for as long as I could. Berlin in particular repelled me – all the more strange since I later came into close and lasting association with Berlin. But is the conductor of the Berlin Philharmonic concerts really concerned with Berlin? Is he not dealing only with a small section of the metropolis, a small part of the Berlin public?

There are a few places, such as Vienna, which cannot be put into any category, because they have their own particular local character. But in general it will be found that the various cities are all similar, according to their own type. Thus – and it is important – one can speak of a metropolitan character in musical matters, which remains the same everywhere. One can speak of the benefits which are typical of the metropolis, one can speak of its characteristic advantages and disadvantages. As it has a disproportionately large influence on the so-called 'provinces', it is worth being aware of these qualities. The city's status as a cultural centre gives it a considerable degree of self-confidence that adheres to all its statements and reactions. It thoroughly believes that it has the last word in all cultural matters, thanks to its superior knowledge and routine. Even this first assumption is wrong. The city knows a great deal, it has a wide perspective; but its knowledge is superficial and generally fails to attain authentic judgement. This pressure to know a great deal necessarily involves being superficial. Great art is not served by superficial knowledge. It only begins beyond it.

In place of real knowledge, in which, quite apart from their incapacity for it, people in the city are not even particularly interested, slogans appear. They fully occupy the foreground of metropolitan concerns. They can be reduced to a few watchwords, which are, however, not spoken directly, but rather used consciously and unconsciously all over the place and, so to speak, crowd the air. These watchwords, these slogans, change according to era and generation; their history has not yet been written, although they represent an extremely interesting object for mass-psychological study. This results from the fact that the metropolises with their characteristic atmosphere have not yet become old, and are also used to responding to everything in the world with scepticism and humour – everything apart from themselves. They take themselves terribly seriously, in fact their arrogance in this respect knows no bounds. Indirectly, metropolitan culture with all its prejudices and slogans occurs entirely in the unconscious, the subconscious. It has no control and therefore no distance from itself, but instead it makes its massive claim, hence the considerable damage which art suffers as a result of this claim.

The watchwords and slogans which regulate the behaviour of the city in artistic matters all have a moralistic character – based on a morality, of course, that the city can understand. One of the most important principles of this morality is, for example, that a work of art may not be boring, that is, that in artistic matters one must be able to speak, discuss and think. Excessively great, excessively intense and selfless devotion to the work is undesirable. In spite of this one knows what is good, or rather, one wants to know this, but as for experiencing it – no, that is too strenuous, that involves too much renunciation. One wants – and this is the real content of all metropolitan morality – to feel, in the face of all things, that one is the superior city-dweller. Thus it comes about that the true battles for new works of art are *not* fought out in the metropolis.

I am – in Germany and abroad – a German artist, that is, a representative of the Germany that manifests itself in German music. One can reject and boycott German music as '*made in Germany*', but one cannot play Mozart and Beethoven and reject those who live and die for them.

But the message which Beethoven directed at mankind in his works, and particularly in the Ninth Symphony, the message of goodness, of trust, of unity before God, seems to me never to have been more necessary than it is today.

Keyserling has a practically virtuoso cleverness. Opposition to him cannot actually attack what he says, for most of that is correct, but rather the way in which he says it. By saying that awful things are the result of associations – he calls it counterpoint and so on – by saying that associative thinking has trained people for the greatest virtuosity imaginable, he deprives what he is thinking of a large part of its reality and its weight.

If a Hindemith suite had come about in the same effortlessly positive way as one by Mozart, it would meet with no opposition. But unfortunately in Hindemith the reasons for many things are to be found in evasions. A work of art is always something that is found; its newness and originality are not based on the fact that something old has been avoided, but that something new has been found.

1944

Stravinsky does not take the living as his point of origin, as he has usually stated, but rather the artificial organism of the doll, the machine. The Russian revolutionary devotion to the machine finds a voice in him. Germany has got beyond this. Germany is struggling from the machine to life, and therefore it much prefers Bruckner's 'stupid' music to the 'clever' music of Stravinsky.

Bach, Haydn, Mozart, even Schubert and Schumann represent a particular age and are consumed as its representatives by our cultivated connoisseurs. That is not true of Beethoven. Here the sum does not quite work out, and they call it individualism. They themselves only want to enjoy historically, to be only observers, they spurn the benefits they could take from this comfortable situation.

At least half of all the so-called aesthetic observations of our time serve the purpose of making life under the same roof as overwhelming greatness more tolerable by trivializing it indirectly. All of us, without knowing it, have played our part in this habit.

Being original means being one's own person, that is, different from the rest. But if everyone is original, as they are today, then no one really is. The greatest courage is needed today if one wants to write simply. Writing a real melody today is 'original'.

I notice that all of my thought revolves around a single point: How is one to respond to the rule of one-sided intelligence today; that is, I too am, as far as I can see, an artist, and seek to justify the artist's existence. Why all these efforts! Why not simply live as an artist! These efforts are, in the end, nothing but the pressure exerted by my environment, nothing but a concession to this environment.

Wagner and Brahms – the last period during which Germany was able to live and work from within. Pfitzner more will than ability to do this,

Reger inflation, Strauss playful virtuosity. Hindemith, attempt at a synthesis largely abandoning the soul. Without this capacity to work from within, true productivity is impossible.

To understand the meaning of all tragic art one must have a feeling for life that does not see cleverness as the *ultima ratio* of all things. Only the non-intellectual person in this sense – non-intellectual in what concerns his actual existence, not, say, his 'conviction' – is capable of true tragedy . . . which is why those who still understand it have become rare today.

For the artist, form is the vessel of insubstantiality. Without it he could not rid himself of his emotions. The virtuoso, on the other hand, possesses not form in the deeper sense, but a 'signature'. He is the individualist.

In this sense the problem of form is the central problem for every true artist, and will always remain so.

If the public is no longer capable of seeing the swan, the riding Valkyries, the dove, etc. in Wagner, that means that it no longer sees the saga in the flesh, but a realistic or symbolic play, such as intellectuals make for themselves – the opposite of Wagner's idea.

Pfitzner and Strauss have a much more superficial sensitivity than Bruckner does. This is also the reason why they do not acknowledge him. They cannot see that this shortcoming in Bruckner includes within it a disproportionately greater virtue. Bruckner's whole personality is much more unsettled than those of the others, and therefore basically more productive, despite all the shortcomings in terms of his ability.

The crucial thing in later life is the extent to which the composer's techinique is connected to inspiration. If it becomes as high-handed as it does in Strauss, it is capable of a long and comfortable life, but from within it is capable only of a modest renewal. In the later Verdi too (*Falstaff*) there is a great deal of technique, which our soothsayers admire, and if Wagner did not have his poetry, which repeatedly lends wings to the musician in him, he would have deteriorated much sooner in his hugely developed technique. The ideal case is Brahms, and even more so Beethoven, of whom one can say that the inspiration is technique and technique inspiration, where no note is written which cannot also be expressed as pure inspiration.

Nations as living communities are the bearers of art. It is entirely a child of love. First the church's great and extensive community of love, then the nation . . . If these should disappear, to be superseded by something that has lost its soul, a community of interest and no longer a community of love, then art will indeed become homeless, baseless, redundant.

The concept of sublimation for the expression of true artistic nobility is false.

There are people who appear secure because they are insecure. And there are those who appear insecure (or imagine that they can do this) because they are secure.

The means of working for 'eternity' as an artist: turning a work into an organism, a world. Every style passes on, but real works remain. For precisely this reason they are works, because they are *more* than their style. Science lives on styles, but people live on works.

Difference between schema and form. The schema of sonata form becomes more strongly apparent as a schema in the blurred and faded Bruckner, precisely because it is often introduced *contrary* to the sense of the movement, than in the much stricter and clearer Beethoven.

In terms of structure and devotion, R. Strauss is equal to the greatest. In this he is as unobjectionable as Bach and Mozart. But what one must object to is *what* he has to say, the essence and content of his personality. Here he cannot be placed on a par with the great composers.

Ambitious people who are weak in substance come up with the greatest achievements of the will. Whether they can play both volumes of the *Well-tempered Clavier* or the *Elektra* – it makes no difference. The overrating of such achievements belongs to the image of our age.

When composing, the will to structure must be just as much alive as direct emotion, the 'will to feeling'.

The various orthodoxies – Bruckner, Brahms, then the moderns, Stravinsky, Debussy – go no further than the material of a composer. Their true significance is revealed only once the age of the orthodoxy is past. Many such orthodoxies, e.g. the Bruckner orthodoxy (and that of

Bach, for his part), appear very late. But this does nothing to alter the fact that they are orthodoxies.

Nature has crises, but there are reasons for these, nature does not make leaps, it only works in sequence.

That sacred and great Titanism that seeks to preserve the rights and freedom of the individual within the bonds of the law. All its expressions, for all their painfulness, have something profoundly peaceful about them. It is the true vehicle of tragedy, whenever and in whatever form it may appear (Michelangelo).

Modern art no longer goes in straight lines. It does not take a stance, it avoids development. It negates the past so as not to be oppressed by it. That is, perhaps, a 'way out', but not a way. Here and there it certainly finds a little flower by the wayside. But by and large it pays dearly for this flight – it is nothing else – with excessive abstractness, which bears within it the germ of death.

There are only two kinds of people: the responsible and the irresponsible, those who are concerned with things as a whole and those who are attached to detail, those who desire the harmony of power according to the harmony of God, and those who desire passion for its own sake, those who form, who know passion but also know of God, and those who are only revolutionary, who lose themselves in upheaval, in passion itself. The former have passion, and therefore seek to dam it up, to give it form. The others seek passion because it intensifies their feeling of life.

The end of the nineteenth century and the beginning of the twentieth is the age during which intellectual connoisseurship reached its peak, and in which, as a result, the phenomenon of the mind, which had taken form among the greatest artists towards the end of their lives, is directly registered and rationally understood. Only as a consequence of this are Mahler, Rilke, etc. possible. Later – Hindemith, Stravinsky – abstractness is worked further into life.

I can only bear one kind of art-history, in which the original relation to art, that of admiration caused by a sense of the divine, takes precedence over the vanity of recognizing connections. The art-lover is a higher being than the art-connoisseur – as long as the former does not simply remain a lover. Art history and true art appreciation differ in the same way as church and religion. Only in so far as one remains the necessary vessel for the other . . .

'Modern art' since 1900 is abstract. Abstraction is its death, it must be overcome. The mind must be reconnected to the material. The concept of progress in itself is an abstraction.

Burckhardt's 'power is evil' sums up a man who saw more deeply and more flexibly than others into the texture of historical reality.

All art which seeks originality has given in to death from the start. Originality is a concept that applies to the dead object. Imagine originality in religion or love.

Originality is a concept of literati and art-historians. The artist does not want to be 'original', he wants to express himself.

The forces of the past are also forces for order. Order itself is not a force, but it liberates forces. Indeed one might say: without order, the deepest and best forces of man continue to lie fallow. But anyone today who uses the order of living tradition as a support against a world of chaos as represented, for example, even by atonal music, must either be a harmless, trivial and hopeless idealist or . . . bear within him the knowledge that he is writing for eternity.

In judging an artist one should differentiate between the intellectual superstructure that is pervasive and individual to him, and the substance itself. In Beethoven this superstructure is very small, the substance enormous, in Bruckner the discrepancy is even greater. In today's artist it is generally the other way around. A great 'intellectual' attitude and great intellectual abilities can mask quite a weak and false substance (and generally do so).

It is certainly gratifying that in the present day an event such as the Lucerne Music Festival is possible at all. Among other things it seems to be to be above all a brilliant testimony of the great solidarity of Swiss musicians.

An orchestra that assembles in its ranks musicians from all the cantons of Switzerland, conductors and soloists from all the various Swiss orchestras – and, consequently, artists from the most diverse schools –

and is still capable of producing a homogeneous ensemble tone that is up to the greatest orchestral tasks, seems to me to merit the pride of the Swiss musical profession.

I am pleased to be able to work with this orchestra.

For myself I am one of the most convincing proofs that the real Germany is alive and will remain alive. The will to live and work in me is, however critically I view myself, that of a completely unbroken nation.

Today, one no longer waits for one's age to come, one no longer fulfils one's age; people now chase after their age, they cling to it.

The pernicious inheritance of Romanticism is the 'art of inspiration'. Overcoming it is a task that has been taken up anew by every individual artist since Beethoven.

Envy and talent (Pinder),* degree of talent – about which nothing can be done – unfortunately also dictate the degree of envy, of resentment, of the inability to acknowledge the merit of others, or even to measure up to it. The greatest person is the one most free of envy.

About 'artists among themselves'.

The most unbearable thing of all is when talented young scoundrels pat the very greatest artists benevolently on the back, and go peddling their greatness from door to door (e.g. Pinder, Rembrandt).

The prison-house of great art: It is not great art that is the prison, but the world. The prison is only the historically trapped view of it. Historical awareness and love cannot be united, and only love liberates, it alone means life.

Man has become too clever. He cannot accommodate this cleverness within his life.

We, that is the art historians, believe that the age is always right, and that one is therefore always right if one does what the superficial vision of the age demands. Apart from the fact that one would first have to determine what the age really demands, ages can also be wrong. A cock-eyed mass convention can come about just as easily as mass

---

* Wilhelm Pinder (1878–1947), art historian.

hysteria. But history repeatedly reveals the extent to which such a convention can swallow up everything that is valuable and independent.

Morality of historical thought: preference for youthfulness, if possible budding childhood in art. A manifestation of old age in the people of today. Admiration is reserved not for the power of the artist, but for the favour of the 'epoch'.

Bruckner accommodates a property that is widespread today: planning on a large scale outweighs planning on a small scale, indeed it is, to an extent, carried out to the detriment of the latter.

In all theoretical findings proposed by individuals one must always differentiate between the objective and the subjective part. The latter suits the theory to the needs of the person holding the belief, and can to a large extent falsify everything that had been properly seen in an 'objective' way.

To categorize and dismiss a phenomenon such as Michelangelo, in a complacent and superior way, as a 'tragic figure', takes an unusual degree of jaded hard-heartedness which has still managed to avoid the real tragedy of existence.

The error of the intellectual, particularly the German intellectual (in a certain sense the German of an earlier age), is to think on an excessively large scale, in politics as well as art (Marées). They forget that living on a small scale and planning on a large one must be *united* if it is to become reality.

Rilke goes a step further than Nietzsche. If Nietzsche has the fantasies, bursting with health, of the weakling at his desk, Rilke is the artist of humility, of the harmonization of man, but – of the man for whom harmonization is the only way of overcoming life. An absolute 'end'.

Brahms' greatness lies in his strictness. Each of his works, whether large or small, sweet or tragic, is bound together as if with iron bonds.

In contrast to Brahms, Reger is one of those who do not continue classical music but presuppose it. Music with *presuppositions* not based in the music itself has no lasting life.

Why are there so few good biographies of great men, particularly in the nineteenth century? Because those with a thorough intellectual training today are already in the state of not seeing the task of writing a biography of someone else as being above them. So from the very beginning there is a topsy-turvy situation.

The real and final malady of our century is conceit. Christianity knew why it placed humility before God at the centre.

It is not enough to have the individual properties of a great master. Even for the very greatest, greatness always lies in the combination as a whole. A single quality missing, and he would cease to be who he is. There is therefore no sense in appropriating or copying individual qualities. The total attitude to the world at its source – that is the only thing in a great musician that can serve as an example to us.

1944–45

There are 'early' and 'late' people (according to Spengler), independent of age, health, talent, achievements. Art is only accessible to people in an intermediate stage. The 'early' is too dull, the 'late' too clever for it. There is never any communication between people who are at different stages, between early and late people. They have different needs, and each believes that the world resembles himself. Today's world is not so uniformly 'late' as the Buschors, Pinders and others wish to perceive, since this is the way they are themselves.

The characteristic of the 'late' man: no longer wanting or being able to find himself in art. It is the first clear sign of self-renunciation, of decline. They seek out the art of the past that is very much in the past (that is, Bach and Mozart), not the past to which one is still attached by tradition. At the same time they make an overly clever, confused art that no longer expresses the whole person. The two things are connected.

1945

Of course it is my position that I really know National Socialism and not only from outside, like most people here in Switzerland, but am among those who experienced it over a period of twelve years. I know how many people there were, for example, who had to become party members in order to be able to exist at all. I know what the system of force and terror was really able and bound to achieve – for each person, for each people. And I know how far removed the German people really was from this terrible phenomenon to which it had given birth. Otherwise I would not have stayed in Germany. My remaining there is the best proof of the fact that there is still another Germany, and whoever denies this should at least wait until this other Germany is able to speak once more. That people do not believe in its existence is due to the fact that National Socialism has silenced it so thoroughly. Anyone who does not hear that voice should be assured that it was silenced. The violation of truth went so far that listening to a foreign radio station brought the death penalty. And such punishments were actually carried out!

So my judgement of the artists who did not protest, who participated because they could do nothing else, who took orders from the state, who took jobs from this state, is different from the way they may be judged here on the outside. But I myself was placed by fate in the situation of being able to be more honest than anyone else in Germany.

The method of 'an eye for an eye' is that of the base person. If someone slaps me in the face, I must under all circumstances slap him back. I take his point of view instead of maintaining my own, and blindly think of revenge instead of my duty, instead of justice. That was Hitler's position – now it is that of the allies.

True heroism, particularly tragic heroism, is always something individual, limited to the individual, responsible person. National Socialism, which cultivated heroism as a mass incitement, as a mass emotion, could not stand the responsible uprising of the individual.

Hence the divided feelings provoked by its decline. Stupidity, blindness, but above all mass-incitement all have too much say in this.

Is it through coldness, decadence, poverty of feeling that I work, that I can work in these terrible times?

I have never understood collective responsibility. Anti-Semitism just as incomprehensible as Nazism. It is an invention of the Nazis. But as the Nazis began to wipe out cities, a weapon which the others then copied and used against them, anti-Semitism was answered and imitated by hatred of the Germans, and contrary to all reason, contrary to all realistic feeling, all Christian principle, all justice an entire people was made responsible for all the transgressions committed by a criminal clique and its organs, using all the means of terror and lies and provocation at its disposal.

Things have a life of their own, and the soul has a life of its own. That is the end, the result of cultural development, of history. All earlier culture, all religion and finally all art is concerned with restoring the soul to things, and restoring living and objective reality to the soul. The 'self-development' of the soul, as it was imagined in the days of Franz Marc and Rilke, is a German error, an excessive introversion. Rilke was, on top of everything – more than he intended – still a poet, to his good fortune.

Those outside have no idea of the hatred that this system has long provoked amongst upright Germans, while those abroad still knew nothing of it. It was a mixture of hatred, contempt and the inability to take anything seriously. One was certainly – precisely because this was the feeling of the Nazis – gradually forced towards the latter, but in a different sense, of course, than many believed.

Hitler was hailed as the unifier of Germany. As such he was, by and large, successful in Germany. No German will ever be able to see why Germany should not have what all other great peoples possess, England, France, Russia, etc.: unification. Even rearmament was based on the fact that the others had rejected general disarmament.

The other development which finally led to war with the whole world was something quite separate. Here the German people did not follow him, and he needed all his set-pieces of lies and distortions to convince them that only the wicked Jews, only the wicked English, Russians, etc. were repeatedly to blame. This can only really be judged by someone who has lived in Germany. For Hitler's propaganda has increasingly silenced the real Germany. The terror is the *sign* of this. It was necessary, it was imperative. I would like to know how another people, any other people, would have behaved under this crossfire of terror and the most skilful lies. Of anyone who condemns Germany today, one can only say that he does not know Germany. Since for twelve years Germany has been mute.

The Treaty of Versailles – as has been said often enough – with its basic principle of the degradation of Germany, was the stepping-stone to the rise of Hitler. What is happening today is the same thing, but even more intense. Anyone who makes the entire people responsible for all the horror of the concentration camps is thinking along the same lines as the Nazis. They first declared and practised mass responsibility in the Jewish question. But these people are doing something even worse: The dishonouring of an entire and great people – a people whose inner nobility can complete with that of any other people, for it produced Goethe and Beethoven and innumerable other great men – is not only dangerous, it is terrible. The German people will never allow this to happen. In that case it would be better to be honest and consistent and exterminate it completely.

There is a danger that the conviction of the Germans of the deep reprehensibility of Nazism could be overturned. Demand from it everything that is right, every reparation, every obligation, but do not dishonour it. Do not connect the people itself with these horrors.

Originality in contemporary music works consciously and expressly to the detriment of the organic. Today's generation still does not know that an art which is not organic is in reality neither meaningful nor necessary, nor even possible in the longer term. This is the real crisis of all modern artistic intentions.

The accumulation of complications has a simplifying effect on emotions. It summarizes them. Keeping to simple lines has an enriching effect, because each line is experienced separately (for example, in instrumentation, Tchaikovsky in contrast to Strauss). The greater force lies in the universal, always in *simplification*.

Why is connection in the work of art so important? Because it and it alone represents the power and greatness of the creative process. The individual case on its own never does this, having always a degree of 'chance', of 'luck' attached to it.

If I think of how Hindemith or Strauss, for example, play some wonderful phrase in Beethoven or Brahms, with what cold, relaxed superiority. I know: They have never understood the real level of warmth and sincerity in this music. But that is also decadence, just as much as exaggerated sincerity *à la* Schumann.

The individual way of overcoming demons: clarity and rightness of thought. The collective way: religion and love.

Every individual must combine clarity of thought and love within himself in order not to fall prey to the demons. But clarity of thought also means above all: not ignoring love. And love means above all: not dispensing with clarity of thought, but applying it in all cases.

Pfitzner's mind is extremely dialectical and journalistic. It grasps the surface very vividly, but without satisfying the deeper connections within the construction. This is noticeable in his compositions as much as in his essays.

A critic tried to explain the fact that people do not repeatedly return to the more recent compositions as they do to the older ones, by saying that they are not familiar enough and not played sufficiently often. But that is precisely what needs to be explained. What today's productive minds lack is the ability to limit themselves simply to the individual case. They cannot do it, because they are intellectually aware of too many similar cases. Knowledge destroys faith – the same thing in every case!

The situation whereby little café literati chuckled over Goethe, Newton was corrected by his school physics master, etc. is typical. It is repeated over and over again.

In music particularly in the case of Tchaikovsky.

It is the task of the daily press to emphasize mediocrity to an excessive degree. Otherwise it would be too much in the shadow of that which is truly good. But it is not rare for the press to exaggerate in this endeavour.

The higher intelligence in artistic matters is expressed by one's being able to entrust the decisive function of judgement to feeling. But it takes infinitely more intelligence to write a Bruckner symphony, or indeed one by Tchaikovsky, than a piece by Hindemith or Stravinsky. Atonal music represents the slide of the intelligence into the lower regions of simple 'combinations', etc.

I was able to do more for true Germany and, as a result, for peace and the arts of the world here than anywhere else.

Every artistic effect is an effect of space. Anyone who does not enter that space cannot experience the effect. This should be said above all to those historians who attempt intellectually to identify spaces as such and then play them off against each other, to do justice to the fact that there are *different* spaces. Justice is only done to the richness of nature in one space, however: by allowing it to work on one unintentionally and appreciatively. But this seems to be the most difficult feat of all for the contemporary man obsessed with intellectual power.

Proof of the existence of God: infinity of space, infinity of time. Endless variety of creation. Contemporary man understands the latter least of all.

The step from Wagner to Schönberg represents not progress but catastrophe. We are in the middle of this catastrophe. It is important to consider the natural powers of growth. This involves not allowing intelligence to become impertinent and sanctimonious, the artist being allowed to develop naturally, to construct, instead of chasing after an unproductive sensational originality.

Music is impossible without 'responsible melody'. Where no starting-point has been established, nothing can move. Consequently nothing moves of its own accord, even in Hindemith, despite all the notes.

Hindemith's success lies in his being a power for order. This can be seen in his life as much as in his art. Unfortunately, however, substance in him has been dispelled to such an extent that while his music certainly proceeds in an ordered fashion, there is basically nothing left to order. The first great example of European *chinoiserie.*

It is said that feelings of religious devotion, elation, etc. 'are not a part of the age' because they are not to be found in Stravinsky. They have seldom been 'a part of the age'; they are a question of level, the deeper stratum of life.

If, in modern art, the ordering principle seems so much less considerable than in former times, it is because the much more strongly controlling intellect needs chaos as its opposite in order to escape itself, and thus to give itself at least the appearance of being 'creative'. This is also the deeper reason for the underrating of the great simplifiers, of Brahms and Tchaikovsky (not to speak of earlier ones), and the overrating of complication, of Reger, Hindemith, etc. In the case of simplifiers, such as Brahms, the intellect believes it has reached the end when it has not even got to the beginning.

It is a part of nature, a part of straight and clear relations, to be responsive to correspondences. Consistently avoiding them is a profound intellectualism which basically seeks to (and must!) escape itself.

Wagner wants to realize – Nietzsche wants to fight. Wagner wants to hope and fulfil himself and life. Nietzsche is already standing next to him with all the clever comments of the outsider which can be of oh! so little help to the active person.

My authority as an artist, that is, as an advisory artist, spared Vienna a great deal. The whole thing was an affair of the moment. Later, under Schirach, they passed on to regular matters. In individual cases I have consistently worked against National Socialist terror and racial politics, and what I was able to achieve here justifies, in my eyes, my having remained in Germany. One thing I had to accept, of course, and let wash over me: National Socialist propaganda. I was exposed to this propaganda more than others. For all its boasting, National Socialism had little self-confidence: It loved to exploit for its own ends greatness which had the stamp of others and other ages. They made propaganda with me because I was already famous before, just as – *mutatis mutandis* – Wagner and Beethoven were claimed for National Socialism.

The important thing for all truly great effects in 'music' as a material is the effect of form, the 'hearing of form'. This is impossible in modern music with its modern and atonal means. It follows its own rules, becomes complete in itself. One day it will therefore simply be possible to pass over it to 'the important business'.

Contemporary music provokes astonishment, curiosity, irritation, perhaps respect, admiration, but not love. It is not rare for the composer to provoke a love that is close to sympathy. Sympathy with someone who has a destiny like that of Tantalus. But the art itself, the music does not exist for love and joy.

What is organic? Two things are included in this word. Something living in itself, discreet, a living, individual essence, a world, a cosmos, an atmosphere . . . and at the same time something embedded in the flux of organic occurrence, in the flux of generations, which consequently contains access to the infinite within its finitude and thus points beyond itself. The one is as important as the other, in fact the two belong most profoundly together.

The inorganic way of feeling and thinking misses any awareness of both. Everything organic is always and in every case profoundly related to religion. At the same time it is free, independent, proud, for it is also what Goethe calls the highest happiness of the earth's children: personality.

The taste of the average man is not familiar with *sfumato* in interpretation. Hence neither colours nor formal powers come to life. The ideal is photography – that is, 'literal' reproduction.

When Mussolini speaks of 'living dangerously' and Schönberg of 'boldness', they mean the same thing. There is no dangerous living in our contemporary organized life, and there is no boldness in modern music.

The crucial thing is: How could National Socialism claim to the world at large and finally even to the Germans that it was Germany, when it was not Germany but its opposite, at best a profoundly misunderstood Germany?

Those who became emigrants or demanded that one should emigrate, believed one thing of Hitler in particular: that he represented the German people. They believed that one had to leave a Nazi Germany. But this is precisely what is incorrect. Germany was never a Nazi Germany, but a Germany ruled by Nazis.

Synthesis as a consequence, as a product of analysis, is often not true synthesis. True synthesis is always something mystical.

The meaning of all tradition is a concentration of the spiritual. The essence of all 'progress' is distraction, power, and as a result the leaving of one's own centre. Hence, anyone who no longer has a centre of his own hurls himself into the arms of progress.

Form or formlessness, tradition or progress – today these are often called the alternatives of the modern art industry.

Through the high level of both intellectual and physical communication, we have become used to seeing the assembly of excessively large complexes. As a result our entire psychology becomes insecure and often completely wrong. 'Twentieth-century man' exists only in a very few common characteristics. Not even Nietzsche's German exists, let alone the German of National Socialism. Certainly collective natures exist, but only in certain areas. What really does exist is people working with these concepts to a previously unknown degree, that is 'politics' and 'literature'!

The crucial difference between modern music and all great art is that in the former the category of *naturalness* is no longer valid. Without it there is no real, that is, no binding, inevitable artistic statement.

Today the world is entering a new political stage. The age of unlimited expansion and conquest is past. It is now a question of making the known earth useful. Likewise in art. Here different standards also come into play. Pioneers such as Liszt, Schönberg and others are no longer overrated. The age of the pioneers, that is of the cheap laurels, is past. Only now does the true, the actual test come, where it is no longer a matter of dealing in 'progress', but in real values. A complete revision of history is needed!

What is necessary: 'scientific' proof that nobility really exists and that it is biologically 'necessary' (Soloviev).* Today's world is in fact thoroughly convinced of the opposite.

The only art perceived by the average public as being 'new' and 'timely'

* Vladimir Sergevich Soloviev (1853–1900), Russian philosopher of religion.

is that which passes beyond the level of consciousness of the age, which gives the intellect some hard nuts to crack. Where this is not the case, however strong intuition may be – Brahms, Tchaikovsky are not recognized, obeisance is not done to them. The recognition of an artist today does not mean that he expresses something that corresponds to our emotion, but that he is cleverer than we are.

I will be attacked a great deal over these performances. To deprive someone of the true basis of their work is actually the worst, the truly existential attack. I should therefore like from the outset to bring everything to the level of discussion that this subject basically deserves, beyond all politics. Something that naturally forms a part of this, and in which I must ask my audience to go along with me, is the pitiless stripping-off of well-loved illusions and ideologies, the ability to look truth in the face. That is hard today!

The period in which the historical importance of a work of art takes precedence over its human and artistic importance is nearing its end. A complete reversal is needed. Schenker! Similar efforts in National Socialist Germany have been condemned to perdition. Apart from the fact that art basically served only as a supplement to politics, here the whole movement was one of comfortable mediocrity, a true re-action, a renunciation of any advance.

1946

Symphonic music
(Written while in detention in Innsbruck, 6/7 II.)

Impossible without orientation, the beginning of a passage over a certain distance, the development of a path, development in general, destiny that has a beginning and an end. Bach still has no destiny, he is free of destiny, celestial and hence *not yet* symphonic. Wagner is devoted to the demons of the world, to the colour of the world; he turns earthly things to music in their physical reality, his music is placed within a tragedy of a material and poetic kind, not a musical one. It is no longer musical destiny, *no longer* symphonic.

This orientation depends on the following: the fulfilment of the moment within a larger process. Each individual thing has its own function (local colour), and this within the development of the whole. The two meet and intersect at each moment. First of all there is the beginning. Even Schumann drew attention to the beginnings of Beethoven's symphonies. Consider those of Bruckner, which are among the most beautiful and the greatest known to the world. Then the so-called main subject. This can stand as a beginning (subject: Beethoven: Eighth Symphony; Brahms: Fourth Symphony; Schumann: Third Symphony), it can appear as a quotation (Beethoven: Fifth Symphony), that is, beginnings are as various as nature itself, but – they are beginnings, that is, they establish a point from which further developments can progress. This in itself is remarkable: This orientation must, in the symphony, which in musical terms corresponds to drama and tragedy in literature, come into effect from the first note onwards. It is the truly fate-laden aspect that attaches to all truly symphonic events. If many pieces of music can be described as a flower-garden, then in the symphony the *path* is not the only thing, but still the most important. It is not always easy at first to grasp the fact that every detail has its function within the whole, and is not only 'arranged' within this whole, but often has an effect on the whole that goes far beyond its individual importance, from the point of view of the audience, or rather of the person who (like all interpreters) gets to know the piece as a finished object. Whether something is a suite, an overture, a *divertissement* or sonata in the old style, a musical fantasy or, on the other hand, a symphony, cannot at first be recognized. Only as the piece progresses do the differences reveal themselves to the person who knows what a symphony is. It must be said at this point that true symphonies in the sense meant here are rare indeed. Within the whole of great musical production there are only very few who can or who even want to write real symphonies. What I mean by symphony here is closely bound up with the form of the 'sonata'. I do not want to go into considerations of form here, and would just like to say: The 'sonata' is primarily connected to subjects, namely to the fact that musical content is manifested at a particular moment, in a particular place, in a particular phrase. This is not true of all music. The symphonic subject, for example, is different from that of the fugue, which keeps returning and does not change within itself. The sonata subject can never return twice without being completely changed. The fugue subject helps the piece unfold, while the sonata subject experiences its own fate, by and within itself. The fact that it must lead somewhere is related to orientation, something that is in no way obvious. Themes from suites, for example, are not continued but spun out, until the beginning of a new theme or pattern. Of course there are very many transitions between the suite and sonata – by far the majority of nineteenth-century sonatas are a part of this. The true symphony or sonata in the symphonic sense meant here (as manifested above all in Beethoven's music), is above all the *energy of becoming, inexorability and the force of forward motion.* There is always something fatalistic in the symphony, something redolent of the single-minded purpose or aim of tragedy even where it is apparently, as in Schubert or Bruckner, strolling 'amid the flowers'. The idylls are here too, but they remain episodic.

This single-mindedness of purpose, this clear and unmistakable cohesion of the whole can only be created through real *laws*, based in nature. In music, this law is tonality. Here I shall say only this: In any case the symphony, and symphonic thought, are unthinkable without tonality. Only in observing the deeper laws of tonality – laws which run extraordinarily deep – does one attain that complete relaxation, the counterpart and precondition of that great symphonic tension that carries the music away across vast tracts. Without tonality, real symphonic music is unthinkable. All attempts to use modern atonal or polytonal means (or the use of 'islands' of tonality) are condemned to failure from the start, as they are carried out with invalid means. True masters – Reger, Hindemith – have never even tried this.

There are people who say that tonality is dead – one must be aware that this means that the symphony is also dead. But what *would be* dead along with it: nothing more or less than the language of destiny, the organization of the clarity of natural development. In any case, it is easy to say – and it corresponds to our contemporary historical and materialistic thinking – that tonality is dead – I do not believe it, as tonality is no more dead than language is, both being only a means of expression, and not expression itself – but one should be aware at the same time that as a result the natural values of clear and organized development are also 'dead'. At least in music. And there arises the question – which cannot be brushed aside – of whether it is still really worth the trouble of making music. Quite undoubtedly, tragic, fateful symphonic language corresponds to western thought in a profound sense. But one thing is certain: the symphony has come into being and cannot be reversed. Even if we still restrict ourselves in such a consciously theoretical way to the most immediate present, as critics and musicians do today, almost desperately in many ways, the situation is still completely altered by the fact that the symphony does exist. One solitary Beethoven symphony by its very existence expresses more about possibilities and realities, which are not to be denied by any theory, and gives the lie from within to the bulk of modern production.

In the last few decades the unconscious relation to the symphony/sonata has been pushed into the background by the all-too-brightly illuminated theories of the day. The fact that it is not dead is revealed by programmes, by practical musical life. If orchestral concerts are of any importance, it is because of and with the symphony; the role which it plays is unmistakable. In modern concert life, one could only manage without it in exceptional circumstances. But just how litte one knows about its real essence is revealed by the performances, the aesthetic concepts, the attempts to continue it with invalid means, etc. One can say that tragedy is dead, the symphony is dead, great art and monumentality itself are dead – people say that everything is dead that is not themselves. Whether something is really alive can only be gauged by someone who does not wish to escape it from the start. If one stands by evolution and decline, the real dramatic and plastic values required for any future, and the biological values of tension and relaxation, struggle and pacification, if one still believes that one should affirm and continue to experience tragic guilt as well as the power of salvation, one must affirm the symphony. Of course there are those who are too tender, too sensitive still to be able to do that, or those who are too clever. They may be right with regard to themselves – but they should not tell us that they and they alone represent the 'modern soul', as they tiresomely persist in doing for their own self-defence and self-enhancement. If anything expresses it, it is the symphony, the last completely autonomous musical form.

In relation to many parts of the *Valkyrie* one can say: The degree of clemency and the artistry here scorn all conceptual thought.

The artist's material life and his true intellectual and spiritual life are completely different things. By material life in art I mean the fact that artistic life goes on, that artists live and work for an audience, which for its part more or less submissively accepts their work. In all this, true intellectual and spiritual life is only quite minimally involved. Hence one solitary work truly born of the soul takes the whole 'industry' and everything pertaining to it, turns it upside down and renders it superfluous. On the other hand, however, this whole industry, seen from a lofty standpoint, only exists thanks to a very few true works and values. It is here that the profound tragedy – in this sense correctly seen by Romanticism – of all truly spiritual life is made plain. A phenomenon such as Chopin is terribly threatened – from a material point of view – and yet it is equally a huge source of strength for all eternity.

In the process it becomes apparent that the Romantic vision of the threatened superman, the 'genius', the spiritual man is not 'Romanticism', as it might seem if one looks at contemporary life, but reality, not superficial reality, of course, but profound reality. The danger today is that the more acutely superficial reality is seen through the modern means of science (psychology, etc.), the more does profound reality fall outside the range of vision of contemporary man.

As a mass, man has no higher qualities, no virtue. This is entirely a matter of individualism.

Sensory presence, 'weight' of existence, is just as much a part of health as clear and decisive attitudes on all matters of intellectual or material property.

Essay!

Coriolanus overture, Beethoven, the shortest piece! R. Strauss – the longest comparable piece.

The mania for bending history according to the needs and ambitions of the self is general today. The great artists who did not do this throughout the nineteenth and twentieth centuries, Brahms, Goethe, etc., can be counted on one hand. Either they are completely unhistorical or, like Stravinsky, Wagner, Strauss, etc., 'conscious' falsifiers of history. Even if we can overlook this in them, it is bad that those whose task is objectivity, the 'historians', do the same today. The historical age of Buschor, Preetorius,* etc., is just such an assault on history to the greater glory of the self. The productive state of the artist is characterized by the following: Here I stand, I can do no other, that is, being entirely fated to be ruled by one's own desire for expression and one's own condition. Even today this is still being imposed upon some.

In the recapitulation of Bruckner's symphonic movements, the free and inadequately valid character, seen by some as exemplary, gets its own back. He is incapable of repeating, like Beethoven or even Brahms. So what does he do instead? – Hence the gap presented at this point by the first movements in particular (Fourth, Seventh Symphonies).

Modern music lacks two things for me, which actually come down to the same thing: clarity of expression and universality of character. The former is caused by the prevailing lack of cosmic and organic feeling, the latter by an unbounded individualism, which, however much people might complain otherwise, continues to hold its own. The modern composer hides behind originality.

Pfitzner's particular style of wanting forcibly to impose an intellectual picture on to the external world! There is something 'National Socialist' in the very tendency.

In modern harmony – such as that of Reger – *richness* is a consequence

---

* Emil Preetorius (1883–1973) was chiefly famous as a stage designer, producing sets of great elaborateness and historical detail. He was responsible for most of the costume and stage designs at Bayreuth during the 1930s when the sets were spectacularly grand.

of *insecurity*. The security of sequential stages naturally produces simplicity.

Bach – Menuhin. Because the violin is a singing instrument, objective performance is in order here.

The danger in the monumental work of art is fatigue. This is related to simplification, which can easily be felt to be overly simple and then ceases to be understood in its true sense as a duty, by the listener as well as the interpreter. The only things that can be of any help here are the use of the imagination and working one's way through the organic connections, immediately revealing the 'meaning' of these apparent simplifications.

When they realized that all their feelings were false and falsified, they began to demand that art be without emotion.

The excessive intellectual clarity of people today corresponds to the tendency among contemporary artists to make their impressions vague. It is true everywhere: If the artist only expresses himself vaguely enough, the others are forced to interpret, to read into the work. It has reached the point where vagueness and depth are identified as being the same thing. Of course, recognizing the depth of clarity takes real 'depth', which is rare.

Money, power, fame – all inventions of inner weakness, of mistrust, inventions of the unproductive person! To the person who is productive in himself they have little to say.

Hermann Hesse: Sincerity is a good thing, but it is worthless without love!

The innocence of the work, that is, its 'organic' independence, is the only way to counter all kinds of subjectivity. In the work, everything that is only the ego is objectified and perfected, but not, so to speak, by having non-egocentric content. The content of Mozart's music is just as egocentric as that of Beethoven, unless one rejects tragedy as being too subjective, as happens today.

It is not for nothing that the ruthless clarity of Toscanini's playing is taken as representative today.

Community can make up for the lack of organism in the individual work – e.g. in Byzantine or Gothic art – but only up to a certain point. The fact that there are limits to this, that participating in the style of the age does not *in every case* relieve the artist and his work of the need to strive for and possess their own organic value, not seeing this, not *wanting to see this* is the true failure of all art history. Above all it is also the failure of the aesthetic of the age, seen here in its art-historical aspect.

There was a great theorist: Schenker. The thing that really ruled him was the concept of *Fernhören*. Article about Schenker!*

Casals has discontinued his collaboration. I fear that Casals overestimates the importance of this step for the course of world events just as he overestimates the effect of my conducting for the Siemens workers – which he holds against me – in prolonging the war. I am particularly surprised by the fact that he of all people, the incomparable great artist, my honoured friend, at present clearly sees music, his sacred art – like all of today's politicians – as nothing but a political demonstration. Does it really prolong the war if the worker, in his tormented existence, is reminded of his divine origins through the message of the great masters? I have never given up and shall never give up the task of conducting for workers, wherever and however it may happen. For Bach, Beethoven, Schubert and others can never have the effect of prolonging a war.

The symphonic 'form' of the Germans, sufficient unto itself, relies on a capacity for deep relaxation, deep harmony from within. This is a real 'ability' which can be replaced by nothing else, and which makes up the indispensable value of German music to the world.

For Rilke, Proust, etc., tragedy, that is, all tragic experience, simply means intellectual backwardness. They think the same of religion itself.

To make conformity the centre of one's thought, as does Kolbenheyer,†

---

* Furtwängler honoured this undertaking, and the brief result can be found in his volume of essays *Ton und Wort*. The concept of *Fernhören*, literally 'far-hearing', was crucial for Furtwängler. What it means, roughly, is the hearing of the climax or conclusion of a work from the beginning – something that uniquely characterizes Furtwängler's performances, and remains mysterious and inimitable. For Schenker, see footnote to page 77.

† Erwin Guido Kolbenheyer (1878–1962), prolific racial theorist and novelist, who travelled widely before the Second World War propagandizing for the Nazis. Not surprisingly, he was forbidden to publish for five years after the end of the war.

for example, leads to completely incorrect conclusions. For the most vulgar is always the most capable of conformity. The whole of the struggle of the vulgar against the superior happens in the name of greater conformity, and today, in the age of conformist thinking, it is difficult to prove the necessity of the superior at all. It is 'permitted' to exist, in order to serve the ends of the vulgar – at best.

Music is – as contemporary man has forgotten – not a sequence of notes, but a struggle of forces.

The world believed that Hitler's Germany was the demon whose conquest would make everything better again. Now, with horror, it sees that it was only the first embodiment of this demon, which still rages.

The thing that has outstripped the 'natural' for us, is the 'new'. But one cannot dismiss the fact: The new quickly becomes old, but the natural always stays natural.

Nothing great in science and art has ever been achieved without belief in the freedom of science and art.

Fernhören demanded *große Form*, was its initial premise. With contemporary means, *großbe Form* is impossible, it is an absurdity. That is also true for reproduction. In spite of this, even among out contemporaries it mysteriously remains a kind of ideal.

Intellectualism means: illuminating with the harsh spotlight of the intellect things which must be hidden and stay hidden. The lack of any feeling for how far intelligence should go – so far and no further – and where the realm of instinct begins, is the real sign of the beginning of decadence. As a result intelligence finds itself in the strange situation of having to protect itself from itself – our situation.

Listening which scrutinizes and listening which is productively receptive to the piece of music are two different things. I make my music exclusively for the latter, i.e. expression comes to the fore. This calls for a fundamentally different attitude and a fundamentally different technique.

There are people who never forgive one for being successful. For them success is the counter-argument against all value.

In music – in performance as well as production – we are in an unprecedented period of technical richness, and of emotional poverty which must also be unprecedented. The one depends on the other, produces it, conditions it.

Evaluations of history

The evaluation of Mozart clearly based on the fact that his material affects him least because of the form of his age. Wagner and Brahms temporarily victims of their closeness to their material. Today Hindemith's material is in vogue. It is not difficult to guess how long that will last. But definitive proof only follows afterwards.

Rejection of Handel by the age of Mozart. Mozart by the Romantics, etc. But never has the simple material point of view been stubbornly taken to such an extreme as today.

Our own time is concerned with the methodology of life, of desire, of emotion. It is believed that will precedes knowledge, but that desire can be achieved, or at least intensified (via this methodology) by knowledge. This is incorrect. The central core of man, of *every* man, whoever he may be, remains his religious connection to God, to his God, who can of course take different forms. Only the man conditioned by today's American-European civilization attempts a life without God, using 'method'. This is why he is so keen to learn methods. He himself is unaware of how empty and hollow his life has become.

Music and reason

In art, as in all things human, the rationally comprehensible and the irrational must be mixed together. The one must bear, cover and protect the other. The natural state is for reason to control the surface, and irrationality to remain in the background. Foreground and background of the work of art are like foreground and background in human life. The monstrous process of rationalization that is permeating the European-American world, indeed the whole of the known world, most profoundly threatens this natural state. The over-rationalized person, worn out by his own intelligence, demands that irrationality be immediate. The background should be perceptible in the foreground. Cubism, Dadaism and Expressionism of all kinds, atonality, which leads to the rejection of all ordering functions within the tones, are part of this. This results in the abolition of the course of nature, which always proceeds in a strictly rational way on the surface, only to appear all the more irrationally in its backgrounds.

All of life is made up entirely of a mixture of the conscious and the unconscious. The emphasis on the one hand corresponds to its spilling over on the other. The one can be suppressed as little as the other. Nor can either be forced. The goal remains the same: to reach oneself, to express the unconscious. It can only be achieved in a natural way: to expose the conscious to consciousness, and allow the deeper level, the unconscious, to shine through. Every true work of art has a double existence: rational foreground and irrational background. If no attention is paid to this relationship, if one already abandons reason in the foreground in order to penetrate the irrational, one is cheating oneself of the category of the natural. And one does not reach the unconscious, which cannot be attained by force or by theory. It has its own profound sense, whereby the roots are in the dark bowels of the earth, while the trunk, the leaves stretch towards the sky. The same process which, in a different form, is also expressed in organic existence, cannot, as over-intense theory and intellectual short-circuiting demand – the most indicative characteristic of the last few generations – be ignored or even rethought.

The past is conquered by reason. But the future is burdened by it. It is as if man, under the overwhelming burden of his own reason, were to collapse groaning.

While visual art is best suited to the correct understanding of monuments, in music an intermediate link is added that makes analysis easier: interpretation. Interpretation as such occurs in terms of the consciousness of the age. But it also relates to objects from the past, the most curious imbalances can arise. Works which were intended to be dynamic are interpreted statically, painterly works are reproduced as drawings. But it is particularly the relationship to reason, the awareness of culture that is expressed in interpretation. Literal rendering, excessive technical control, and increasing loss of the awareness that there is anything in the background. The withering of classical literature is plainly a part of this. But the fact that this means more than simply the withering of an era, that the possibility of enigmatic music in general declines with it, is not seen by those involved in modern music. In a certain sense one can say: the stronger the reason in the foreground, the more irrational, the more infinite the background (Beethoven). In contrast to modern efforts.

Mengelberg – Beginning of the Ninth Symphony. Incomprehension of the background. But one might ask: In what way should Beethoven actually express the cryptic sextole?

General intellectualization has taken hold of interpretation – the music itself is becoming superfluous – the machine is taking the place of the living being – and one day the overly perfect machine will bore us . . . Art is no longer necessary, no longer the expression of the subconscious, it is finished.

Today we are clever and unprejudiced enough – one might also say brave enough – to predict this with our eyes open. Does this fact imply the possibility of confronting this process? We should stay with all those creators and their followers who are aware of the danger and seek to deal with it.

As a conductor I must consider musical development as a whole, the whole of the musical audience. I cannot play only for those who have had enough of familiar music and want to hear something new at any price. But neither can I make music only for those who reject everything new from the very start. In my programmes as well as my performances I must take music where it is most alive, and must consequently often remind individuals, especially composers, that I am not there for them alone.

The crucial question for the conductor – apart from his occupation itself, where only the proverb: *Bilde Künstler, rede nicht** applies – is that of his programmes. In the years after the First World War, shortly before I succeeded Nikisch in Berlin in 1923, I once tried to learn everything through the exchange of programmes that existed at the time. In those days the situation was as it is today. People finally no longer wanted to hear the same works over and over, they wanted to feel that they lived in the world and not only in Germany. They wanted to know the whole richness of the literature, and wanted above all to let the present, the new forces have their say. The consequence at first was that the classics and the great Romantics, apart from a few seldom played minor works, disappeared almost completely. That along with the good new works, an enormous amount appeared that was merely new.

---

* *Bilde Künstler! Rede nicht!/Nur ein Hauch sei Dein Gedicht* (literally: Artist speak not, but create! Let your poem be but a breath.) This is the epigraph to the section on art in Goethe's 1815 *Collected Works*, vol 2, p. 163.

Between composer and conductor there has existed for years that kind of tension that often occurs between the members of particular intellectual occupations. It should come as no surprise that for example the historian, who sees everything in relative terms, that is, historically, and the creative artist, who sees and must see things from within himself, that is, egocentrically, are natural opponents. Something similar is true of the composer and the conductor. Not while they are working together, but while one is reproducing the work of the other.

Different in every historical situation. The conductor really feels the pulse of the age. He must evaluate in a truly responsible and far-sighted sense, he cannot speak up for anything, but has to tell people what to do, and that certainly breeds hatred. It is the height of ridiculousness for people to say of me, who has performed everything . . . that I am 'reactionary'. But I of all people could not dedicate myself to a one-sided and unconditional propagation of the *new* music to the detriment of the *old*. Not allowing either one or the other to grow, but rather letting the one grow out of the other, and allowing both to speak in terms of the real life inherent within them, is the task that is, of course, seldom understood by the partisans of either side, and one receives no thanks for carrying it out.

The boundless appetite for change in modern musical life – one of the special signs of decadence.

1947

(Hölderlin) Germany!

Was lebt, ist unvertilgbar, bleibt in seiner tiefsten Knechtsform frei, bleibt eins. Und wenn Du es zerstörst bis auf den Grund, und wenn Du es bis ins Mark zerschlägst, doch bleibt es eigentlich unverwundet, und sein Wesen entfliegt Dir nur siegend unter den Händen!

[That which lives cannot be rooted out, remaining free in its deepest servile form, remaining one. And if you raze it to the very ground, and if you crush it to its very marrow, it yet remains unharmed, and its essence only flees victorious from beneath your hands!]

These illusions were based in the self-development of the material. There were dreams of liberation through atonality. As the material has not developed any further over twenty years, as it cannot do so, people still cling to the same illusions, but not with anything like the enthusiasm and conviction that were there before. One gradually sees the unprovable need to pass beyond the stage of desires, resentments, etc. Still even today – especially since these illusions have been able to don the cloak of politics – anyone who penetrates these questions more seriously and soberly is vilified.

Isolation is not German – on the contrary. But neither does it bring strength, it is not a sign of strength – on the contrary. The Nazis had curious concepts of what was German – Beethoven – Gounod – Brahms – Dvořák – Lehár, etc. All of their evaluations, in as far as they are official, are partly determined by Hitler's megalomania, partly by the most primitive political considerations. It is not even worth contradicting them, and the only significant thing was the terror with which they were imposed.

Decadence begins where a concern with art does not stem from religion and the joy of life, but from a desire for knowledge. Strictly speaking all science, applied to art, is already decadence.

The excessive and one-sided claims of intelligence amongst people today have made us lose our immunity to the seductions of intelligence. These consist in seeing science even in those things which are not a part of it. 'Quietly honouring the inexplorable' seems to be difficult to us.

The greatest French musician is the Pole Chopin.

Essay

Wagner and Beethoven

Wagner's understanding of Beethoven is deeper than that of Strauss and Pfitzner (*Missa*). Understanding 'beyond itself' characteristic of the all-encompassing nature of Wagner's mind. If we read *Über das Dirigieren*, our first reaction is: What is he getting so excited about? Today we know the answer to that much better. But in Wagner we are dealing with something completely different: a question of level.

Bartók: an over-abstract mind, a composing intellectual phantom. Metronomization to the point of nths of seconds is an abstraction. All of music has been seized by the same thing. Powerlessness, hubris of the abstract!!

For thirty years contemporary music has gone under the sign of dissolution. It is only natural that the future will bring the contrary trend, of 'connection'.

Laws of dissolution – laws of connection. Both in their own way eternal and static. Eras generally have their own character, but this has nothing to do with value. On the contrary. Every true work of art has a balance; that is the essence of art as it is of everything that lives. The great exceptions. Complete devotion to one side, which condenses into politics today, comes from heightened intellectualism and heightened communication and suggestibility. Strange phenomena are produced . . .

Even Buddha fears the virtue of the minor poets (Japanese proverb).

The monumental is human. Neither is it strange to the mass age. But to modern music – the so-called new music – it appears to be unknown.

People agree to an extent about Bizet and Puccini, but not about Beethoven and Brahms. Why? It is not people who are so 'diverse', but their *prejudices*.

1947

In our humanity, languishing in the prison-house of its own intellect, its prejudices prove more powerful than the greatest and clearest values. There is barely any point in attacking the prejudice with which the world sees a composing conductor. Hindemith once said to me: 'If you want to be taken "seriously" in the world as a composer, you must give it up.' Is that true? Well, I have 'given up' conducting but I have not renounced it, and still want to be taken seriously.

The prejudice against conductors who compose is based on the idea that they exploit what they have learned as conductors in their compositions; the one occupation grows out of the other. This is incorrect . . . On the other hand a conducting composer is very easy to imagine.

There are people who declare that love is 'finished'. This kind of resentment, which has held too much sway in the world since the very beginning, cannot stop us agreeing with those who still believe in love. The same is true of tonality!

1948

Universality of expression . . . that requires one thing above all: the will and the strength for monumentality, or rather, for simplicity. The simplicity of childhood, of Haydn and Mozart, is closed to us, their successors. But conscious simplicity, the capacity to take content to its simplest form, to concentrate it, is today, as it always has been, a creative commandment.

Essay: The temple and the low dive.

Previously, originality to the detriment of naturalness in music was seen as indecent. Today the situation is reversed. No one dares to be conventional any more; the most disagreeable form of convention. No one wants to be what he is. Everyone wants to seem more than he is. No one wants to accept responsibility for what he is. The whole thing is a sham that is not worth dwelling on.

Instead of observing that we are dealing, after all, with a piece of music that has evolved, in which echoes, even if they are there by chance, are just as unimportant as they are in other evolved pieces – otherwise one could say that all of early Beethoven consists of echoes of Mozart and Haydn – instead people are concerned – always a favourite party-game for critics and 'connoisseurs' – precisely with hunting out those echoes! What some people have found there is truly astonishing. Of course it is as clear as day, all the things that could have flowed unintentionally from his 'practice' into the pen of the professional composer. That's the only way it could have happened!

I am not concerned with whether something seems new, but with whether it 'touches the heart'! The heart, that is, the whole person, is something I think I know a little about.

After long years of work and self-examination I have brought a symphony to the public ear. A part of the press has, because this is its way, promptly pronounced its judgement upon it. Indeed this judgement, which dealt partly with things, influences, etc. which are, with the best will in the world, not to be found in it, was quite obviously prepared beforehand. Allow me, then, to say some words about my 'case' as a composer.

It is understandable that the public should not believe in a man, whom they have previously known only as a conductor, as a composer. This is due to the view, fundamentally quite correct, that these are two completely different and incompatible things. Dedication to a finished work that is already formed beforehand is something different *in principle* from the creation of a new work. It is therefore impossible to be a conductor and a composer at the same time, so to speak. The combination of the two is absolutely wrong. In my particular case let me say, therefore, that I was a composer certainly much earlier and much more exclusively than I was a conductor. That only very late, in relative terms – and at first entirely with a view to earning my livelihood – did I think of conducting. That I still always thought, even later on, about composing – even if this was squeezed into the remaining quiet summer months – as the main thing. Which is why for many years conducting has taken up such a disproportionate amount of my time . . . this is not the place to discuss this development.

It is quite beyond doubt that any real creation must be a breakthrough into new territory – even for the creator himself. If it is not, it becomes repetition and routine, the work of an epigon. But the real question is what is meant by the *new*, whether it is something material, such as a new harmony or rhythm, or a development of the mind, as often occurred over long periods in history. So, for example, the Beethoven of the Eighth Symphony in 1812 had introduced hardly any new material compared to the Haydn of sixty years before, and Brahms in 1890 was using more or less the same devices as Schubert and Beethoven in 1820. Of course today, many see Brahms as trivial. Indeed we cannot imagine the new coming about in any way other than emerging from the material, being manifest in the material. Anyone who does not introduce new devices or at least use those contemporary devices that differ *in principle* from those of the past, does not count. Every simple triad is suspicious. We behave like monkeys who are interested in what they hold in their hand only in so far as it is edible.

In response to this I should like to state most categorically that that which is 'materially' new, a new harmony, rhythm, etc. has only ever interested me 'historically', that is in a very limited way. That we have reached an age where musical material appears to be exhausted, and can no longer be significantly extended. The gaze which is fixed on the material, which believes in the material alone and expects everything from it, has brought us endless unhappiness. When people speak of the end of music today, they mean the end of its material development. As if the mind did not have infinite possibilities. Of course each new formal evolution of the mind will not pass the material without leaving a trace, but the extension and renewal that are possible and necessary today are not produced by the material, are not dependent on it.

As we now believe only in the material, we have become, in terms of the intellectual essence of music – even the works of the past – as ignorant as children; we ignore it and no longer know anything about it.

Of course the mind depends on one thing: that people, that is the audience, not deprived of the security of their judgement by pre-packaged concepts, should reach their own judgements. My music is meant – in this it is like all the living music of the past – for a real audience.

In America – journalist – there is said to be no tragedy, but only *prosperity* or its opposite. I am of a different opinion, and even find that our contemporary life is the greatest of all tragedies. It is possible that some of this consciousness should have rubbed off on my music. Anyone who takes offence at this should turn to different music. But they should not claim that I am writing the music of today.

We all face the same audience. Our claims are of absolutely no consequence. Wait for what this audience has to say. Give it the chance to listen.

One may be in doubt as to the *what* of my music. Not as to its *how*; for it is a whole, not an assembled construct. But the claim made by those critics who always enjoy the merry game of 'find the echo', that it is influenced by this and that, is not correct!

There are people who bear the destiny of the West – they will understand Wagner, Beethoven, Michelangelo. There are some who have no destiny, who are born beyond destiny, facetious drones of the human race, cheeky, cynical, clever and spiritless – might one not say that they have no 'soul', that they do not know what Europe was and still is?

For over sixty years, the Berlin Philharmonic has been Berlin's first orchestra. It was involved in and partly responsible for the unparalleled rise that city once enjoyed – particularly as a musical city. In fact, one might say it had a very significant part to play in it, being Germany's definitive concert orchestra for over fifty years.

Today, under different conditions, robbed of the Philharmonie, the site of its former effectiveness, it is more than ever a symbol of Germany's unbroken artistic will, in the narrower sense of sorely tried Berlin. I feel personally bound to this orchestra, and confidently hope that the Berlin Philharmonic may continue to remain the saviour of German music into the future. I personally hope that soon – that is in the autumn – I shall once more have the opportunity to play with them as in the old days.

The unnatural is collective, nature is individual self-responsibility. There are many reasons for the unnatural, most of them shallow, but some very deep. Nature knows only one reason: Man is the standard of man. A solid foundation. Now more than ever we are shaken up by isms of all kinds, or perhaps we should say: terrorists. There will come a time when the self-sufficient attitude of the late Pfitzner will be more important.

From the form as well as the content of your letter of the . . . it is plain that in the Furtwängler case you are not concerned with establishing the true state of affairs, or with truth and justice, but only with maintaining your own prestige. You do not go into uncomfortable facts which I have raised. Instead you introduce new accusations: How does it affect my 'case' if the French government, in June 1939, turned down a visiting operatic concert with German singers? (The fact that it had nothing to do with me was proven by the fact that the French ambassador in Berlin made me a Commander of the French *Légion d'Honneur* in July of the same year – an honour which was not to be made public in Germany, on Hitler's orders.)

And how is the fact that I conducted in Austria even after the *Anschluß* relevant to my case?

Is the person who is bound to the state neither financially nor contractually, but who has been in a position to refuse to participate in official occasions, to take part in propaganda films and to conduct in occupied countries, more free than those who did all these things but who today conduct in Switzerland with impunity?

Do they wish to conclude from the fact that I was, it is true, unable to prevent the emigration of the Rosé Quartet to London – particularly as I was not in Vienna at the time – but in any case later, when I went to Vienna in response to that city's cry for help, saved the lives of half-Jews and those who were married to Jews, do they wish to conclude that I was one of the most 'deadly' figures of the Third Reich?

Unfortunately I had not been clearly enough informed that you – as I now know – have for many years allowed your life to be governed by hatred to the detriment of emotion, indeed of thought. May you be granted the profound satisfaction of feeling that you are in a position of judgement over entire peoples and individuals. I prefer to think of the biblical proverb: Judge not that ye be not judged. Why did I come to you? – well because I still had the old E. in my memory. I would have spared you – and myself above all – that painful hour, had I known how untrue to yourself you had become.*

What I wrote about prejudices still holds even apart from the particular instance of the performance of one of my own works. It is of general importance; we are all much more subject to the power of prejudice than we are ourselves aware. So where do those failures of judgement come from, of which musical history repeatedly tells us, the nonsensical overrating and underrating of individual musicians and groups?

Above all, however, specialist knowledge is no protection against prejudices. However valuable it may be – it contributes little to the productive formation of judgements. On the contrary: It was always the orthodoxy of specialist-trained musicians who rejected Wagner, Bruckner, Strauss and whoever, and it was the judgement of the untrained public that carried these masters through. Let us not forget that music speaks to the whole person – far beyond any specialization. Let us not try to be cleverer with our heads than with our hearts.

The feeling of infertility in music in our time has become strong and undeniable, even among those who outwardly proclaim the contrary and feel that they are the artistic avant-garde. We lose our good conscience if we cultivate progress, as we still did after the First World War, when the first great wave of atonality arose. Nothing is more urgent, quite apart from the usual 'slogans', which are only 'election speeches' for parties, working hypotheses aimed at making composition

* Letter to Eleonore Mendelssohn.

possible, than objectively and rationally establishing what is actually the case and the extent to which possibilities for development actually exist. Neither must we lose that rationality that made development, movement beyond the present state, possible in the first place. Above all we want truth – truth about things as well as about ourselves.

If we consider the past we shall see that periods of great material progress alternate with periods which experienced relative stasis in material terms, but instead enjoyed great intellectual development. Bach's material was created by his antecedents, and what he added to it was a significant intellectual development. The coincidence of material and intellectual development is a modern postulate, but it in no way corresponds to history. In this it resembles the life of the individual. Here one might say that one third consists in the appropriation and individual moulding of the language of the age, a second in material innovation, the last in a type of intellectual development best characterized by Freud's term of sublimation. So there are actually two kinds of development which fertilize and replace one another, in such a way that the emphasis is always on one or the other. Bach, like Beethoven in his late period, carried out achievements in sublimation; the same must be said of the Romantics, Schumann, Brahms, Bizet, etc., while the great Wagner, late Reger, Debussy and recent developments in general have been one-sidedly devoted to the material side.

England

There are people who take offence at the fact that the conductor who plays concerts abroad with the Vienna Philharmonic was born in Germany. Would the same people also take offence at the idea that Beethoven, Brahms, Hebbel and R. Strauss were not born in Vienna and therefore deserve to be rejected from the Austrian point of view?

We are willing to be taught about Italian music by Italians, and about French music by Frenchmen. It is somewhat astonishing that the English want to teach us how to play the Viennese classics and Beethoven.

But another, more profound problem is concealed here. Nowhere does the routine of modern playing, further extended by the influence of radio and the gramophone, have a more fatal effect than in the performance of great absolute 'classical' music, created from purely musical forms. Here Europe really is entrusted with the care of the 'holiest possessions'. The term 'literal' rendering is being turned into a motto. But there can be no question that the performance of Beethoven symphonies, as they were cultivated and realized (previously by

Weingartner, for example) in Vienna, is less literal than the style of performance to which people outside seem to have become used in so many ways today! The difference is that one still has, or strives to have, the breath of life about it, while the other, according to which classical art means outmoded art that no longer affects us, has come to terms with mechanical and rational routine from the very start, with the tinned-food taste of everything 'classical', and indeed is not happy without this taste.

To give the baby a name, they invent mottos such as that of 'literal' rendering. As if it were only in England and America that the classics were performed in a truly literal way. But there can be no question of the way in which, for example, Beethoven symphonies have been cultivated and played in Vienna since Richter, Weingartner and others, being less literal than contemporary performances in England and America. One crucial difference is certainly: In Vienna Beethoven is alive, he is the city's own flesh and blood. In America he is – with all due respect – one of the Viennese classical composers who lived 150 years ago and basically no longer affect us. They can therefore be enjoyed only as preserves; for us they still have the scent of blossoming life. From this fundamental difference in attitude, all the other differences emerge of their own accord.

And in any case, in America, where this state of affairs originated, they are much more aware of it today than they are in many European countries.

1949

It is curious that people today are reassured if they can arrange things temporally and historically. They are incapable of enjoyment without this knowledge. It is the inability to enjoy the moment; but it is also the inability to enjoy the sequence represented by a series of moments. It is the lack of vitality, which is no longer 'alive', but seeks to protect itself from everything, seeking, that is, to *know*.

If only so many uncontrolled things did not coexist within us – then that which *is* controlled would no longer be worth the effort!

If Herr Strobel* thinks Beethoven's Ninth Symphony is a mediocre work, and considers it his task, freely adapted from Stravinsky, to take us Germans and 'wash Wagner out of our ears', that means that we Germans, however we do it, will have to witness the digging away of the very well-springs from which we live.

If the creator Stravinsky represents such abstruse opinions, that is of interest if one wishes to know the Stravinskian aesthetic. He is Stravinsky, after all. But if the German music writer Strobel claims such things – his writings used to be read differently – then . . .

Modern music

The entire discussion has been sent off on the wrong track. Instead of being intoxicated by music, we seem nowadays to live intoxicated by words. Here, as everywhere else, the question is very rational and precise: to what extent is there a correspondence between what comes out of the notes and what we put into them? To what extent does the resulting performance exist in an objective and not merely a subjective way? The very great danger of subjectivism must be objectively ascertained. The formation of sects, words, the elimination of the controlling public. I feel that this elimination is going too far.

---

* Heinrich Strobel (1898–1970), musicologist and spokesman for neo-classicism. Not to be confused with Otto Strobel, Bayreuth archivist and the leading Wagner scholar of the first half of the century.

Looking for something that objectively existed within the notes, I arrived at the cadence. The cadence, as mentioned in my little book,* has been misunderstood in many ways. It is an extraordinarily broad concept. It lies at the basis of all European music up to Stravinsky and Debussy and Strauss. In this context, one should think not of harmonic doctrines, but of the consequences as they appear in compositions on a very large scale. If one objects to the word cadence, one should remember that in music there *must* be something that objectively expresses a beginning and an end, a process and development, that is, there must be something that gives it a form. The problem of form is and always remains the artistic problem *par excellence*.

It is entirely ridiculous to claim – as they keep doing, tendentiously – that I reject modern music lock, stock and barrel. I should never forgive myself if I did not respond most sympathetically to the solutions and efforts of Stravinsky, Honegger, Hindemith, Bartók and many others. But it is also true that I do not wish to deny my own judgement on their works any more than my judgement on old works. The important thing is what I hear, what emerges from the music, not what I think or read about it. In correct and judicious contact with the public, modern music too will have its indispensable life.

Also, if I am especially concerned with the nurturing of old music, it is because this seems necessary to me today. We will make modern music our own if it is appropriate. It is *its* business to convince us. It will do so to the best of its ability, for it has the support of living people with vested interests. Old music has no such advocates. If things go on like this we will soon be faced with a massive Herculaneum and Pompeii . . . buy it, in order to possess it. In this context, something about my programmes: If I play on a tour – a concert in every town – the programmes must primarily be concentrated and monumental. And if, on this, my first journey after the terrible war in Germany, along with old works, I think of the recently deceased Pfitzner and the eighty-five-year-old Strauss, that does not imply a rejection of the young composers. Or is – as sometimes almost appears to be the case – a contemporary conductor reproached for playing a Beethoven Symphony in the first place? Is there so little understanding of the signs of the times, of the needs of the soul?

I express reservations about certain devices in modern music,

---

* Furtwängler is referring to the book translated as *Conversations with Furtwängler* (Boosey and Hawkes).

reservations shared by everyone (Ansermet, Hindemith, etc.), and am cried down and maligned as an arch-reactionary. This is, in itself, all the same to me, I can put up with some things, but unfortunately, it is incorrect. What is expressed is something completely different: a general envy of the performer.

The important thing is that this is a case of an opinion using terror to make its point, as if there were only one possible way of making music today. And the way in which this should be done is a matter not for artists but for theories.

But it seems to me, and to some others, that it is time for the recognition of the essence of tonality, the extension of tonality and of consistent atonality. There can be no doubt of the biological superiority that I have identified. What we used to see as musical life is still based on it, and it appears that musicians who have struggled to their very core with atonality . . . Tonality is not the past, but the future.

There can be no doubt that Bruckner has not become general property in the same sense as Brahms, Wagner or even the later Strauss. This is because he takes things for granted in the listener that are not universally given. There is an extensive literature which is, however, of little use to those who approach the subject from outside. Certainly a work such as the Eighth Symphony cannot be imagined without the dual basis of a mystical and all-encompassing religious sense, and also of a magnificent Baroque heroism. Even if they stretch the classical form of the symphony, which developed from improvisation, to its limits, both are still profoundly human and a great and stirring tribute to human creative powers.

Deeper reasons for literal rendering and excessively quick tempos. The internal weakening of the relationship to great music as a whole, which naturally precedes or preceded its dethroning.

Contemporary man cherishes the complication of the complicated, timeless man the complication of the simple. This is also infinitely more 'complicated'.

The intellectuals among our contemporaries are very suggestible and sensitive. Because of their excessive cleverness, they are tired of the simple, complex music that has been made up until now, and call for a new music that corresponds to themselves, calling the more vehemently the less such music already exists. A shame, because nothing shaken together in a test-tube, no method or game-like rule (twelve tones) can replace conception through boundless love. I stick to the old, modest way, and make music as it has been made over the last few centuries. I am as I am – and completely secondary to this is what anyone thinks he must demand of me as a result of theories.

People today reject the definitive aspect of the cadence, that which is in harmony with itself. But they themselves are wishful, yearning, wandering and therefore uninterested in other kinds of experience. They are so uninterested that they no longer feel at peace within themselves, and can only cherish the happiness of life and creation in other ages, a devotion which is the dubious compensation for their own miserable restlessness.

Something else that was said on the subject – our contemporary world is, in fact, entirely a prisoner of its impetuous craze for progress. This madness is like an endless spiral, for what is new today is inevitably old tomorrow. It has often been said and is still the case: We have forgotten one thing in the process: ourselves, humanity. It is simply no longer the time for writing 'bold' music – the concept itself is the most naked, the most primitive example of the terminology of progress – no longer the time for being 'new'. But it is, in the end, very much the time for being authentic in a human way, simple – in short, to be the way we are. Instead of attempting with all our might to flee ourselves into a barren concept, we should try with all our might to find ourselves, if we do not want to lose ourselves completely. What is Romanticism or Modernism? There is only one opposition: authenticity and deceit. There is more of what we need in one single natural melody than in all the theories about the 'new', which only remains new as long as we are unfamiliar with it. Of course, these natural melodies call for grace, while all the others require nothing but will and intellect. But these are two a penny these days . . .

The development of European music is unified and coherent. I was able to attempt to perform old works in such a way that they would appear contemporary, for I was in search of the human being in them. And if I now come forward with my own contemporary work I am also attempting, within the scope of my powers, to speak of the human being in all of us. As a result of this alone, a connection with the old works becomes apparent; I should have to see a denial of this, for the sake of craze for novelty of a tired world addicted to originality or the avoidance of originality, as a betrayal of myself!!

A number of celebrated American artists have protested my visit to America.* They do not even want me to be allowed to stay there for a few weeks as a guest. This protest by artists against another artist is something completely new, a monstrosity in the history of music, a slap in the face to all previous concepts of ideal solidarity among artists, of the function of art in uniting peoples and serving the cause of peace. They have acted in quite a personal way against me, so I too shall become somewhat personal.

At the head of list I see the illustrious name of A. Toscanini. What can have caused him, the great man, who stands above oppositions, to take part in this short-sighted and ill-founded protest? Was he not the one who, in 1936, invited me to New York as his successor, and a few months later in Paris hurled reproaches at me for not accepting this post despite overwhelming opposition? And at that time it had long been clear that despite resigning from my official posts I would remain in Germany. Certainly he suddenly said a year later, when I successfully conducted along with him in Salzburg, that one could not perform Beethoven in an oppressed and a free country at the same time, while I was of the opinion that Beethoven makes his audience 'free' wherever he is played. But what is the reason for his refusal to let me conduct today, in free and democratic America? Four years after the war? I am faced with a puzzle! There is also Arthur Rubinstein†, whom I do not know, but who plainly does not know me either, for he should know that I was the one artist who remained in Germany and *emphatically* intervened on behalf of Jews until the very end. Then I see Herr Brailowsky** and Herr Isaac Stern††. Have these two not condescended to play, in the past year, at

---

* In 1948, Furtwängler was invited by the Board of the Chicago Symphony Orchestra to conduct a series of concerts, and accepted. Immediately there was a storm of protest, and many musicians stated that they would never appear again with the CSO if the invitation was not withdrawn. It is still unclear who was behind the protest, which accomplished its aim.

† Arthur Rubinstein (1887–1982) was certainly one of the ring-leaders of the protest; he never performed in Germany after the war.

** Alexander Brailowsky (1896–1974), a French Jewish pianist, whose career was cut short by illness, and who was equally hostile to Furtwängler.

†† Isaac Stern, whose career as a violin virtuoso was just getting under way. At Lucerne he was friendly to Furtwängler.

the celebration concerts in Lucerne, although they must have known that I am definitively employed here as a conductor? Then I see my old friend Gregor Piatigorsky,* the long-haired solo cellist of the Berlin Philharmonic. I watched the beginnings of his rise with my own eyes, and even shortly before the war, when it had long been clear that I was staying in Germany, we associated in a most friendly manner in Paris.

When they are in Europe, do they have a different conscience from the one they have in America, which permits them to do in Lucerne what they would have to refuse in Chicago?

What is the reason for all this? The whole thing is organized. This is a boycott which has been introduced with a particular aim in mind. Individuals, I have been told, received anonymous telephone calls threatening to make their lives in America 'impossible' if they did not take part in the Furtwängler boycott. And this also explains why the refusals of all the conductors and soloists invited by the orchestra in Chicago all arrived on the same day. The orchestra was simply placed in a difficult position.

If one considers that this boycott is based entirely on accusations which were thoroughly refuted in a one-and-a-half-year trial against me, which was certainly not organized and carried out by my friends, one involuntarily wonders: So what are the *real* reasons for this trial, for this kangaroo court, this calumny against an artist respected in the whole of the rest of the world? Might it have something to do with my being a German? Is it not the task of art and artists to unite peoples and serve peace, not to perpetuate hatred yet again, four years after the end of the war?

I shall save myself the answer.

Herr Strobel thinks it wrong of me to invoke standards other than the purely musical. Precisely this is something he should be proud of. That musicians take themselves seriously is understandable. That others should do so is the important thing.

From its origins after the First World War, the new music unfortunately claimed all too often to be a music of the future, which

---

* Gregor Piatigorsky (1903–76), great 'cellist who for many years played in the Berlin Philharmonic Orchestra under Furtwängler. Though his name appeared in the protest, it may well have been without his consent – this was certainly the case with some of the names on the list. For a detailed account of the whole matter, see Dan Gillis's *Furtwängler and America*.

was to be understood as an 'historical development'. But historicism, particularly in Germany, is on the point of reducing itself *ad absurdum*. Not a music of the future, but one of the present . . . And this is true of only a small part of the new music. The extent to which it becomes so is a decision not of the musician in us, but of the 'human being'. The human being is more important than tonality, atonality, twelve-tone technique and all the technical problems put together.

1950

Magic Flute

Today more than ever, and also with regard to the work of art, we feel the need to define, to classify. We attempt to recognize the types that underlie the various works and put them in context. We wear ourselves out trying to discover whether the *Magic Flute* is more of a fairy tale or a stage-consecrating drama, more of a *Singspiel* or more grand opera, more popular entertainment or *opera seria*, more freely fantastic or masonic, and we have to have an 'opinion'. Whichever opinion we decide on is the one by which we will organize the performance, whether as director or musician, singer or actor.

Let it be said straight away: All classifications, all attempts at typification break down in the face of a work like the *Magic Flute*. It is neither one thing nor the other, neither light nor serious, neither fantastic nor strict, neither tragedy nor comedy, it is – so to speak – all these things at once, all these things in one. Our urge to classify might have tried to recognize a new 'type' here, if the work had not remained on its own, *entirely sui generis* as a type and a work of art in the history of the opera. The *Magic Flute* is life itself; all classification breaks down here. It is a terrible misunderstanding to claim to see in it – in reference to the Sarastro scene – a stage-consecrating play *à la Parsifal*. But it is just as perverse to describe the comic scenes – in reference to Papageno – as a Viennese pub farce. Sarastro's seriousness is more relaxed, more human, nobler, but certainly, by virtue of this, no less deep than that of Parsifal, and no more than this are Papageno's melodies simply 'Viennese' in the sense of the later Viennese operetta, since Mozart was not Viennese, in fact not even Austrian but – as is becoming increasingly apparent – a cosmic phenomenon, simply Mozart, entirely *sui generis*.

If one wishes to get the bottom of the *Magic Flute*, one must probe further than the types named above, even if it outwardly appears to contain something of all of them. It uses devices from all of them; but these devices are merely the foreground, merely devices. Everything is also symbolic, but symbolic as life itself is, both real and unreal, fantastic and realistic at the same time. So it happened that in the *Magic Flute* such heterogeneous elements came together, individual parts which were so essentially different were nevertheless (thanks to the unique genius of Mozart) welded together as a unified whole, a living work, as never before in all of world literature. For – and this is the most remarkable thing – it is not a conglomerate of various individual parts, but, from the artist's point of view, it is unified from beginning to end like no other work, the most mature, the most thoroughly formed, the most balanced of Mozart's works.

What is at the root of it, where do we find a basis for our understanding of it, the points of departure for its performance?

This much is certain: they are incommensurable. Less than any other work of operatic literature is the *Magic Flute* what it seems to be at first glance. Its whole colourful exterior is more pronounced than in any other work. It is all of this, and yet it is not all of this. All these heterogeneous elements, the wisdom and humanity of Sarastro and the folly of Papageno, the blossoming love of Tamino and the pain of Pamina, the choirs of priests and the trios of ladies and boys, the expression of the most esoteric and sacred things and the unrestrained and yet 'classical' folkloric elements – all of this draws its cohesion, its unity, its style from the humanity of its creator. It is Mozart's blood that courses through the whole work. A thoroughly simple and thoroughly real and yet enormously pure sense, as modern science would express it, an extraordinary 'sublimation' without the merest hint of exaggeration, of decadence, wonderfully pure, without the merest hint of isolation or flight from the world – the only way that the work could become as it is – opera, surface down to the last fibre, and yet down to the last fibre a consecrating play, a mass of life, a consecration of life, an injection of vitality into everything high and noble. The simple, sweet humanity of Mozart, this 'Christ of music' as one great musician once called him, does not speak, in any of his works, more completely, more comprehensively or more naturally than it does in this miraculous work.

At a time like the present, when artistic development is being questioned in so many ways, the monument of great and unbroken humanity that Sibelius has erected with his music is all the more valuable. It is with admiration that the world remembers this man who has done so much more for his country than it is generally granted to a musician to be able to do.

It should not be forgotten that the past contains a number of wonderful masterpieces, and the present a number of experiments. It is possible that the past, that is, the self-contained harmonic conception of the world, corresponds to mankind, and that modern art corresponds to the world, as the man of the atomic age imagines he understands it. But apart from the fact that this is incorrect as well – does mankind not count? Is it permissible or even possible for us humans to abstract from 'mankind', to ignore and lose ourselves? . . .

Hindemith

I have been sent your lecture about Bach. What you say is so different from the twaddle that was so often put before us in the *Bach-Jahr*.

Ernst Jünger declares at one point that the value of recent literature basically depends on its relation to the main hypotheses of our contemporary life with regard to nihilism. By nihilism he means the attitude which undertakes to reorganize the world on the basis of reason, which takes it upon itself to deprive it of wonder, of astonishment, of the unpredictable, and to arrange it mathematically, that is, to give it a machine-like organization, to make it visible, reduced. When Jünger says that this spirit has for generations had no more pressing concern than the naming, examination and overcoming of 'nihilism', he is doubtless right. And I know today that all the concerns that have plagued me since the beginning of my musical career have been related to this thought.

In musical life, nihilism is very much in evidence. As elsewhere, it is good to be aware of it. Musical life means above all that music is capable of creating life, that is, communal life, life as communality. The work of art in general, but especially clearly in music, is as much a product of communality as it is a creator of communality, that is, it depends upon communality, it presupposes it. It presupposes those values that can create communality because they originate in values that transcend the individual, mere calculation. We can recognize nihilism by the fact that it attacks music here, in the core of its being.

1951

Tiburtius

As I take it that you, Herr Senator, are concerned, in the regulation of matters involving the Philharmonic Orchestra, not only with overcoming the difficulties of the moment, but also in superior planning from a wider perspective, I should like once more to present my position to you.

When, at the beginning of the 1920s, I succeeded A. Nikisch as director of the Philharmonic Concerts, I was concerned with restoring the great German symphonists Beethoven, Brahms and Bruckner to their rightful place within German musical life, and thereby giving this musical life a stance, a direction and a character which it seemed at the time to be in danger of losing. Along with this, of course, there was also the appropriate nurturing of the music of living composers. Regardless of the musical directions which come into conflict precisely here – from the conservative to the extremely radical – all the considerable works of this kind have been heard in the context of my concerts by virtue of their historical and artistic significance. I was able to do this because the administrators in question – first of all the concert director Wolff, then the various directors of the orchestras, the last of these being Herr von Westermann – worked together with me smoothly and sympathetically.

Since then, times have not improved. The general confusion, not so much that of the audience, which never changes, but rather of the powers involved in the music business, has become even greater since the Second World War than it did after the First. The activity of agents and virtuosos has continued to proliferate since then, and men with clear perspectives, beyond that of the mere virtuoso socialite who occupies the foreground of today's musical life, have never been so necessary as they are today. In order to make my own contribution to this, I have entered into discussions with Berlin.

I must point out that if a director is chosen who does not meet my requirements, any further contractual connection between myself and the orchestra would seem to be impossible. I therefore think it better that we should agree on the choice of director *beforehand*, allowing that you still set some store by my working for you the year after next. Of course if this should not be the case – I could not tell from your letter – I should like to request a clear statement on the matter.

If one speaks about music, one runs the risk of talking past it. There are no common premises; without these there can be no fruitful discussions. What I say, for example, may not be understood; what cannot be understood might as well not be said. For this reason I have, in the past, said very little of what I could have said from my own experience. Repeatedly, I have the experience of not being understood – not merely half understood, not merely incorrectly understood, but not understood at all. I therefore wish to attempt to make myself understood from another angle. I shall make a particular work the basis of my performances – if possible one that everyone knows. I do not see the work as an end in itself, but rather as the source of all my observations. It represents that common premise, so absent in the past, which must precede and underlie any living exchange.

In any case it must be a work that is not only important, of striking weight, that is not only, if possible, generally familiar, it must also be a work of such clarity and definition in its features that the things which concern me here can be clearly demonstrated and read from it. To this end I shall first of all choose the first movement of Beethoven's Fifth Symphony.

Why two pauses longer? (Weingartner's theory, the nadir of theory as a whole.) Theoretical thought, particularly in music, has developed very little. There is a lack of natural control here, control by 'experiment'. Scientific progress is brought about by the constant mutual influence of creative theory and the controlling experiment. Here I am attempting to give you a concept of what experiment means in music.

Here it is a case (the 𝄐 – question) of a failure of architectural thought (or feeling) in music. Weingartner's mistake was the mistake of a superior kind of musician, a musician with classical training and experience. The mistake of a musician, at any rate, who was no stranger to architectural thought in music. And still there are these colossal errors. The small extent to which this thought is actually known in any depth, precisely by those who pride themselves upon knowing it, is also revealed by other examples which are too instructive not to be mentioned here. (*Pastoral*, Heuss, etc.) The beginning of the *Adagio* of Beethoven's Fourth Symphony. Here we can immediately see the importance of correct knowledge for the performer in such cases. The logic of emotion is just as compelling and inevitable as the logic of thought. It is in the nature of things that the latter should continually win through against all the nonsense that people spout. This is less true in the emotional sphere because the opinion of an outmoded Romantic era, that emotion is a 'matter of taste', is still current. At any rate, the primitiveness of musical architectural thought among people like Halm is astonishing. This man who, as a major writer on music, is actively occupied with the truly promising beginnings of an independent understanding of things, is still just as incapable of dealing with even simple cases.

Let us now proceed with our performance of the Fifth Symphony. Look at the first part, three entirely different types of content. *Fertile* contrast: this provides the starting-point for the developing subject.

All very hard facts, nothing to do with mood. Is this the classical composer? Not a Romantic, at any rate. It has nothing to do with these historical concepts. It is the sculptor, or rather the dramatist, who is speaking here. Everything is development, everything is revealed during the course of the action. So what is one to say to those who turn this fertile action into a comfortable account of things, who hide behind literal rendering (their own ignorance) – for – and this is a truth fundamental to all performances, of which composers in particular, in conflict with performers, must be reminded: Nothing can quite emerge during a performance that was not 'there to start out with', that is, in the mind of the performer. The dissolution of the contrasting character of the phrases into a pretty and general obligingness, which does nobody any harm but also says nothing to anyone – the development of the art of performance – from the point of view of the critic – from responsible and characterful performance into contemporary 'faultlessness', which can then be glossed over with a flourish as a 'modern' development.

Wagner himself always stressed that the poet was primary in him, and the musician, so to speak, received the poet's instructions, carried out the poet's intentions. Whether or not this is the case, in Wagner's complete works the musician certainly does not take second place. Only through the musician does his work receive its living surface, its flowing, full-blooded presence. And if Wagner, remaining true to himself, always referred to the importance, in performance, of clear and plainly comprehensible words – the language of the poet – this is conspicuously apparent in the building of the Festspielhaus in Bayreuth with its concealed orchestra – we must still say today that a performance of the music that is both clear and true to the sense of the music is no less important for the final effect, and the reason for the large number of inadequate performances of Wagner's works is that the musical and poetic aspects do not seem to be attuned to one another, or to be properly balanced in terms of their content.

Certainly a performance of the *Götterdämmerung* cannot do without the stage; and we can never seek to substitute a concert-style performance of the music for a scenic and theatrical, total performance of the work. A real performance of the *Götterdämmerung* is possible *only* in the theatre. Nevertheless, a performance in which justice is done to the *music*, and in which the music is not, say, made banal and impaired by the false theatricality of the exaggerated 'gestures' of singer-performers, is important today – and particularly today, when many people are having to rediscover Wagner. And anyone who only knows the work from total performances will be astonished to notice how much power emanates from this music if it appears on its own, as the sole vehicle, so to speak, of the events as a whole.

The worst thing is that today's methods make the act of selection more difficult, if not impossible. But in order for our music to develop successfully, everything depends on this selection being carried out naturally. We allow ourselves to be told what we have to find good and bad, asking all and sundry whether or not we should find this or that beautiful (or rather '*passé*' or 'not *passé*'). For all our Teutonic thoroughness, we rely on outside information (whether it be historical, scientific or social facts or even only the opinions of others) at the one point where *our* opinions and decisions matter. The decision of what we are to see as good and bad – even in art – is something that cannot be taken from us in the long term, something indeed, that *cannot and must not* be taken from us.

In our age of heightened communication, tours by whole orchestras have become a commonplace. As a result, even here, in the sphere of orchestral music, the apparatus, the thing that performs – here in the form of entire orchestras – has taken centre stage. This is in response to an unproductive, formulaic and unserious need for variety on the part of the Moloch public. The main thing is no longer the music that is played, but who plays the music. Whether such tours are to be hailed as an enrichment of musical life or lamented as a trivialization, a fragmentation, is another question. In any case they are a part of the age and we must come to terms with them.

Not only cultural philosophers, not only biologists, have for a long time been able to read the state of health of a culture or an individual out of the 'morality' proclaimed by that culture or individual, from what it sees as desirable and as contemptible – in other words to see this morality as one of the main sources of his intellectual allegiance. If we apply this method to the world of art, of artists, we discover a richly productive source in the process; for in few areas does morality – at least displayed morality – play such an important part as in the field of art. Our entire musical life is drenched in morality; and if everything that was written and read every day from a moral point of view were true, there would have been no musical 'life' for a very long time, and only demands, programmes, postulates, trends – that is, theories.

Any musician who dares to descend to the 'depths' of real musical life, that is, instead of theory, pedantry and chatter, in order simply to make 'music', is bombarded by the preachers of morality.

There are the conductors, for example; they will undertake a tour at the head of an orchestra, say, as has recently become accepted form once more. It must be clear to everyone that such a tour needs to be financed. And that a tour such as this is not possible without a crowd-pulling programme. But if the programme includes one of those monumental and familiar symphonies by Beethoven, etc., which according to the experts – in this case particularly the agents – pull the crowds, the press will always feel obliged to point out how morally inferior such a programme is, how it is obviously dictated solely by the conductor's concern for his own success, and how the poor critic and with him the intelligent sector of the audience are forced for the so-and-so-manieth time to hear the old familiar symphony whose files have long been closed.

It would be wrong to take it for granted that this is the position of individual 'critics'. Individuals may give it expression in a particularly pronounced way, but only because it actually corresponds to the attitude of the age. This is a part of the 'morality' of today's 'public'. But nothing is more telling, nothing provides a deeper insight into the actual condition of our musical life than the pointedly involuntary expressions of this 'public morality'.

To stay with our example: What is the meaning of the fact that the choice of a Beethoven symphony in itself is seen as a morally reprehensible concession to the public, aimed solely at one's own personal success?

The meaning is this:

1) The files on Beethoven are closed. He does not pose any problems for contemporary people, we have known for a long time how he is to be performed. He is 150 years old, has nothing to do with our modern life and our modern feeling for life, and is only to be seen historically.

2) For the people of today, Beethoven's symphonies mean a comfortable and therefore an immoral source of enjoyment.

3) We go to concerts not for the sake of artistic enjoyment but for a continuation of our education, our development.

Here Beethoven is only one example of many.

It must be said: The most important thing for practical musical life is in so far as it concerns the *future*, that the great selection process should continue smoothly, that is, the process that introduces the true and the productive and accords it a place while at the same time unmasking and discarding the false, the expedient and the mendacious. This process occurs before what is known as – and this must be said again and again – the audience. Without the endorsement of this audience – in the broadest sense – it will not work. It is not the connoisseur – where are the connoisseurs today? – not the expert, least of all society, least of all is it the audience, equally exposed to every external 'impression', every true or false suggestion, that seems – but only seems – to make the decisions today. But neither is it those who hold this audience in contempt, those who, recognizing the shallowness of the audience's impression, believe they can use their subjective connoisseurship to criticize, without needing to come into contact with a higher community. It is – and this must be said again and again – this higher community itself that cannot be avoided. One may also call it the audience [*Publikum*] – there is no other word in German – without identifying it with the usual, non-judging external 'audience' that fills a large part of our theatres and concerts. It is, of course, a wider, a larger audience that then truly makes the decisions. It is the human being in us that makes the decision, not the connoisseur.

The selection process of which I spoke at the start is nothing but the process of bringing the artist directly to *this* 'audience'. We see, however, that all available means are repeatedly used to prevent precisely this. Partly by those who deal with the worse instincts of the Moloch audience. And partly by those who think they can launch an assault on this audience with their minds and their theories. Some enjoy too great a complicity with the audience, while others believe they can do without it completely. The audience's idea of a higher community is the *artistic conscience* of contemporary man. The pursuit of it – it must be said again and again – means above all following one's own judgement, giving room to the human being within ourselves. But if the selection process no longer works today, it is because we are no longer brave enough to stand by our own judgements. What we have been told to find good, we find good, in order to remain progressive and up to date. We do not live in the present, but in an imaginary future.

For thirty-five years I have been known as a conductor, not a composer. In such cases, the 'world' refuses to take one's compositions 'seriously' from the start, rejecting them – generally with good reason – as 'conductors' music'. In my case I should like to state that I started out as a composer long before I conducted, and that throughout my life I may have considered myself a conducting composer, but never a composing conductor. The two occupations are completely different from one another. If the composer can really receive stimulation from the conductor, then his work is in a bad way. But the reverse is possible. Wagner and Strauss, but also Bach and Handel were conductors; this is even the musician's natural condition. The fact that I withhold my compositions from the public to a fairly large extent in any case has other reasons, and this is not the place to discuss them.

The development of the modern natural sciences dazzles and fascinates us contemporary-thinking Europeans. We are not fully enough aware that the fruits of the mind – religion as well as art, which is still in some way related to it – are based on different laws from the development of the atom bomb.

It must be said that today true 'boldness' does not consist in writing incomprehensible harmonies and rhythms based on an imaginary 'development', but the opposite – expressing oneself clearly and with musical logic.

Personal genius, inspiration, which is the same thing, is to be dethroned, and will be replaced by a method, a style, that is, the 'mass' in some form. It is the most complete chimera: A method that enables one to learn composition. The pipe-dream of all unproductive people.

Those people who believe that the history of music is the history of its means, its harmony, rhythm, melody, etc., are now talking about the 'end of music'. From their perspective they are right, for these means as such are exhausted today. They were already exhausted at the start of the First World War. In spite of this it is not true that European music is finished. It will only be finished when European man is finished.

I demand of modern music:

1) that it should be written for living people of flesh and blood, not for mental gymnasts;

2) that it should take into account the natural laws of all organic formation, the laws of tension and release;

3) that it should apply to the people of today, not those of tomorrow or the day after tomorrow, that is to a *real human being*, not an imagined or even a prescribed human being;

4) that it should express what it has to say with the greatest possible clarity. Anyone who has something to say can risk expressing it clearly. The professional obscurantism or camouflage of so much new music is not 'depth' but a lack of productiveness.

Classical music is that music in which form is conditioned by inspiration and inspiration by form. Where inspiration predominates, and is therefore only insufficiently formed, the music is Romantic, and where form predominates, leaving inspiration in the background, it is pre-classical. Love of the Old Flemish Masters, Baroque music, etc. for this reason. Modern music is the music of mass man, in which a method is intended to replace the living man, and a system to replace inspiration. The fight against inspiration, which is called subjective, Romantic, etc.

Nietzsche's battle against Wagner is also the battle of the modern intellect against the man of imagination. The will to power of the intellect the most profound fundamental reason, as Nietzsche himself finally admits. In order to achieve this, the imagination, joy in life, must be anathematized – as prefigured by Wagner in Alberich, in a way that can never be marvelled at enough. Wagner equates imagination with the goddess of love. Nietzsche, himself receptive to the imagination and love, only began his rebellion with *Parsifal*. For Wagner it was only natural to bring religion on to the stage as well, for the stage was also reality. It was here that Nietzsche made his break, here that it became clear that Wagner was actually a play-actor. Although he was not insensitive to the power of Wagner's imagination, he nevertheless had to sacrifice this whole imaginative world to his intellectual hunger for power. The will to power, which in this intellectualized world leads to the authoritarian state and finally to the atom bomb . . .

I use all the means which I feel to be natural. What this naturalness is – visual artists talk about 'nature' – is certainly something that my own feeling tells me better and more clearly than the cleverest intellectual deductions. In this, the most important respect, a deeper instinct speaks in the artist, one which he must constantly heed. It must therefore be of little consequence to me whether this 'naturalness' works in agreement with other developing tendencies such as the novelty of the material. It is more important; it alone provides the opportunity of speaking to the *people* of today. And this is the only crucial thing. Experts, musicians . . . well, they play their music among themselves, they praise one another for as long as it lasts. One day they themselves become aware that they cannot do without people, meaning the audience, and that even the most 'correct' theory is a poor exchange for the living, warm person whom they have lost. I even risk the most terrible insult that could by hurled at a musician in contemporary Germany – I risk being 'Romantic'.

It can be seen again today, for example in the Hindemith case. As soon as the individual has a really constructive, that is a restraining effect, he is restricted by the community that has lost its restraint. The 'bold' person is not the one who encourages fashionable excesses. He is only driven. It is the one who restrains them. There is no more difficult, more thankless task than that of confronting the community *in the name of nature*, particularly if it is organized and uses entirely amoral methods of combat.

If a community achieves something valid, it is only when it does not *want*, but *is*. Conscious creation is only achieved by the individual, the responsible person. Everything created by the community is by and large unconscious, and this is the source of its value. As people today are conscious and 'want', communal achievements have lost their value. Here the responsibility of the individual, which in many cases was previously unnecessary, finds its mission. By itself, a community is not capable of the conscious restriction of freedom – the master is revealed by limitation. It is the moral achievement of the individual.

What is needed is a music that is not new or previously non-existent from the point of view of its material, that is, 'modern' in this sense, but one that expresses *modern man*. The history of recent musical developments has shown often enough that the two things are different.

In all great art, the foreground, the vision of the 'whole' is simple, while the background is infinitely complicated not to say irrational. In contemporary art, on the other hand, the foreground is excessively complicated, the background often inexpressibly primitive. Contemporary art seems complicated – but it is a mathematical complication, and this is never complicated compared with a work of art. There are naïve people and peoples – it may depend on their level of development – who pray to machines. As an artist, the machine says nothing at all to me. The intellectual possibilities of the finest machine are, compared to those of the living being – the true work of art – nothing short of ridiculous. All of this contemporary art is not too complicated, but too simple.

1952

The Vienna Philharmonic rose to world prominence as the popular orchestra of the Vienna scene long before the highly cultivated orchestras of today's capitalist world came into being. As a truly popular orchestra, consisting exclusively of musicians from the Viennese school, it will continue to maintain its prominence in time to come.

Subsidiary phenomena, such as the recent polemic that has been circulating against Beethoven and Wagner (with Stravinsky at its head), are geared towards a further curtailment of musical life. They start out from the idea that man is a thinking machine. That is not so today, nor will it ever be so.

The artist – and he alone – has the great advantage of being able to express himself directly. He confronts humanity directly – naturally the humanity of his age and his cultural circle, but humanity nevertheless. He has the particular ability of expressing what this humanity is and what weighs upon it. He also has a huge burden of responsibility.

What means does he have at his disposal to carry out this task? More than anything else he needs a language in which he can speak and make himself understood.

The tragedy of the intellect is that it cannot on its own understand polarity – the need for the simultaneous coexistence of obligation and freedom, etc. It only ever sees one side of things, and exaggerates. This is revealed by the whole of musical history.

A living work cannot be destroyed by thoughts and theories. But neither can its living nature be defended by thoughts and theories. It has been shown that the spark flashes across, that living music finds a living audience, beyond all the know-all attitudes of our age, so unhappily trapped within the unshakeable concepts of its overdeveloped intellect.

But I should like to say one thing: As far as I can see, there has never been any great art that was not natural, that is, art which could not to a high degree have been placed under the category of the natural. It is not originality in itself, but originality combined with expression that is the urgent and entirely compelling aspect of the true work of art. There remains the question of what the individual feels is 'natural', and to what extent this changes according to people and eras. Here one must say, quite categorically, that every single one of us is born with the knowledge of natural feeling, just as much as the knowledge of the natural and healthy functions of our bodies. And if in biology today, in the doctrine of the healthy body, we have come much further than we have in the doctrine of the healthy mind, healthy feeling, this does not mean that knowledge is not coming into its own here too, and beginning to make its presence felt.

Each individual has within himself an infallible standard of what is and what is not natural in music. He must only learn to perceive it, he must hear the voice that speaks within him, he must learn to trust himself and his own feelings. If he asks his own internal voice, he will know immediately what it means to be 'natural'. With the strength to bear a work of art he will also receive the courage to be himself. Anyone who says: 'We may, we must, we may not . . .', etc. will never reach the deeper nature within himself, will never reach 'nature' itself, that is, that which means 'naturalness' in music as in any art. That can only be achieved by someone unconcerned with theories, who says: I feel this way, for me this and nothing else is compelling, convincing. Only the person who feels from within, who, untouched by 'influence', dares to feel what he really feels, knows what – even in art – is meant by nature, the natural. He is the one for whom the artists have written, carved and made music.

1953

Musical life – as an expression of our relationship to art in general – goes on changing and developing inexorably. This is barely noticed by those who are right in the middle of it, and who know nothing but the present. It is different if one has consciously lived through it – as I have – for a number of decades. The changes are all interrelated, it is a great developing process – and yet it manifests itself in the most diverse ways.

The striking thing is how much the criticism of the day has changed in character. Certainly, much depends here – as everywhere – on the individual personality. So it is all the more surprising that even the self-contained and independent person is not uninfluenced by it.

It used to be an unwritten rule that it was criticism's task to record the actual *meaning* of the artistic event, whether of a productive or a reproductive kind, to grasp and express this meaning. What was sought was a kind of 'résumé', an impression of the whole.

It is only to be hoped that the thinking person of today is developing so far in terms of his own thought that he also leaves room for the feeling and instinctive person within. This alone will be the true cleverness of the future, in art as well as in politics, in the most personal as well as the most universal matters. Then we shall understand what it means, today, in possession of all the means of the musical development of the twentieth century, to want to write 'naturally'.

What I want to reach is the 'soul' of modern man. One can only speak to the soul with the language of nature, with a 'natural', not an artificial language. Art that speaks to the soul is quiet – it seeks only to exist, that is, it does not engage in politics, either negatively or positively. It is self-contained, only apparently recalling the past. For it does not finds its orientation in the past, either positively or – as in today's fashion – in a consciously negative way, protesting, desiring to overcome the past.

We now live in an age characterized by the withdrawal of the question of value. Organizations, machinations, trends, in short all the things that spring from desire, are overwhelming existence, and the standards for true values are lost (Beethoven, Bellini).* It is the inflation of music – if it goes on like this it will be the beginning of the end.

Irony makes reality bearable for the unproductive person. Without it he could not bear his own image. It is just as much an evasion, a falsification, as false Romanticism.

One sign of unproductivity is that it will not allow the nature of God to prevail. If I cannot enjoy it, it cannot be there to be enjoyed. Hence irony; hence even the most divine blossom such as Mozart is trampled underfoot.

Bruno Walter and R. Strauss, very different characters, both told me that they would like to *agree* with *Cosí fan tutte* in the way in which it is *meant*.

The balance between reason and irrationality, intelligence and emotion, conscious and unconscious: Because our daily life has become more conscious, it does not mean that nocturnal life has disappeared, but simply become more difficult to grasp, something that has made it all the more effective. It is the subject of depth psychology, which is not a science in its own right. Iceberg . . .

The situation of 'needing to make new things' is so strong that no one even notices the banal jigsaw-puzzle character of the tone row.

---

* The context is sufficiently vague for it not to be certain whom Furtwängler is referring to, but I take it to be the Venetian painter rather than the composer of *Norma*.

1954

Essay: Ninth Symphony.
It is always good to be honest with oneself, even if not everything that emerges is agreeable.

If one considers our contemporary musical life, it is striking that there are few things about which we are as vague as we are about our relationship to our own music. A great confusion prevails today in all matters of the intellect. But nowhere is this confusion greater than in music, which only a few generations ago represented the centre, the pride of European man.

Most of all a confusion in the sense of *value*. The confusion that attacks the centre and therefore leaves nothing untouched. This issue would be very simple if everyone thought about what he felt and found within himself. The remarkable thing is that this seems to be the hardest thing of all. There are people who tend to see this from the moral point of view, and lament the prevailing lack of courage. And it is true: There seems never to have been a greater lack of respect, of inner truth, of the courage of one's own convictions. There has never been more cowardice, self-disavowal, consideration of the opinion of others, of experts, etc. But the whole process cannot simply be seen from the moral angle. Seen from this point of view it would be as good as hopeless. But there is something else: It is the awareness of being faced with facts which we are unable to deal with; the feeling that one must conform to a reality of life which terrorizes us and which we cannot escape. We have created this reality ourselves, it is reality as the age of technique, that terrible pressure for progress, for development, that has taken hold of us and which no one can escape. We imagine, in all seriousness, that an art which has become unhuman and unnatural to its very core, if it only corresponds to certain primitive ideas of development, could express something *about us*. As never before, we squeeze ourselves into a corset of our own making, and really believe that an art which has no meaning for its *own* time could have a meaning for times to come. For an artist today there is only one accusation which is absolutely fatal, and which makes him and any effect he might have completely impossible – the accusation of being reactionary, of having something to do with the healthy human understanding of the old art – old art being all art before 1900.

It is time we became aware that the only development which has any significance is the one that does not find itself in conflict with us, which is thoroughly natural and not thoroughly unnatural and which is capable of addressing the soul of the *whole* person of today; that, in a word, categorization under the heading of progress is not more important than honesty towards oneself.

We have thus reached a situation whereby the force for progress comes to contradict honesty towards ourselves. Force for progress: That means the intellectual level of the present, a level which has been attained, even in art, through technical thought which is alien to art, but which no one is capable of denying. Nobody wants to be the fool today. But does the fool see that, as a result, we have ceased to be honest towards ourselves?

One such idea – which actually ushered in our own age, the 'mass age' – is the idea of progress. Another is the idea of the 'new', of new art, new music, which has lost its connection with the past. The one overrates, the other underrates the importance of 'development'.

There is a type of thought that takes man as its origin and moves on from there to circumstances and situations: European thought until the present day. And there is a type of thought which starts out from circumstances and situations, in which man is only an object: thought which is increasingly taking control today. This thought is produced by the mass, not by man as such. The latter has entirely swallowed up the former. We are all terrorized by this mass, which consists of ourselves. We are terrorists on the one hand and 'heroes' of conformity on the other.

We must be careful not to slip into theorizing. That happens so quickly, it is frightening how easily, particularly in Germany, people have learned to think and talk pessimistically. Is it not as if all the gods and the great world religions had suddenly died? The terror of despair. Not long ago the world was rich.

One advantage of music is that we can feel the pulse of 'musical life' more easily than that of artistic life, because music is divided into production and reproduction. Certainly these two are mysteriously connected, but development as a whole is equally visible in both.

The common denominator that connects us with our past is the fact of our humanity. And that which connects us with our future – if it really is our future – must also be our humanity. We are people, and this is our limitation – our strength. It is time for us – after the theorizing that pessimistically leads to the abyss – to become aware of it.

Here they talk and talk; he is silent. There the almighty racket of oh-so progressive and fine-sounding theories. Here active silence, silent action. There chatter about the future; here action in the interest of maintaining the future. (Nothing says more for the importance of Schönberg's mind than the fact that he found the connection from Wagner to Brahms.) Brahms knew what Goethe knew: that there can be no development without man, beyond man. As a result he became the arch-enemy of all false illusions.

Tonality is nothing but the architectural structuring of time. For this reason it should not be discarded. It would only be exhausted if we were no longer capable of producing the reality of time and space, the reality of architecture, and no longer saw and heard it, but only thought about it, if architectural art itself were exhausted. It is exhausted if we do not look and do not hear. A natural melody says – even today – more than any theories.

On the one hand the will to chaos. On the other, the tendency to 'separate oneself off', and not for the sake of higher cosmic unity, of a more profound experience of community, but of increased arrogance.

Man is imprisoned by his intelligence. The problem of the mass plays its part in this. Not the simple person, not the truly clever person. The matter can be totally reversed: Anyone who has forgotten how to respect, who is no longer capable of devotion or admiration, is in prison. The prevalence of cheap irony, so widespread today – the way in which the unproductive person disposes of the productive person – know-all attitude of *Kunstwissenschaft*, etc. – this is all part of the prison of one's own intellect. Sometimes it creates the impression that science exists in order to suppress and destroy everything that is productive in its own time. This is already the crucial drawback of freedom, of the joy of life.

It is compensated for by the awareness of working on the rebuilding of culture. But a deeper awareness tells us that renunciation of the joy of life, self-renunciation, amounts to our death-sentence. Only a work of art written for its own sake has the prospect of any historical significance. Conscious history-making, as in Schönberg, has deeper reasons behind it. The foreground is untenable, despite all the cleverness applied to it; it is condemned to collapse.

With this work I sought to provide neither a mythical and mathematical construction nor an ironic and sceptical consideration of the age, but nothing more or less than a tragedy. I am not a Romantic, and not a classical composer, but . . . I mean what I say. Even today that still seems to me to be man's purpose – anyone who thinks it 'out of date' need not listen.

Composer and conductor

From the point of view of music, the treatment which prevailed in former times, which saw no separation between productive and reproductive musicians, is entirely right. If I have conducted, throughout my whole life I have done so as a 'composer'. I have only ever conducted music that gave me pleasure, with which I could identify; the prosaic accounts of the 'musical peddlers' were nothing to do with me.

Even if I attempted to point out and formulate some state of affairs, I did so as a composer, as a productive musician. That was my solid starting-point in every case.

*Symphony**

1) Fate.
2) The life force.
3) Beyond.
4) The struggle goes on.

---

* This, and the previous entry but one, refer to Furtwängler's Third Symphony in C minor, of which the manuscript has pencil-headings by Furtwängler with the titles listed here. He subsequently removed them. He wasn't satisfied with the finale, and the Symphony has usually been performed in three movements, but the only available commercial recording is of the complete work.